E. Thissen

The Russian Revolution

AN ANTHOLOGY

The Russian Revolution

★ ★ ★ ★ ★ AN ANTHOLOGY

Edited by M. K. DZIEWANOWSKI
Boston University

THOMAS Y. CROWELL COMPANY

NEW YORK · ESTABLISHED 1834

Contents

The Russian Revolution

AN ANTHOLOGY

Introduction

The Reverend Billy Sunday, addressing his gaping flock in Nashville, Tennessee, warned them against the Bolsheviks: "If that gang got in control, the laws of nature would be reversed or suspended. Cats would bark and dogs crow. The sun would rise in the West and set in the East. Yesterday would be tomorrow . . . "

Although Reverend Sunday's predictions were perhaps somewhat exaggerated and the Bolsheviks did not upset the laws of nature, the Russian Revolution has been one of the most dramatic and thorough upheavals in history; only the Chinese revolution, and perhaps the Cuban, of our day rivals it in radicalism. (In one respect, however, Reverend Sunday proved correct. On January 31, 1918, the Soviet regime introduced into Russia the Western, Gregorian calendar which was thirteen days ahead of the old, Julian calendar; for thirteen days yesterday *was* tomorrow.) If the

extreme fears pertaining to the Revolution did not quite materialize, neither did the great expectations. Who would now subscribe
to the ecstatic line of the American poetess, Amelia Burr, who on
March 28, 1917, wrote in the *Outlook*:

> *Throughout the troubled earth*
> *Prophetic rumors run—*
> *It is travail of the birth*
> *Of Freedom's youngest son!*

There is no doubt, however, that the upheaval achieved in
Russia in 1917 was a Revolution with a capital "R": a seizure of
state power by a party "of a new type," dedicated to a new
philosophy of history, and determined to achieve a thorough re-
construction of human life, not only in Russia but eventually
throughout the rest of the world. And indeed, the Revolution
shook the world to its foundations. Its expansion has been impressive—about one-third of humanity now lives under various
Communist systems which claim to be heirs of the Bolsheviks. Our
way of life has been challenged by what happened in Russia in
1917. Our dictionary is now sprinkled with terms borrowed from
Communist jargon: Bolshevik, Soviet, Stakhanovism. Whether
one considers communism as the inspiration of the world or its
bad conscience, familiarity with its triumph in Russia is a must
for any serious college student of history and politics.

The main purpose of the present anthology on the Revolution is
to present to American students seven selected passages from
outstanding writings about its crucial phases or aspects. The term
Russian Revolution is understood here in the narrow sense, that
is, as the period from the fall of the Tsarist regime which, according to our calendar, took place around the middle of March, to
the Bolshevik seizure of power at the beginning of November, but
which the Communist regime of the Soviet Union still celebrates
at the end of October. Thus, we are dealing here, roughly speaking,
with about eight months or so of the fateful year 1917, and thus
both the causes and the civil war that followed are outside our
consideration.

The Russian Revolution is now one of the best documented events of modern history. The bibliography of the Revolution is enormous and growing. Its fiftieth anniversary has contributed a new crop to the thousands of volumes dealing in one way or another with the fateful year 1917. Nevertheless, before World War II, relatively few professional Western historians dealt with the subject in a systematic and comprehensive way. Until the postwar period the interpretation of the Revolution and its aftermath was largely left to journalists or former diplomats, as a sort of extracurricular hobby. In the first group one should mention John Reed's brilliant and colorful (although frankly partisan) book, *Ten Days that Shook the World* (New York, 1919), Morgan Philip Price, *My Reminiscences of the Russian Revolution* (London, 1921), and Claud Anet (Jean Schaeffer), *La révolution russe*, 4 vols. (Paris, 1918–1919). In the second category one should include the rambling and often naïve memoirs of the United States ambassador, David R. Francis, *Russia from the American Embassy* (New York, 1921), the reminiscences of his British counterpart, Sir George Buchanan, *My Mission to Russia and Other Diplomatic Memoirs*, 2 vols. (Boston, 1923), and the highly literary but heavily edited diaries of the French diplomatic representatives in Petrograd, Maurice Paleologue, *An Ambassador's Memoirs*, 3 vols. (London, 1923–1925), and his successor, Joseph Noulens, *Mon ambassade en Russie Soviétique, 1917–1919*, 2 vols. (Paris, 1933). It is interesting to note that among the high-ranking diplomats one finds not only less sympathy for the Bolshevik cause but also less understanding of both the mechanics of the revolutionary process and the socioeconomic conditions in Russia during the Revolution. In the diplomatic diaries often facts of importance were handled in a cavalier fashion. For instance, to Paleologue Lenin was "an anarchist"; Francis could hardly distinguish Bolsheviks from Mensheviks. Again, in contrast to the people occupying exposed and responsible positions, the minor and unofficial diplomatic representatives displayed more political perspicacity and were generally better informed. The best book in this category is the highly readable account of an unofficial representative of Great Britain, R. H. Bruce Lockhart, *British Agent* (New York, 1933). It is also noteworthy that the best interbellum general treatment of the crucial event was penned not by a professional historian but by a journalist and publicist turned historian, William Henry Chamberlin, *The Russian Revolution*, 2 vols. (New York, 1935).

Numerous writings of leading participants in the great events, later anti-Communist emigrés, from a special category. Here one should mention, first of all, the three books of the prime minister of the Provisional Government, Alexander Kerensky, *The Catastrophe* (New York, 1927), *The Crucification of Liberty* (New York, 1934), and his latest, less rhetorical and more balanced, *Russia and History's Turning Point* (New York, 1965). One of the earliest attempts to cope with the year 1917 is the highly personal and disappointing account by the leader of the Kadet (Constitutional Democratic) Party, and the first foreign minister of the Provisional Government, Paul Miliukov, *Istoriia vtoroi russkoi revoliutsii* [History of the Second Russian Revolution], 3 parts (Sofia, 1921–1924). Also significant are the works of the two Socialist members of the Provisional Government, its minister of agriculture, Victor Chernov, *The Great Russian Revolution* (New Haven, 1936), and its minister of posts and telegraphs, Iraklii Tseretelli, *Vospominaniia o fevral'skoi revoliutsii* [Reminiscences about the February Revolution] (Paris, 1963). Most of this category, with the possible exception of Chernov's *History*, is characterized by subjectivism and lack of comprehension for the play of socioeconomic and revolutionary forces that had undermined the Provisional Government and helped to bring the Bolsheviks to power. They all represent individual pleas disguised as history. Even the brilliant work of Leon Trotsky, *The History of the Russian Revolution*, 3 vols. (New York, 1932) falls into the same category. One of the few people involved in the events who managed to achieve considerable detachment was an independent Socialist, N. N. Sukhanov, author of a seven volume memoir, *Zapiski o Revoliutsii* [Notes on the Revolution], published in Moscow in the early 1920s.

The post-World War II period, with its mushrooming interest in all things Soviet, has brought an avalanche of books about the Revolution. The works of Chamberlin and Trotsky have not only been republished, but also made available in paperback editions. The same has happened to the two outstanding treatments of the fall of the Romanovs, Michael T. Florinsky, *The End of the Russian Empire* (New Haven, 1931) and the classic of historical reportage, Sir Bernard Pares, *The Fall of the Russian Monarchy* (New York, 1939). In addition, Edward H. Carr, another journalist-turned-historian, published his monumental *The Bolshevik Revolution, 1917–1923,* 3 vols. (New York, 1951–1953), which also is now available in paperback. Research establishments devoted to Russia and the Soviet Union, such as the Russian Research Center of Harvard and the Russian Institute of Columbia University, have produced numerous valuable monographs on the subject. Short histories of the Soviet Union, with heavy emphasis on the revolutionary period, abound; J. S. Curtiss, *The Russian Revolution, 1917* (Princeton, 1957) is probably the best of them, but Joel Carmichael, *A Short History of the Russian Revolution* (New York, 1958), is also good. Monographic treatments of various aspects of the revolutionary process and its outcome are so numerous that it is self-defeating to try listing them. Biographies of Lenin, Stalin, and Trotsky have also proliferated at a rapid pace. David Shub, B. D. Wolfe, Isaac Deutscher, Louis Fischer, Robert Payne, Stephen Possony, and Adam Ulam have written the most outstanding ones. All of them devote a great deal of space to the year 1917 in Russia, on which the present anthology focuses. The recent appearance of the first systematic scholarly treatment of the Revolution by a Russian monarchist, George Katkov, *Russia 1917* (London, 1957) has been a highly controversial but refreshing event—it has marked a break in the Liberal-Soviet dialogue on the Russian Revolution that has hitherto dominated the historiography of the field. The anniversary also produced a crop of symposia of all kinds, the most distinguished of which was that edited by Richard Pipes, *Revolutionary Russia* (Cambridge, Mass., 1968).

Consequently, the choice of material for the present anthology has been a difficult task. The two guiding principles in this respect have been first, to provide the student with excerpts that are both historically significant as well as readable and second, not to seek a consensus of opinion but to give some idea of the existing variety of interpretations. In his interesting essay published in *World Politics* on the fiftieth anniversary of the Revolution, Professor James Billington of Princeton has listed as many as six different approaches to the event. They can be reduced, however, to four basic attitudes. Soviet historiography, with a few minor and timid exceptions, views the Revolution as heroic and inevitable: the infallible Bolshevik Party, led by its omniscient, charismatic leader, the great Lenin, acted as an instrument of irresistible social and economic forces. They won, and no other outcome was conceivable. Reed's book and Trotsky's trilogy are striking examples of this attitude. This position has also been shared to a larger or smaller degree by a few Western scholars, some of them Marxist and some simply impressed with the victors, their ruthless determination and their achievements. A good example is E. H. Carr. Non-Soviet historiography has been split into three basic groups. To the first belong those who attach a great deal of importance to the element of spontaneity and to accidental factors (such as Robert V. Daniels, *Red October* [New York, 1967]). The second group consists of those who see conspiratorial factors as of decisive importance (for example, George Katkov, *Russia 1917. The February Revolution* [London, 1967]). To the third category, which is by far the most numerous, belong those who avoid attaching any particular emphasis to single factors and oscillate in what Billington calls, "the suspended judgment position." Pares, Sukhanov and Chamberlin, in one way or another, represent this approach. Thus, all main schools of thought are represented in the present anthology.

The basic structure of the anthology is essentially chronological. Since the triumph of the Bolshevik Party in Russia was preceded by the overthrow of the Tsarist system and establishment of the short-lived, liberal Provisional Government (March–November,

1917), the present anthology opens with an eyewitness description of the downfall of the Romanov dynasty by the late dean of British historians of Russia, Sir Bernard Pares. This account of the spontaneous February–March upheaval in Petrograd is followed by a reappraisal of the Liberal Revolution by a Russian monarchist, George Katkov of St. Anthony's College, Oxford. Then comes a description of Lenin's return from Switzerland to Petrograd by an independent Socialist observer, a brilliant journalist, and participant in the events, Nikolai N. Sukhanov. Another turning point of the Revolution, the attempt to replace the Provisional Government of Kerensky by a military dictatorship of General Lavr Kornilov, is evaluated by W. H. Chamberlin. The capturing of the seat of the Provisional Government, the Winter Palace in Petrograd, is described by one of the leading protagonists of the drama, Leon Trotsky. The mechanism and the meaning of the Bolshevik triumph is analyzed by one of the leading American scholars specializing in Soviet history, Robert V. Daniels, author of the recent book *Red October*. The first days of the Bolsheviks in power is described by John Reed. Thus the authors of the selections in the present anthology come from all major schools of thought and are far from agreeing even on the events they describe. Indeed, reading their divergent accounts one may be sometimes reminded of the Japanese movie entitled "Rashamon," in which a rape and a murder are described by four eyewitnesses—each version is so different that one actually believes he is watching four different stories.

Besides the great Bolshevik leader Trotsky, at the time of the Revolution second in importance only to Lenin and the most important rival of Stalin, the reader will meet an independent Social Democrat, a Menshevik Internationalist who later submitted to the Bolsheviks and cooperated with the Stalinist regime, N. N. Sukhanov, and a founding father of the Communist Party of the United States, John Reed. Along with these three Marxists the reader will find an early American sympathizer of the Soviet cause who, under the impact of his experiences as a foreign correspondent in the USSR, grew disappointed with communism and wrote one of the early classics on the history of the Revolution (W. H. Chamberlin). The wide spectrum of approaches presented here is completed by the British scholar of liberal views who was an observer of the pre-revolutionary Russian scene and an eyewitness of the events, Sir Bernard Pares, and the independent American student of Soviet history and politics, Robert V. Daniels. Thus the views represented here range from those of a leading militant Bolshevik to those of a Russian monarchist. Three authors directly participated in the events described (Trotsky, Sukhanov and Reed), and one of them helped to shape them in a decisive and dramatic way. Four are outside observers (Pares, Chamberlin, Daniels and Katkov), but the first of these was an active and perceptive eyewitness.

Notable by their absence in the present anthology are professional present-day Soviet historians. It is significant that, despite the passing of over half a century, and the spending of impressive sum of money on research, Soviet historiography has been unable to produce a single comprehensive and scholarly treatment of both the Liberal and the Bolshevik phases of the Revolution. The best books on the subject written by a Communist historian working on Soviet soil have been M. N. Pokrovsky's collection of essays printed in 1924, *Ocherki po istorii Oktiabr'skoi Revoliutsii* [Sketches on the October Revolution], and E. N. Burdzhalov's recent work, *Vtoraia Ruskaia Revoliutsia* [The Second Russian Revolution] (Moscow, 1967). Between 1924 and 1967 there is little worth mentioning. Most of the historical output of the Stalinist period was brazenly propagandistic, outright polemical and, generally speaking, of little scholarly value. De-Stalinization aroused some hopes that a thorough revision of the historiographic errors of the "previous period of the cult of personality" would be undertaken by scholars of the younger generation. In 1956, some bold attempts in this direction, undertaken by the associate editor of the leading historical journal *Voprosy Istorii* [Problems of History], E. N. Burdzhalov, were quickly stifled by the Party. His removal from the editorial staff of the journal in the spring of 1957 after the publication of a revisionist article questioning the decisive role of the Party in the revolutionary process, showed the optimists that Soviet historians would not be allowed to reopen and reexamine objectively questions that, as *Pravda* put it, have "long since been decided by the Party," or to cast "doubt on indisputable facts." Thus, the principle of *partiinost'* or absolute loyalty to the Party has been reimposed on the historians by the omniscient and infallible Party. A fuller discussion of Soviet historical publications on the Revolution is presented in the special issue of the journal *Kritika*, vol. 4 (1968), while Western writings are analyzed by R. D. Warth in *Slavic Review* 26 (June 1967): 247–264. The essay by James Billington, already mentioned, is also helpful.

Thus, regrettably, even the last few, somewhat freer and more relaxed years have produced little of lasting scholarly and literary value, comparable to the works of Trotsky or Sukhanov, and worthy of inclusion in the present anthology. Also absent from the present anthology is the monumental and scholarly *Bolshevik Revolution* by E. H. Carr, certainly one of the most significant achievements of Western Sovietology. But Carr's professed determination "to write the history not of the events of the revolution but of the political, social and economic order that emerged from it" does not fit the purpose and structure of the present work. Nevertheless, students interested in Carr's deterministic approach, not far removed from the Soviet interpretation of the revolutionary process, are advised to consult Volume 1, Chapter 5 of his work.

Being complex and controversial, the Revolution puts the historian's skill severely to task. Some of the controversies are fundamental, some are of a minor, technical nature. Besides the difficulty of ascertaining what really happened and how it happened, there is the problem of interpreting the real meaning and message of the Revolution. Was Russia, owing to her peculiar historical development, "sentenced to Bolshevism by fate," as the Soviet historian M. N. Pokrovsky believes? Or did she stumble into communism by accident? Was the Revolution plotted and planned, as George Katkov seems to suggest, or did it happen spontaneously? Was the Revolution the majestic culmination of an historical process (if not its actual termination), or a ghastly catastrophe?

Has it been a blessing to suffering humanity, or the Pandora's box which has opened an avalanche of misfortunes, including the Fascist coup in Italy and the Nazi upheaval in Germany? These essays, of course, have not been selected to answer such questions, but rather to raise them through a juxtaposition of viewpoints.

Among the minor problems encountered by any student of the Revolution, there is the unavoidable issue of the calendars. Until February 1918, Russia used the Julian calendar, which was in the twentieth century thirteen days behind the Western or Gregorian calendar. Hence, what the Russians call the February 27 revolution, the downfall of the Tsarist regime in Petrograd, is for us the revolution of March 12; the abdication of Tsar Nicholas II, which according to the old style calendar took place on March 2, for us occurred on March 15. Lenin returned from Switzerland to Petrograd on April 3 according to the Julian calendar, but on April 16 according to ours. Finally, the Bolshevik Revolution, which according to the Julian calendar was carried out on October 25, for us was accomplished on November 7. In order to avoid confusion both dates are given by side. Another minor problem concerns the name of the Russian capital. Present-day Leningrad, where the decisive events took place, from the founding of the city in 1703 by Peter the Great until the outbreak of World War I, was known by its Germanic name, St. Petersburg. In 1914, under the pressure of nationalistic feeling, which swept the country after the outbreak of hostilities, it was given the Russian name of Petrograd, which it retained for a decade, until after Lenin's death.

The excerpts composing the present volume have been edited as little as possible. For readability, the original editorial footnotes were removed and replaced by editorial notes which explain briefly the background of important events and introduce unfamiliar personalities. There has been no attempt to make the spellings of Russian proper nouns uniform from selection to selection, as there is often more than one acceptable way of transliterating Russian into English. In footnotes, I have employed the spelling used by the author of the selection.

1. The Fall of the Russian Monarchy

SIR BERNARD PARES

Great happenings often stimulate eyewitnesses to produce vivid, intensively alive accounts. So it was with the Russian Revolution. Among the witnesses of the downfall of the Tsarist regime a place of honor should be awarded to the distinguished British scholar, Sir Bernard Pares, professor of history at the universities of Liverpool (1908–1918) and London (1919–1936) and author and translator of several books on modern Russian history, politics and literature.

The acquaintance of Sir Bernard Pares with Russia was long and intimate. Up to World War I he spent three or four months of each year there, and as he put it, "sought out anyone who had played or was playing a part of any importance in public events, not for a newspaper interview, but for materials for history." Yet, happily, his

SOURCE: Bernard Pares, *The Fall of the Russian Monarchy* (New York: Alfred A. Knopf, Inc., 1939), pp. 440–470. Reprinted by permission of Alfred A. Knopf, Inc.

accounts usually combine the vivacity of a newspaperman's report with the thoroughness and accuracy of a scholarly paper. He passed most of the war with the Russian forces at the front, and described this unique experience in a fascinating book entitled Day by Day with the Russian Army. At the same time he followed the political life of the country by means of frequent interviews as well as of a thorough analysis of printed materials. Eight years of research and study resulted in the publication of his classic, The Fall of the Russian Monarchy: A Study in Evidence (New York: Alfred A. Knopf, 1939 and 1961.)

The excerpt given in the present anthology forms Chapter 15 of the book; it contains a detailed description of the events in Petrograd between March 8 (February 23, Old Style) and March 15 (March 2), events which brought about the overthrow of the Tsardom and its replacement by a liberal Provisional Government. Its members were selected by the middle-of-the-road parties of the Russian Parliament or Duma, a parliamentary coalition known as the Progressive Bloc. The Bloc had been formed in August 1915, after the severe setbacks suffered by the Imperial Army on its western front. The Bloc included deputies from three moderate parties, the liberal Kadets (Constitutional Democrats), the conservative-liberal Octobrists (those moderate conservatives who pledged themselves to defend the Constitutional Manifesto of October 1905), and the Progressive Nationalists (a more conservative group of fierce patriots). These parties constituted about three-quarters of the Fourth Duma elected in 1912 on a franchise biased to favor the propertied classes.

In their appeals to Tsar Nicholas II and in their speeches, members of the Bloc, led by a learned historian, Professor Paul Miliukov (1859–1943), urged the monarch to remove the incompetent bureaucratic government and to appoint a new government more representative of the public at large. The Bloc called for elimination of "the distrust of the public initiative," and for enforcement of the rule of law. This was to be achieved by repeal of the worst of those measures inspired by racial, religious, and class discrimination (including some anti-Semitic legislation), and by changes in local administrative bodies. Less military interference in civilian affairs and more active cooperation of all citizens in public life were also urged. When the Tsar rejected their demands, the parties of the Bloc, which earlier in a show of patriotic enthusiasm had supported the government, now turned toward open opposition and vitriolic criticism of the allegedly criminal and treasonous misconduct of the war. Disappointed with the Tsar and his administration, accused of tolerating pro-German influences in the Duma and of plotting a separate peace with the Central Powers, some members of the Bloc became involved in conspiratorial activities, including plans for a palace revolution which could place on the throne one of the grand dukes who would pursue the war with more vigor and prove more hospitable to the demands of the Bloc.

In the meantime the country, exhausted by thirty months of bloody and unsuccessful war, was flooded with rumors about alleged treason at the top, of negotiations for a separate peace and of scandals in court circles. These latter included the activities of Grigory Rasputin (1872–1916), who had gained ascendancy over the empress because of her distress over her sole son's hemophilia, an illness which Rasputin could control with his remarkable hypnotic powers. More and more often, doubts were expressed whether the struggle could be brought to "a victorious conclusion," as the government had repeatedly promised. Industrial strikes were increasingly frequent. There was no general shortage of food, but high prices, communication difficulties, and faulty distribution tended to create this impression locally. This was especially the case in Petrograd, a frontier city surrounded by an agriculturally unproductive area.

The story excerpted here from The Fall of the Russian Monarchy begins on Saturday, March 8 (February 23), 1917, when Tsar Nicholas II, after a brief visit to Petrograd, returned to supreme headquarters at Mogilev on the upper Dnieper to resume his duties as nominal supreme commander in chief of the army.

★　★　★　★　★

On the very day of the Tsar's departure (March 8) [February 23], while the Duma violently attacked the food policy of the Government, disorders broke out in the city, where already thousands of workers were on strike. Crowds wandered about the streets, calling for bread and peace and singing the Russian version of the 'Marseillaise.' There was some looting in the poorer parts to the North of the Neva, and on the Nevsky Prospekt itself there were conflicts with the Cossacks.

On the ninth (Friday) [February 26] the disorders increased, and in the northern wards the crowd began to sack the bakeries. It has since been declared that there were really supplies of bread in the city for several days, and that the trouble was due to the extremely tardy distribution; the bakers, in their turn, complained that they could not get the necessary fuel for doing their work. The Cossacks were brought into play to assist the police; but . . . there was still a certain amount of good humour, and in reply to the crowd the Cossacks shouted back: 'We won't shoot.'

Rodzyanko got into touch with the Prime Minister. An urgent meeting of the Cabinet was held, though so far the only question seemed to be that of the food supply. Protopopov[1] was again absent; but by invitation Rodzyanko[2] and the Mayor of Petrograd were present. They insisted that the food distribution should be committed to the town council, to which the Cabinet readily agreed, though there would necessarily be some little delay in organizing the change. The Cabinet also decided to seek the co-operation of the Duma; and two of its members, who could command respect there, Pokrovsky and Rittich, paid a visit to it and talked with Basil Maklakov[3] and others. The Duma men made it quite clear that they could not support any Cabinet where the members were not responsible to the Prime Minister for the unity of their policy, and this was reported to the Cabinet.

On the Saturday (March 10) [February 25] the crowds were even larger. They bore red flags and shouted 'Down with the German woman' (the Empress). The police fired, and there were a hundred wounded. Police patrols paraded the streets. The Cabinet met again, and sat till five in the morning. This time Protopopov was present. The Duma's answer was reported. Nearly all the Ministers were only too ready to be replaced by men whom the

[1] A. D. Protopopov (1866–1918), a Duma deputy, friend of Rasputin, and Rasputin's choice for the post of minister of the interior (1916–1917).
[2] M. V. Rodzyanko (1859–1924), speaker of the Duma and a leading member of the Octobrist Party, a group which split from the liberal party, the Kadets (or Constitutional Democrats) and formed a party of their own pledged to defending and consolidating the constitutional system as established by the October 1905 Manifesto.
[3] B. A. Maklakov (1870–1957), a leading Kadet member of the Duma.

country would follow. They communicated this wish by the long telephone to the Emperor at Headquarters, but they were commanded to stay at their posts. They begged him to return. They also decided to prorogue the Duma not at all out of hostility to it, but on the ground that it could hardly work in the existing conditions, and as they had offered their resignations, time would be required for the appointment of a new and popular Cabinet.

It was really something like a repetition of the situation in the summer crisis of 1915, when the majority of the Cabinet, who were in favour of a popular Ministry and offered their own resignations, had considered a similar friendly prorogation, which Goremykin[4] managed to convert into a hostile one; but it was hardly to be expected that all this would be understood by the public.

Even before the War, it had been the practice for the Emperor to leave with the Prime Minister during his absence blank orders of prorogation or of dissolution, where in case of urgency the date was to be filled in by the Premier, and originally these dates had been settled in consultation with the President of the Duma, a practice which had latterly been abandoned. Golitsyn[5] had in his possession such 'blanks,' both for prorogation and dissolution. Protopopov, though he afterwards protested that this was not so, according to the evidence of his colleagues had throughout stood not for prorogation but for dissolution.

Protopopov told the truth when he compared himself and the Emperor as persons who both evaded plain speaking where possible, and in his report over the long telephone to Headquarters we know from that side that he quite failed to bring home the seriousness of the situation. Even in Petrograd itself the question was still in the first place one of food; and the Emperor, away in the wilderness of a small provincial town, had no means of judging the situation. In reply to the nerve-wracked [General] Habalov,[6] the Emperor at 9:00 P.M. sent a telephone message: 'I com-

---

[4] I. R. Goremykin (1839–1917), an old bureaucrat, former prime minister.
[5] Prince N. D. Golitsyn (1850–1925), the last prime minister of Imperial Russia.
[6] Military commander of Petrograd.

mand that the disorders in the capital shall be stopped to-morrow, as they are inadmissible at the heavy time of war with Germany and Austria. Nicholas.' By this message he signed his own dethronement. It is significant of the complete disorder that the War Minister in Petrograd was never informed of this telegram till after the Revolution. Habalov showed the telegram to Protopopov. He himself was in dismay, and from this moment completely lost what balance he had, but he saw no way of disobeying the order.

On Sunday, March 11 [February 26], the people of the capital read the posters in which Habalov announced that crowds were forbidden and that if they gathered, he would open fire. The crowds were huger than ever; the troops fired four or five times and many persons were killed. The Pavlovsky regiment mutinied and killed its colonel, but it was disarmed for the time being by the crack regiment of the Guard, Peter the Great's Preobrazhensky. By the evening order was restored, and Protopopov even made a tour of inspection through the quiet streets.

In the course of this day there were urgent Cabinet consultations. Its meeting of March 10 had ended only at four o'clock in the morning; but the War Minister, Beliayev, who as such was specially responsible, consulted the Premier in the morning and asked for another meeting in the evening. The Cabinet met at nine o'clock and sat till 2:00 A.M. Protopopov, who was present, spoke at great length, but very vaguely, though it was clear that he strongly desired the dissolution of the Duma.

But the worst was now to come. The Volynsky regiment of the guard had at first participated in the firing on the people, but in disgust had retired to its barracks. Here there were heated discussions, and in the end the regiment mutinied and killed one of its officers. At this time most of the regiments in the capital were short of officers, and these were nearly all either wounded men or those who had successfully escaped being sent to the front. Habalov's own deputy was away ill, possibly by design, and of the colonels next under him, the two senior were not to be found.

On receiving the order of prorogation, the Duma had refused

to disperse. For all that happened there in these hectic days the best record—at once the most objective and the most picturesque —is that of Shulgin.[7] On the eleventh [February 26], he, the Conservative, urged the others to get ready as soon as possible their own list of new Ministers; as we know, it had already been drafted; he was also the first to recommend the inclusion of Kerensky,[8] but no action was taken. 'We had not the courage,' he writes, 'or rather the saving cowardice, to think of the gap yawning.' On the other hand Kerensky, young Labour leader, in the early thirties, was in his element. 'We must do something,' he said. 'Are you going to do something?' He only insisted that the power should not be given to bureaucrats, that is, those already associated with the official world. Another Labour man, Skobolev [a Menshevik], declared: 'You have the confidence of the people.'

On this day Rodzyanko sent an urgent telegram to the Emperor, reporting the disturbances, and ending: 'May the blame not fall on the wearer of the crown.' Nicholas, on receiving it, put it aside with the comment: 'Some more rubbish from that fat Rodzyanko.' At the same time Rodzyanko got into connection with all the generals in the highest commands, asking for their support, which he very soon received from Ruzsky and Brusilov,[9] and later from all the rest.

[7] V. V. Shulgin (1878–), a leading member of the Progressive Nationalist Party and author of the lively memoirs, *DNI* (Days) (Belgrade, 1925).

[8] A. F. Kerensky (1881–), a prominent lawyer and leading member of the moderate Socialist Labor Party, vice chairman of the Petrograd Soviet of Workers' and Soldiers' Deputies and first minister of justice of the Provisional Government. In May 1917 he became its minister of war and navy, in July prime minister, and in September, following the attempted coup d'etat of General Kornilov, Kerensky became commander in chief. Kerensky published several books on the Revolution, the most recent and comprehensive being *Russia and History's Turning Point* (New York: 1965).

[9] General N. V. Ruzsky (1854–1918), commander of the northwestern front; it was at his headquarters that Nicholas II signed his abdication. In October 1918 Ruzsky was shot by the Bolsheviks, together with other generals and high officials.

General A. A. Brusilov (1853–1926), commander of the southwestern front; led the victorious Russian offensive against the Austrians in April 1916; appointed supreme commander on May 22, 1917, he was replaced on July 18, 1917, after the failure of the July offensive ordered by the Provisional Government. His memoirs, published in Russian in 1929, are available in English under the title *A Soldier's Notebook, 1914–1918* (London, 1930).

On the Monday (the twelfth) [February 27] the Volynsky regiment, whose barracks lay not far behind the Duma, was out, and that was the turning point in the whole story. Three hours before they came out, the leaders of all the groups of the extreme Left were conferring in Kerensky's quarters. The representative of the Bolsheviks, Yurenin [Yurenev],[10] declared: 'The reaction is gaining strength, the unrest in the barracks is subsiding. Indeed, it is clear that the working class and the soldiery must go different ways. We must not rely on day dreams and preparations for revolution, but on systematic propaganda at the works and the factories in store for better days.' This confirms Kerensky's picturesque statement: 'The Revolution came of its own accord, born in the chaos of the collapse of Tsardom.'

The regiment came out with only one officer accompanying it. . . . Their invitation to other units went round like a snowball. Kerensky, the moment he heard they were out, telephoned to a friend to go straight to them and direct them to the Duma, and that is where they went, and not only they, but regiment after regiment as it joined them.

Habalov had news of the Volynsky about 6:30 A.M. The regimental commander was at this time a sick man, and Habalov sent a substitute and went himself to the regiment. It had by then drawn itself up outside its barracks fully armed, and had already been joined by a company of the Preobrazhensky from their neighbouring barracks and a number of factory workers. Great crowds were coming over the Alexander Bridge from the Viborg suburb in the northeast, which contained the Finland Station and a number of ammunition factories. The insurgents marched towards the Duma and wrecked the barracks of the gendarmes and the School of Ensigns. Habalov formed a column of reserves, which he had very great difficulty in obtaining—6 companies with 15 machine guns. It was to push down towards the Duma and confine the revolt to the loop of the Neva which almost surrounded it. The column was commanded by a badly wounded officer from the front, Col. Kutepov, the same who in 1930 was

[10] The author is mistaken; Yurenev was at that time a Left Menshevik.

mysteriously kidnapped in Paris. No news came back from this column. The Assize Court near the bridge had now been sacked and was on fire, and the firemen who arrived on the scene were driven off by the crowd. Two detachments of the Moscow Regiment endeavoured to isolate the Arsenal but were overwhelmed and the Arsenal taken. A huge crowd filled the Sampson Prospekt and the troops quartered there stood doubtfully in front of their barracks. By noon 25,000 were arrayed on the side of the revolution. The military forces were now divided, and fighting went on the whole day. Government troops were firing with machine guns on the Nevsky, but the military headquarters were captured and as many as twenty of the police stations; all these were set on fire. By the evening Habalov only had under his control the central part of the city, where he drew up his small remaining forces in front of the Winter Palace: three companies of the Ismailovsky (from the other end of the city) and three of the Chasseurs of the Guard. One commander after another had replied to his requests that if he sent him his few dependable units, the rest would break away at once. An appeal to the garrison at Kronstadt brought the same answer. He was joined for a time by some of the Preobrazhensky and strangely enough by the Pavlovsky which arrived with its band playing. He had hardly any shell or cartridges, and access to the northern factories was of course out of the question. Some of his officers were already urging him to make his peace with Rodzyanko. The fortress of St. Peter and St. Paul, on the north side of the river, was besieged. There were barricades on the broad Liteiny Prospekt near the Duma. Most of the troops, including the Guards, had now gone over. The prisons were opened and the prisoners set free. Again, there was no sign of general direction other than what has been mentioned. The revolted regiments made for the obvious marks, just as in July 1789 the whole of Paris, without organization, made for the Bastille; and the great wave went over them like a flood. Amidst the blaze of the burning buildings fighting continued on all sides in the evening.

Of this day's happenings, March 12 [February 27], we have a

vivid picture from the Director of Police, Vasilyev. The night before, Protopopov had been supping with him and his family before going to the Cabinet meeting, and Vasilyev was sent for at midnight to report on the police measures taken for the tranquillity of the city.

It was three in the morning [he writes] when I came back home. The Ministers had let me see their anxieties and their discouragement. The feeling of their heavy responsibilities oppressed me, and their nervousness had passed on to me. Crushed with fatigue, I was a long time unable to get to sleep.

At six in the morning the telephone bell woke me sharply; the City Prefect informed me that an N.C.O. of the Bolynsky Regiment of the Guard named Kirpichnikov had just killed his superior officer, Training Captain Lashkevich, the assassin had disappeared, and the attitude of the regiment was threatening. The news crushed me; I now saw how far anarchy had infected the barracks. The murder had taken place on military ground; so I could do nothing direct, and called General Habalov to the telephone. No use; the Governor could not be found, and from the vague answers which were given me, I could not know where he had gone. The N.C.O. Kirpichnikov, who escaped abroad, has later naively confessed that he fled without knowing whether an hour later he would be a national hero or hanged. This remark is a picture of the situation; no one in Petrograd had then the least idea of the turn which events would take.

Through my window I could see an unusual excitement in the street. Soon there passed hurrying military cars; in the distance shots resounded. The telephone rang again, and again the City Prefect gave me bad news; Brigadier-General Dobrovolsky, commanding a battalion of sappers of the Guards, had been killed by his men. Then events moved fast; the Volynsky Regiment, which had risen after the murder of Captain Lashkevich, had chased its officers out of the barracks. The mutineers joined the Preobrazhensky and Lithuanian regiments of the Guard, whose barracks were near their own. They had succeeded in taking the Arsenal on the Liteiny.[11] Soldiers were dashing about the streets armed with guns and machine-guns. A roaring crowd invaded the quarters of the prison of preliminary confinement (before trial) and opened the cells; soon it was the same in all the prisons

[11] Vasilyev writes 'Lithuanian.' The right word is 'Liteiny,' the Foundry Prospekt.

of the city. The police stations of the various wards were carried by the mob. Policemen, who were not able to change into mufti were torn to pieces. The fire finished off the rest. Most of this took place in the Liteiny quarter. I was told on the telephone that the criminals freed by the mutineers had set fire to the offices of the Regional Assize Court of Petrograd; this meant an irreparable loss and the destruction of archives which could not be replaced.

There could no longer be any doubt; the situation was extremely serious. Petrograd had for several days been in the hands of the military authorities, who proved powerless to prevent the murder of officers by the revolutionary troops and to overcome the insurrection. The sequel proved this only too clearly. The mutinous troops disarmed their officers; any resistance meant death. One detachment of engineers, which had remained faithful and was doing all it could to resist the mutineers, was crushed. The insurgents succeeded in seizing the Officers School on the Kirochnaya and disarming its occupants. Their number increased under one's eye. The mob was rushing to the centre of the town, not to miss so fine an opportunity for plunder. The bridge connecting the Liteiny quarter with the Viborg quarter to the north of the Neva was held for some time by police officers armed with machine-guns, but soon they were overwhelmed by numbers. The crowd rushed on the barracks of the Moscow Regiment of the Guard. Some detachments resisted, arms in hand. They were soon overflowed and the Moscow Regiment joined in the revolt.

I was preparing to go to my office and try to see Protopopov, who lived in the main building. As I was getting ready to start, a courier came up and told me that a sharp fusillade made the Liteiny Prospect impracticable. The police were making a last effort to prevent the insurgents from crossing the bridge. The courier begged me not to risk my life uselessly and wait till things were quiet again.

The only thing left to me was to get into telephonic communication with the (Police) Department. My secretary told me they were going on working as usual in the office, though not without great nervousness. As I had several reasons to fear an assault by the insurgents, I gave orders to send all the staff away. My orders came just in time. A little later my secretary rang me up and told me that a furious crowd had made its way into the building. I at once gave orders to burn the books with the personal addresses of the employees and secret agents. As I learned later, the 'free people' had ransacked all the offices. Some of the leaders had tried, no doubt out of personal interest, to find the section of identification of criminals. All the records, photographs, finger-print albums relating to ordinary criminals, thieves, swindlers and murderers were thrown out into the court and solemnly burnt. The insurgents also forced my tills and appropriated the sum of 25,000 roubles of public money. From the Police Department the crowd made its way to the quarters of Protopopov and sacked them. Afterwards, according to eye witnesses, cloaked women of respectable appearance came out of the Minister's flat carrying objects of value. I pass over the innumerable telephone calls which I received in the hours that followed. The Moscow authorities wanted at all costs to know what was happening in Petrograd. I replied to Colonel Martynov, chief of the Okhrana, that a serious mutiny had broken out and I would do my best to keep him informed. The disorder was so great on all sides that neither the insurgents nor the military authorities thought of occupying the telephone exchange. It continued to work normally, maintaining a perfect neutrality and thus allowing both the representatives of order and the revolutionary leaders to coordinate their action. Still it was not long before the employees abandoned their work to get off home as soon as possible, and it became more and more difficult to get a connection. In the end the direct line through to the Winter Palace was interrupted. After that I could not ring up the Okhrana.

I was also surprised to get a telephone call from Protopopov, who had taken refuge at the Marie Palace. I gave him in a few words a rough sketch of the situation, adding that the military authorities appeared absolutely powerless, as the troops were making common cause with the insurgents.

Let us follow the events of this day in the Duma. Shulgin and the Cadet Shingarev, who now lived with him on the north side of the river, made their way thither, with difficulty. On their road they passed the funeral procession of one of the authors of the pre-war prosperity, Alexeyenko, formerly Chairman of the Budget Committee of the Duma. As they crossed the river, Shingarev ironically remarked: 'Both banks recognize us at present.' But as they came nearer through the crowded and agitated streets, Shulgin observed: 'I think our role is over.'

At 11:00 A.M. Kerensky, Nekrasov[12] and Chkheidze[13] asked

[12] N. V. Nekrasov, a leading member of the Kadet Party.
[13] N. C. Chkheidze (1864–1926), a leading Menshevik deputy of the Duma and future chairman of the Petrograd Soviet of Workers' and Soldiers' Deputies.

Milyukov to support an immediate summons of all Four Dumas, including the two first which were elected by general franchise. This might have given the necessary basis for popular support, but Milyukov refused. The news went round that open elections by show of hands were proceeding at various points in the city. These elections were for a new Soviet or 'Council of Workmen Delegates,' such as had intervened in 1905 after the general strike had begun and endeavoured to give it direction. Word came that a crowd of 80,000 was on its way to the Duma. The leaders of groups met in the President's cabinet. It was understood that, as in 1905, Labour would be sure to ask for a constituent assembly, and to this Milyukov was opposed. An officer dashed in, asking for help. Kerensky confirmed that urgent action was necessary if any control were to be maintained, and he was himself preparing to start for the barracks to establish it. 'I must know,' he asked, 'what I can tell them. Can I say that the Imperial Duma is with them, that it takes the responsibility on itself, that it stands at the head of the movement?' No answer was given: but his figure, writes Shulgin, seemed to grow to significance that minute. 'He spoke decisively, authoritatively, as one who had not lost his head. His words and his gestures were sharp and clear-cut, and his eyes shone.' His eloquence, direct and whole-hearted, was essentially that which could take command of a crowd. It was decided to set up a 'provisional committee' of all the leading parties except the Rights. Shulgin was on it, Rodzyanko, Milyukov, Nekrasov, Kerensky and the Social Democrat Chkheidze—in a word it was the committee of the Progressive Bloc with the addition of the two last names. Kerensky, by his authority alone, had managed to create some kind of a guard for the Duma.

And now the crowd arrived, and flooded the halls, so that there was no room to move. It was a great unwashen crowd, and the pressure, though friendly, was overwhelming. As Shulgin amusingly writes: 'Ils viennent jusque dans vos bras.' [14] Most of the Duma members were still mazed, and no wonder, at this sudden happening. It was not fear of death, Shulgin writes, death did not

[14] "They come just into your arms," a line from the "Marseillaise."

seem to matter; they were simply lost in amazement. But Kerensky, as he puts it, was 'one of those who can dance on a marsh,' and this marsh was one that had 'little hillocks on which he could find a footing,' like those on the marshy front from which Shulgin had come; or again, changing his metaphors, that there were 'little hooks' at which he alone could catch.

He seemed to grow every minute. The soldiers who had streamed in consulted him and took his orders without question.

And look! One of the first prisoners of the Revolution, Shcheglovitov [the evasive reactionary ex-Minister of Justice] is brought in. He is in near danger of lynching, but Kerensky strides up to meet him, and says in his vibrant voice: 'Ivan Gregorevich, you are arrested. Your life is not in danger. The Imperial Duma does not shed blood.'

And this was like a watchword, everywhere received with reverence. After all there was someone in the Duma who could command, and Shulgin describes the crowd as standing in the great lobby 'as if in church.' As to the rest:

We did not have an idea of what was happening, and certainly no plan or idea of how to deal with it.

All were feeling as if they were in some strange new country. One of Milyukov's opponents dashes up to him: 'Let me introduce myself,' he says, 'your bitterest enemy.'

In one of the smaller rooms of passage was a group of men particularly excited about something. In the middle of this group was a man in a winter overcoat and scarf rather rumpled, grey-haired but still young. He was calling out something, and they were pressing on him. Suddenly he seemed to see an anchor of salvation; evidently he recognized someone. This 'some one' was Milyukov, who was pushing his way somewhere through the crowd, as white as a ringtail, but clean-shaven and 'quite respectable.' The slightly rumpled man threw himself at the well-preserved Milyukov: 'Paul Nikolayevich, what do they want of me? I have been six months in prison; they have dragged me here, and they say I have got to take the lead of the movement. What movement? What is happening? You see I don't know anything. What is it all? What do they want me for?' I did not hear what Milyukov said to him; but as he got away and drifted past me, I asked him 'Who is that man?' 'Why, don't you know? That's Hrustalev-Nosar.'

It was the famous president of the first Soviet of 1905; the Vice-President Trotsky was still far away in America. Meanwhile, poor old Tory Rodzyanko is saying: 'I don't want to revolt.' But Shulgin, who is even more conservative than Rodzyanko, urges him: 'Take the power, the position is plain; if you don't, others will.'

At night the city was arming. The executive of the new Soviet, hastily and very irregularly elected, had by now established itself in the hall of the budget committee of the Duma; one of the Vice-Presidents was Kerensky. Shulgin was by now convinced that the monarch must be sacrificed if there was to be any chance of preserving the dynasty, and, among other reasons, for this—it was the only way of saving his life.

While all this was going on, the Cabinet was also busy. In the morning some of the ministers met at the Premier's quarters. None of them had expected such quick developments. Habalov arrived before the rest, and it was evident that he was completely distracted and quite incapable of taking any responsibility; Golitsyn observes that his report was a hopeless jumble. The colonels in charge were inexperienced men; and Beliayev suggested that the Cabinet should give Habalov an assistant in the person of General Zankevich, who had held a command at the front. He himself visited the City Prefecture, and could find no plan, organization or presence of mind. Beliayev insisted that the first step must anyhow be to dismiss Protopopov. Golitsyn saw difficulty in doing this without the sovereign's authority, but was prepared to take the responsibility if necessary.

The Cabinet met between six and seven P.M. Golitsyn at once addressed Protopopov and requested him to retire from his post, giving the plea of 'illness,' if he desired; and Beliayev adds the comment that, as a matter of fact they very well knew that Protopopov was 'ill' all along. The man, who was to have saved the monarchy and taken all care of the Empress, makes no objection; this tragi-comical figure passes out. 'Now there is nothing left me, but to shoot myself,' he says, but that was to be left to others. No one says goodbye to him as he walks out. Beliayev makes a haphazard suggestion that he should be replaced at the Ministry of the Interior by one General Makarenko; but someone remarks at once that Makarenko is at the head of the military discipline, and that at such a moment this would be a most unsuitable choice; in fact Makarenko points this out himself. The Grand Duke Michael (the Emperor's brother) has come to the meeting; he and Beliayev go off to the War Minister's residence, and there the Grand Duke speaks direct to Headquarters. He urges that there should at once be appointed a Minister who can command the confidence of the country, and suggests the name of Prince George Lvov;[15] he asks leave to announce the appointment immediately. General Alexeyev,[16] who comes to the telephone, asks him to wait half an hour for an answer. In forty minutes he speaks again, this time on behalf of the Emperor. The Tsar tells his brother to announce that he is coming at once himself, and will take his decision on arrival. The Grand Duke lingers on with Beliayev till two o'clock in the morning, and then sets off home for Gatchina. Meanwhile, the Cabinet has dispersed of itself in various directions and most of its members by this time are already in hiding. Protopopov has taken shelter in a tailor's shop.

In the early morning of Tuesday, the thirteenth [February 28], as soon as the Grand Duke had left, Beliayev went off to the Winter Palace, where the staff was still protected by a few loyal troops, drawn up on the Palace Square. The Preobrazhensky, the Pavlovsky, the sailors of the Guard had all gone. General Zankevich had been introduced to his small command. Attack was out of the question. As it was now known that the Emperor was sending General Ivanov from Headquarters, the only hope was to hold on

[15] G. E. Lvov (1861–1925), close to the Kadet Party, chairman of the All-Russian Union of Zemstvos (or institutions of local self-government, established in 1864). During the war he was active in the Zemgor, or the Union of Zemstvos and Towns, set up in 1915 to help the Russian war effort by mobilizing all available resources.
[16] M. V. Alexeyev (1847–1918), chief of staff to Nicholas II as supreme commander in chief and in May–June 1917 under the Provisional Government, commander in chief and once more chief of staff.

to one last fastness till he arrived. Zankevich wanted this to be the Winter Palace, at whose gates he thought that the last defenders of the sovereign should die fighting. Habalov, now half superseded, preferred the neighbouring Admiralty, so placed by Peter the Great that it commanded a free range down the three great diverging arteries of the capital; but what was the use of a free range with only eighty shells to fire and hardly any cartridges? The little band moved from one to the other, first the Admiralty, then the Winter Palace. The Emperor's brother, Michael, who at this point arrived from the last Cabinet meeting, asked that the Palace should be evacuated, so the Admiralty was occupied again. As there was no water supply or fodder, the few Cossacks were allowed to go. But there was also no food, except a short supply of bread obtained with difficulty and distributed to the men, of whom in all there were about 1500. From time to time single gun shots are fired at the garrison to which there is no reply. At noon the Naval Minister Grigorovich intervenes. The fortress of St. Peter and St. Paul has been taken and will turn its guns on the Admiralty unless it is evacuated in twenty minutes. The troops lay down their weapons and go out unarmed; there was no authority with which a surrender could have been negotiated. By now captured machine guns were dashing along the streets with red flags, and fires blazed up at one new point after another in the city. Police and officers were being hunted down, and urgent appeals for help were made to the Provisional Committee of the Duma. In particular, a group of officers were still defending themselves at the Astoria Hotel. As the early evening closed in, fighting continued in the dark; but the battle was really over.

The centre of direction was now at the Duma, where both the Provisional Committee and the Soviet had their headquarters, and throughout that Tuesday it was flooded out, as before, by invading crowds singing the 'Marseillaise.' Its members were constantly called out to address one deputation after another. Rodzyanko in particular, with his bull-like voice, had to make speech after speech. His bulk and gravity, as well as his office, made him the most suitable spokesman. He was doing all that he could to shout into his hearers some enthusiasm for the defence of the country against the foreign enemy.

By now no government controlled, no officers commanded. The committee was hard at work and appointed commissaries to deal with the most urgent tasks. Appeals streamed into the Duma, and prisoners were dragged thither, mostly from the police, who were still firing from some points of vantage with machine guns down the broad straight streets of the city. These men owed their lives to the motto that had been set by Kerensky. 'For that,' writes Shulgin, his political rival, 'let us say thank you to him; let it at some time or other be reckoned to him.' 'They were pitiful . . . these policemen,' he says. 'One could not even look at them: in mufti, disguised, frightened, humbled like the small shopkeepers whom they used to bully, there they stood in a great coiling queue, which led to the doors of the inner chamber of the Duma. They were waiting their turn to be arrested.' By now the President's cabinet was full of prisoners, and the more important of them were housed appropriately enough in the pavilion set apart for the Ministers.

Suddenly [writes Shulgin] out of Volkonsky's room [the Vice-President's] there was coming something specially exciting; and at once the reason was whispered to me: 'Protopopov is arrested'; and at that moment I saw in the mirror the door burst open violently, and Kerensky broke in. He was pale, his eyes shone, his arm was raised: with this stretched-out arm he seemed to cut through the crowd; everyone recognized him and stood back on either side, simply afraid at the sight of him. And then in the mirror I saw that behind Kerensky there were soldiers with rifles and, between the bayonets, a miserable little figure with a hopelessly harassed and terribly sunken face—it was with difficulty that I recognized Protopopov. 'Don't dare touch than man!' shouted Kerensky—pushing his way on, pallid, with impossible eyes, one arm raised, cutting through the crowd, the other tragically dropped, pointing at 'that man.' This was the arch criminal against the revolution, the ex-Minister of the Interior. 'Don't dare touch that man!' It looked as if he were leading him to execution, to something dreadful. And the crowd fell apart. Kerensky dashed past like the flaming torch of revolutionary justice, and behind him they dragged that miserable little figure in the rumpled great-coat, surrounded by bayonets. A grim sight!

Cutting through 'Rodzyanko's cabinet' Kerensky, with these words, burst into the Catherin Hall [the great lobby] which was crammed full of soldiers, future Bolsheviks and every kind of rabble. It was here that the real danger for Protopopov began. Here they might throw themselves on that miserable little figure, drag him from the guards, kill him, tear him to pieces. The feeling against Protopopov was as incensed as possible. But that did not happen. Struck dumb by this strange sight, the pallid Kerensky dragging his victim, the crowd fell away before them. 'Don't dare touch that man!' It seemed 'that man' was no longer a man, and they let him through.

The Duma was now sending speakers in all directions to restore some measure of control, and men of the most various parties took part in this work. The day passed like a nightmare, writes Shulgin. He felt as if they had all been let down into some deep, sticky hole. Night came, and the hubbub grew less. Everyone camped out as best he could. In fact, as Kerensky has written, 'all Russia was now camping out.' The members slept where they could find room—on chairs or on the floor.

On this day (Tuesday, March 13) [February 28] lorries, crowded with revolutionary soldiers, made their way to Tsarskoe Selo, which was only fourteen miles off. No special steps had been taken for the protection of the palace, though at one moment the City Prefect, Balk, had offered to Protopopov to try to cut his way through. Gilliard [17] has described how after the death of Rasputin the Empress had seemed to be 'painfully waiting for some unavoidable misfortune.' Her confidence had been smashed; but she was not one to break down, and she had found a spur to new exertion in the claims of her sick children. The troublesome Vyrubova,[18] who had been moved into the palace and had also caught the measles, writes, 'I kept seeing her beside my bed dozing, now preparing a drink, now smoothing the cushions, now talking to the doctor.' She had had full reports by telephone of the disorders in the capital. About 10:00 on the Monday evening

[17] Pierre Gilliard, the tutor of the young Tsarevich Alexis (1904–1918), and author of a diary, *Imperator Nikolay II Ego Semya* [The Emperor Nicholas and His Family] (Vienna, n.d.).
[18] Anna A. Vyrubova, a lady-in-waiting of the empress, her principal intermediary with Grigory Rasputin.

Beliayev had urged that she should leave at once, which was of course impossible with the children in bed with measles. She communicated with Voyeikov[19] at Headquarters, and the answer was that the Emperor was coming. In the night Habalov, evidently quite overwrought, telephoned that he was still holding the Winter Palace and begged for food supplies; but soon afterwards he finally moved to the Admiralty, and this line was closed. . . . The railway lines were already being interrupted. It was now that the lorries came; and when they arrived the Empress was perfectly calm and courageous. In the evening rifle shots were audible in the palace. The whole garrison of the little town had marched off fully armed without its officers; but the palace guard had assembled in the courtyard; it consisted of two battalions of the Picked Composite Regiment, one of the Guard, two squadrons of the Cossack Escort, one company of the First Railway Regiment, and one heavy field battery. Songs, music and shots were heard from the town. The reserve battalions of the three rifle regiments of the Guard had joined the insurgents and thrown open the prisons. The night was full of alarms. There was a skirmish with a palace patrol, and it was felt that some of the defending troops were doubtful. Accompanied by her plucky daughter of seventeen, Maria, who was already sickening for measles, the Empress went out into the snow and visited her defenders. It was bitterly cold— 40 degrees below zero—and she had them brought in by groups into the palace to get warm, and served them with tea. She herself brought pillows and blankets for those of the staff of the Court to whom she had given refuge. She slept fully dressed, but rose several times to see that all was well and to give the news that came in. By 2:00 A.M., the noise outside was dying down.

The next morning (Wednesday, March 14) [March 1] the little town was quiet. General Ivanov[20] arrived that day with his small force and had a short audience of the Empress. No more news came in except that the Emperor's train had not been able to get through. The family, as we know, had been completely alienated

---

[19] Voyeikov was the commandant of the palace.
[20] N. I. Ivanov, a military adviser to Nicholas II.

from all the Grand Dukes and no Christmas presents had been sent to them this year; but the Empress summoned the one remaining uncle of the Emperor, the Grand Duke Paul, who lived in Tsarskoe. He came, says Count Benckendorff, at 5:00 P.M. in a very excited state, and a heated talk took place. He wanted her to sign on behalf of the Emperor a muddled kind of 'constitution' which he had drawn up with the Grand Duke Michael. He sent it to her typed out next day, but she gave it no attention. Paul therefore signed it himself with some other Grand Dukes and sent it to Milyukov, who received it with the professorial comment: 'It is an interesting document.' The night of the fourteenth [March 1] passed with frequent alarms. In the course of it, the railway company killed its two officers and started for Petrograd. The battalion of the Guard also left, alleging orders from the capital and leaving its colours and officers behind. An armistice was arranged by which the troops facing each other before the palace donned white armlets and engaged themselves not to attack each other. In the town the wine shops were looted.

Meanwhile the Emperor was starting for the capital. He had committed the task of dealing with the disorders to General N. I. Ivanov, the former commander of the South-Western Front, who, when replaced by Brusilov, had been brought to Headquarters as a military adviser. Nicholas knew that he was acceptable to the Empress, who in several letters had urged his appointment as Minister for War. Ivanov was an old, loyal, and tried Conservative, the typical Russian general of the old style, honest and human and always at home with his troops. He has given his plain and impressive record of his journey. At 8:00 P.M. on the twelfth [February 27] he received his orders to go to Petrograd; two regiments from the Northern Front and two from the Western were to be sent to support him. He, like others, had already urged reform; and for this he had felt that the Emperor was displeased with him. Alexeyev, who was entirely opposed to any forcible attempt at suppression of the revolt, recommended that he should only take with him a single battalion, composed in the main of soldier knights of St. George. In that splendid order of chivalry, established by Catherine the Great, there were distinctions alike for officers and men, and the soldier knights were always the pillar of a regiment in an advance. Nicholas had spoken of the troubles as only food riots, but Ivanov told him that the true cause lay much deeper, and that the garrison of Petrograd was not to be trusted. He proceeded to get into contact by telephone with Habalov, with whom he was even able to converse as late as the morning of the thirteenth, when the Government's troops were on the verge of quitting the Winter Palace. He set out in the early hours of Tuesday, the thirteenth, and heard at the last moment that the Tsar was coming too, though by a different route. They conversed at the station at 3:00 A.M. Ivanov was given full powers to act in the capital, and Nicholas said to him: 'We shall probably meet to-morrow at Tsarskoe Selo.' Ivanov did not fail to get in a last word. 'Remember the reforms.' With only one battalion, he had of course no intention of attacking, and he told Nicholas that if he found the capital still in revolt he would not take his men in, to which the Tsar replied: 'Of course.'

Ivanov and his men travelled by way of Vitebsk on the direct line from Kiev to Petrograd, which passes through Mogilev, where the Headquarters still stood. They reached the junction of Dno very late at 6:30 A.M. on the fourteenth [March 1], and at once they were in the thick of things. A number of soldiers who had come from Petrograd were disarming the officers at the station; the local commander of gendarmes begged his help, telling him that Nicholas was also expected at Dno. Other trains arrived from the capital, simply crammed with disorderly soldiers. The windows were all smashed. Agitators were busy making vehement speeches. A soldier dashed straight at him with an officer's sword in each hand. Ivanov recalled an occasion where he had had to deal with mutinous troops at Kronstadt; he laid his hand on the man's shoulder and called out, 'On your knees!' Old habits held good, and the mutineer was removed.

He proceeded farther north, and reached Vyritsa at six in the evening. Here he heard that the Ministers had been arrested and there was mutiny at Tsarskoe Selo; but he still pushed forward, after attaching a second engine to the back of his train in case he was compelled to retreat. He did succeed in reaching Tsarskoe Selo, where he had anyhow intended to stop, and here he had a short audience with the Empress, to whom he spoke clearly of the cause of the troubles and especially about Protopopov. The palace was still guarded, and he was told that Members of the Duma were now charged with its protection; but his own position was ominous. The town was quiet; but armoured cars, manned by revolutionary soldiers from Petrograd, probably dispatched to oppose him, began to appear. It would have been quite impossible for him to rely on his own men, and his presence could now only be a source of trouble. He received a telegram from Alexeyev saying that order had been restored in the capital, and that there was even hope of saving the monarchy. It ended: 'So it would be best not to attempt anything.' So Ivanov and his troops left the little town, and the whole enterprise petered out ignominiously at a point on a branch line farther west.

Nicholas had also started, going by Orshal, Vyazma and a branch railway at which Likhoslavl joins the main line from Moscow to Petrograd. Had he travelled behind Ivanov by the same direct route, he would have come straight to Tsarskoe Selo. He chose the other to avoid dislocating the movements of the troop trains. His train left Mogilev between four and five on the morning of the thirteenth [February 28]. At Likhoslavl, and also at Bologoe, he received telegrams from the capital. At Likhoslavl he learned that a Provisional Government was being set up under Rodzyanko, and that the Winter Palace had fallen; the City Prefect, Balk, and his assistant Wendorff were reported to be killed; the railways were now in charge of a member of the Duma, Bublikov; the travellers were warned that they would probably not be able to reach the station of Tosno. Revolutionary troops were said to be in Lyuban; a railway officer who had just come through declared that they had machine guns.

The Emperor had two trains, one preceding the other, and when this news reached the first train, it was decided to stop in Malaya Vishera and inform the sovereign, who was in the second. At 2:00

A.M. on the fourteenth [March 1] the second train arrived. Everyone in it was asleep, and Voyeikov, the palace commandant, had
to be waked. He went straight to the Tsar, and it was suggested
that they should turn aside due westward and proceed by Bologoe
to Pskov, the headquarters of General Ruzsky, who commanded
the Northern Front and would have the military firmness and
experience required to deal with such a situation. Nicholas accepted this suggestion with complete calm. Several writers, some
hostile like Guchkov,[21] have commented on his extraordinary
self-command and restraint in critical circumstances, which, they
insisted, were not at all to be identified with apathy; and the
picture given of him at this time is very different from that of
Kokovtsev's[22] last interview. 'Well then, to Pskov.' . . . The two
trains, therefore, turned aside and, passing through the junction
of Dno, reached Pskov on the evening of the fourteenth. It had
been rumoured that Rodzyanko was coming to Pskov, and the
telephone was busily at work between him and Ruzsky throughout
the night of the fourteenth.

This brings us back to the Duma. On the fourteenth there was
still fighting in the city, and fires were still blazing. Officers and
police were being hunted down by soldiers and the mob. Troops
were rallying at the Duma. They included the pet regiments from
Tsarskoe Selo—the imperial convoy, the Cossack bodyguard, the
Tsar's railway regiment and even the palace police. The Grand
Duke Cyril of the Vladimir Branch, demonstratively hostile to his
cousin, arrived leading the sailors of the Guard, who were under
his command; we must credit him with the belief that this was the
only way in which he could continue to keep them in control. The
Soviet had already established itself at the Duma. It was a large
body of about a thousand delegates. Its significance had been
entirely altered by the fact that it was now not merely a Soviet of
workmen members, but a Soviet of workmen and soldiers' dele-

[21] A. I. Guchkov (1862–1936), a leading member of the Octobrist Party and
the first war and navy minister of the Provisional Government.
[22] Count V. N. Kokovtsev (1853–1942), prime minister (1911–1914), and
author of the interesting memoirs *Out of My Past* (Stanford, 1935).

gates. The principle that a thousand workmen elected one delegate was supplemented by a representative from each company. The change was vital; for to all intents and purposes it made the Soviet master of the capital. It sat first in the huge lobby of Catherine;[23] but later it moved into the actual hall of debates, crowding the Provisional Committee and its new commissaries, whose authority it did not challenge, farther and farther into corners of the Duma's own house. The Soviet did a good deal of valuable work in the restoration of order; but its attitude to the Duma and its Provisional Committee was more than doubtful. It did not take the responsibility, but it held the whip hand.

Let us continue Shulgin's lively narrative. As he passed through the streets on his way to the Duma, they looked to him like 'known streets seeming unknown.' Great lorries rushed past crowded with revolutionary soldiers with fixed and pointed bayonets, bellowing as they went by. Shulgin paid a daring visit to the fortress. He managed to keep the peace there and arranged for the transfer of the fortress and the liberation of prisoners. He gets a ride back. He describes those whom he passes as 'men who seemed to come from some other kingdom.' All the time Kerensky maintains his commanding position. 'You can go,' he says in the old way to a man who has just delivered a packet to him; the soldiers retire and Kerensky, throwing it on the table, says: 'These are our secret treaties with the Powers; hide them!' and off he goes in the same dramatic way. As the Duma is crowded out and there is no chest available, the secret papers are hidden under a table. Under another table are hidden two million roubles which could not be stored elsewhere. When Cyril [24] arrives with the sailors of the Guard, Rodzyanko makes them a speech on country and discipline and, 'touched for the moment,' they greet him with a hurrah. Work is almost impossible; people come in from all sides to beg advice of the members. Kerensky is calling for Rodzyanko; officers are being killed, and something must be done at once.

[23] The Catherine Palace.
[24] Grand Duke Cyril.

Some of the invaders almost attack Rodzyanko, who exclaims: 'What a rabble!' They are accusing him of being a capitalist. He thumps on a table and shouts: 'Take my shirt, if you want, but save Russia.' Rodzyanko is in communication with Headquarters, which the Tsar has now left. Alexeyev is for abdication. Rodzyanko wants to go to the Emperor, but no train can be found for him; and the Soviet, scenting danger, demands that he should not go unaccompanied. Meanwhile we find the monarchist Shulgin sending the Labour member Skobolev to arrange things at the fortress.

Now is posted up the famous Army Order Number One, which is one of the first products of the debates of the Soviet; it has already been put up all over the town. As will be seen from its title, it was originally intended for the local garrison, which had made the revolution, but its disruptive message was to break down the front.

March 1st (14), 1917. In the garrison of the military district of Petrograd to all soldiers of the Guard, army, artillery and fleet for immediate and exact execution and to the workmen of Petrograd for information.

The Soviet of Workers and Soldiers Deputies has decided:

(1) In all companies, battalions, regiments, parks, batteries, squadrons and separate services of every kind of military administration and on ships of the fighting fleet there must at once be elected representatives of the lower ranks of the above named fighting units.

(2) In all fighting units which have not yet elected their representatives to the Soviet of Workers Deputies there must be chosen one representative per company who must present himself, with written certificate, in the building of the Imperial Duma by 10:00 A.M. on this 2 (15) March.

(3) In all its political actions the military unit is under the Soviet of Workers and Soldiers Deputies and its committees.

(4) Orders of the military commission of the Imperial Duma should be carried out only in those cases where they do not contradict the orders of the Soviet of Workers and Soldiers Deputies.

(5) All kinds of armament such as rifles, machine guns, armoured cars, etc., must be in the hands and under the control of company and battalion committees and in no case are they to be given to officers, even on their demand.

(6) In line and when carrying out service duties, soldiers must ob-

serve the strictest military discipline, but outside service and the line, in their political, ordinary and private life, soldiers can in no way be reduced in those rights which all citizens possess. In particular, standing to attention and saluting outside service are abolished.

(7) In like manner are abolished the titles used to officers: 'your excellency,' 'your nobility,' etc., and they are to be replaced by addressing them as Mr. General, Mr. Colonel, and so on. Rude behaviour to soldiers of any fighting units and in particular the addressing of them as 'thou' is forbidden and any violation of this or any misunderstandings between officers and soldiers must be reported by the latter to the company committees.

This was the first sign of a positive political purpose. The revolution had been made by the soldiers of Petrograd, mostly recruits. The real army was in the field, facing the enemy. The Soviet could not know what it would do, though those who were living at the front could probably have told it. Officers themselves were in a helpless position: there was no recognized civil authority to which they could turn for orders. It might all still prove to be a simple *émeute* which was ultimately suppressed. It would seem that Chkheidze, who was President of the Soviet, had this fear, for as he lay down to snatch some sleep in the Duma that night close to Shulgin, he murmured: 'It has all failed—I tell you, it has all failed. To save it, we shall need a miracle!'

Shulgin urges Milyukov at once to write down the names of new Ministers, and this chivalrous Conservative pictures the conditions in which his courageous Liberal colleague sets about this task:

Amidst endless talks with thousands of people, plucking him by the arm, receiving deputations, speeches at interminable meetings in the lobby of Catherine, wild journeys to the regiments, discussions of long-phone telegrams from Headquarters; wrangles with the growing insolence of the Soviet Executive, Milyukov, squatting for a minute somewhere on a corner of a table, wrote down the list of Ministers. 'Minister of Finance? Yes, look here, that's difficult. The others all seem to work out somehow, but Minister of Finance' — 'Why Shingarev' — 'No, Shingarev must have Agriculture' — 'Alexeyenko's dead — happy Alexeyenko.' [The Prime Minister is to be Lvov, not Rodzyanko.]

So writes Milyukov

holding his head in both hands . . . [He stood] a head and shoulders above others in mind and character.

Guchkov of course is to have the War Office, and young Tereshchenko,[25] the beet-sugar millionaire, who has thrown himself heart and soul into the Revolution, is eventually to be the Minister of Finance.

Of the two impromptu additions from the left, Chkheidse was offered the Ministry of Labour but refused it. Kerensky was offered that of Justice. As a Vice-President of the Soviet he was aware that it was opposed to any of its members joining the Ministry; but after brief but earnest consideration he consented, and carried its approval. By this he established an all-important link between the two rival authorities.

In the evening arrives a deputation from the Soviet next door consisting of Sokolov[26] (its secretary), Steklov,[27] and Sukhanov;[28] and Shulgin exclaims: 'Either arrest us or leave us to work.' Milyukov is engaged in long debates with these visitors: 'With a stubbornness which belonged only to him, he demanded that the Soviet should issue an appeal against violence to officers.' And Milyukov 'persuaded, entreated and cursed them. This went on a long time, it was endless. It was not a (regular) session. It was like this: A few men, quite worn out, lay in arm-chairs, and the three visitors sat at a little table with the grey-haired Milyukov. Really it was a debate between these four. The rest of us only occasionally replied out of the depths of our prostration. Kerensky dashed in, dashed out, lightning-like and dramatic. He threw in some tragic phrase and vanished, but in the end he too was completely worn

---

[25] M. I. Tereshchenko (1888–?), a prominent Ukrainian businessman, the first finance minister of the Provisional Government and its foreign minister, May–October (November), 1917; a successor of Professor P. Miliukov.

[26] N. A. Sokolov, a lawyer, member of the Executive Committee of the Petrograd Soviet; drafted Army Order No. 1.

[27] Y. M. Steklov (1873–193?), member of the Bolshevik Party and member of the Executive Committee of the Petrograd Soviet.

[28] N. N. Sukhanov (Himmer) (1882–?), an independent Social Democrat, author of seven volumes of memoirs, *The Russian Revolution, 1917: A Personal Record* (New York, 1955).

out and sank into one of the arm-chairs. And there still sat Milyukov, stubborn and fresh, with pencil in hand. He jumps up, saying: "I want to speak to you alone." He goes out and gets agreement again.'

Milyukov's persistent patience and equanimity was, as often before, a marvel: the more so as for four days on end he slept as best he could in the Duma. He did indeed succeed in obtaining an agreed statement from the Soviet. There was to be a constituent assembly based on universal suffrage. The constituent assembly was to settle the form of government. All nationalities of the empire were to be equal (here the Liberal would have no difficulty in agreeing). Soldiers, apart from the requirement of discipline, were to enjoy all civil rights. But more immediately practical, and in the end fatal, was the agreement that the garrison of Petrograd should stay, as it was, in the capital; for the garrison meant the soldiers, and the soldiers were the reality in the Soviet.

Late at night Rodzyanko is called out to make another speech in the snow. However, ' "Mother Russia" works again, and they shout hurrah.' Rodzyanko reads out endless telegrams from Headquarters. He thinks the Emperor must absolutely resign. Guchkov comes back from the regiments, very gloomy; his friend, Prince Vyazemsky, a senior usher of the Duma, has been shot dead sitting by him in his car. Rodzyanko, Milyukov and Shulgin are all for saving the monarchy. 'Russia can't live without it,' says Shulgin. Then if the monarchy is to be saved, and Nicholas' life too, someone must go and bring back his abdication, and this task is entrusted to Guchkov and Shulgin. At five o'clock in the morning Guchkov writes out the text for the Emperor—not nearly as well as Nicholas was to write it himself. The two of them in the early dawn make their way to the station, which they find empty. A train is supplied in twenty minutes, and they start.

According to N. Sokolov, the Emperor had a prolonged talk on the long telephone with the Empress before leaving Headquarters. The agitating reports which he received in quick succession on the train must have shown him that the position was desperate. On his arrival at Pskov he did at last offer serious concessions, which Ruzsky communicated to Rodzyanko by telephone. He was now ready to satisfy the request of his Prime Minister and others to appoint a Premier who had the confidence of the country, presumably Rodzyanko, and to give him full authority for control over his colleagues and direction of policy, leaving to the sovereign as imperial prerogatives only foreign policy and the fighting services. Rodzyanko was himself already losing out in Petrograd, and he replied that these concessions came too late, as was only too evident there. Ruzsky reported the result of his talk at one o'clock at night. The four divisions to be sent respectively from the northern and western fronts had failed to materialize; the two northern divisions revolted between Luga and Gatchina on their way to the capital, and the two from the western front never got anywhere.

Alexeyev, on hearing from Rodzyanko, had on March 14 [March 1] consulted by telephonogram all the Generals in command of Fronts,[29] putting to them the question of abdication. From all five he received the same answer: they all regarded it as indispensable. These answers were all communicated to Ruzsky on the morning of Thursday, March 15 [March 2], and he reported them to the Emperor. He also asked both his two next subordinate officers, Danilov and Savich, to give their opinion, and it was the same. Nicholas was greatly disturbed. They put it to him that, in face of the foreign enemy, this was the only course which could unite the nation. What guided him throughout was the fear of a civil war on his account, and he readily answered that there was no sacrifice which he was not ready to make for Russia. A form of abdication had been sent by Alexeyev, and the Emperor, using his own words, gave over the throne to his son, Alexis, for whom the Grand Duke Michael was to act as regent. This was the programme of the Progressive Bloc and the Duma Committee, and had no doubt been communicated to Alexeyev. The document was dated 3:00 P.M. March 15 [March 2].

The abdication was to have been sent on by telephone to

---

[29] The Grand Duke Nicholas, Caucasus; Sakharov, chief of staff, Rumania; Brusilov, the southwestern front; Evert, the western front; Ruzsky, the northern front.

Rodzyanko by the commandant of the palace, Voyeikov, who was still with the Emperor. But it was now known at Pskov that Guchkov and Shulgin were on their way thither. Ruzsky therefore decided to hold it up till Guchkov and Shulgin had arrived; and it was well that he did so. In the interval Nicholas consulted his own doctor, who travelled with him, Fedorov, asking him if his son's ailment was incurable. Fedorov, a devoted and loyal servant, had to say that it was. Nicholas decided, therefore, to abdicate in favour not of his son, but of his brother Michael. This was, as a matter of fact, directly illegal; the order of succession to the throne had been definitely settled by the Emperor Paul on his accession in 1801, and no departure could be made from it except by a formal renunciation, which in the boy's tender years would not have been in order; nor was he there to make it, as he was with his mother at Tsarskoe. On the other hand, the whole plan of the Duma Committee to save the monarchy depended on the accession of Alexis, as a regency was the obvious way of establishing a constitutional regime. To the country Michael would simply be another Romanov Tsar.

Guchkov and Shulgin, after a bleak journey through the mournful winter landscape of north Russia, reached Pskov at ten in the evening. They were the right men for the occasion. Guchkov would be sure to bring back the abdication, and Shulgin would see that the demand was presented in the most delicate way; his presence alone would make it clear that this demand was universal. Both men have given their accounts of what happened. Guchkov was full of pity at approaching his arch-enemy at the moment of his deepest humiliation. Shulgin was affectionate and deeply distressed, and, above all, awed by this fateful crisis in the history of the Russian monarchy.

In the sympathetic accounts of this scene which both men have given, one feels at once that it was Nicholas who was master of the situation. Here was a part to play which was entirely in keeping with the best and highest in his character. There was no real difficulty about the abdication itself—had he not been abdicating through the whole time of his reign?—and he was returning to the role for which nature had all along fitted him, that of the good loser, the willing accepter of defeat. The whole scene was one of a triumphant simplicity. He greeted them kindly, and in the sitting-room of his train they sat down to a simple talk. Guchkov spoke much too long; and the only gesture of impatience which Shulgin remarked was a look which seemed to ask: 'Is all this necessary?' But Guchkov spoke extremely well. He laid a quiet emphasis on the abandonment of the palace by the picked troops of the Guard, as the proof that there was no other way open. He and Nicholas had one thing in common, a burning Russian patriotism, and it was on this ground that he asked for abdication. The Emperor, speaking in a quiet voice, made no difficulty at all; but he communicated the all-important change which he had made in the order of succession, adding simply 'You will understand a father's feelings.' The two messengers were taken aback; they saw at once the difficulties of the change, and they asked if they might not discuss it between themselves, but they did not insist. The Emperor went for the corrected document, and handed it to them with the dignity of simplicity. The text, which is well known, in its final form runs as follows:

In this great struggle with a foreign enemy, who for nearly three years has tried to enslave our country, the Lord God has been pleased to send down on Russia a new, heavy trial. The internal popular disturbances which have begun, threaten to have a disastrous effect on the future conduct of this persistent war. The destiny of Russia, the honour of our heroic army, the good of the people, the whole future of our dear country demand that whatever it cost, the war should be brought to a victorious end. The cruel enemy is gathering his last forces, and already the hour is near when our gallant army, together with our glorious allies, will be able finally to crush the enemy. In these decisive days in the life of Russia, we have thought it a duty of conscience to facilitate for our people a close union and consolidation of all national forces for the speedy attainment of victory; and, in agreement with the Imperial Duma, we have thought it good to abdicate from the throne of the Russian State, and to lay down the supreme power. Not wishing to part with our dear son, we hand over our inheritance to our brother, the Grand Duke Michael Alexandrovich, and give him our blessing to mount the throne of the Russian

State. We bequeath it to our brother to direct the forces of the State in full and inviolable union with the representatives of the people in the legislative institutions, on those principles which will by them be established. In the name of our dearly loved country, we call on all faithful sons of the Fatherland to fulfil their sacred duty to him by obedience to the Tsar at a heavy moment of national trials, to help him, together with the representatives of the people, to bring the Russian State on to the road of victory, prosperity and glory. May the Lord God help Russia!—NICHOLAS.

Shulgin suggested two insertions. The first was that the new document should be dated at the same hour as the earlier one. The Emperor understood that this was to absolve the messengers from having used pressure, and he agreed at once. Shulgin further suggested that the reference to the Grand Duke Michael should include a public pledge to the new regime, and this too Nicholas accepted, improving on the wording suggested to him.

There was also the need of appointing a new Premier, and the Emperor no doubt assumed that this would be Rodzyanko. He simply turned to them: 'Who do you think?' They replied, 'Prince Lvov,' and the Emperor, in a curiously suggestive tone said: 'Oh, Lvov? Very well, Lvov.' He recognized that Rodzyanko was passed over, and that the man chosen was the head of the Zemstvo Red Cross, which he had learned to regard as the prospective organization of revolution. The appointment was made in the form of a message to the Senate, the highest legal authority in the country.

The Emperor stood up, and he and Shulgin had a few words of conversation in a corner of the compartment.

The Emperor looked at me, and perhaps he read in my eyes the feelings which were distressing me, because in his own there was something like an invitation to speak, and my words came of themselves: 'Oh, Your Majesty, if you had done all this earlier, even as late as the last summoning of the Duma, perhaps all that—' and I could not finish. The Tsar looked at me in a curiously simple way: 'Do you think it might have been avoided?'

Even his enemy Guchkov could feel only the deepest pity, as he noticed how those around him, who were the Emperor's own men, showed a complete indifference to his fate. We cannot be surprised that Nicholas wrote in his diary that night—the very economy of words made it the more impressive—'All around treachery, cowardice and deceit.' The isolation was complete.

While the messengers were away, very much had happened in Petrograd. Order had been comparatively restored; but now that the masses had their own voice in the Soviet, things were moving at a breakneck pace to the left. The deed of abdication and the appointment of Lvov as Prime Minister had been dispatched in advance of them by telephone, and the names of the new Ministers were now published; Guchkov was to find that without his being consulted the Naval Ministry had also been entrusted to him. To one of the deputations which in constant succession were visiting the Duma, Milyukov committed the new Government to the principle of constitutional monarchy. He was at once shouted down. The crowd would have no more Romanovs. Guchkov, immediately on his arrival, was invited to address the railway men in a hall at the station, and was faced with a demand to hand over the deed of abdication. Shulgin, addressing another audience in the station, had announced the accession of Michael in words of fervent patriotism, and had even obtained a fairly vigorous hurrah; but he was directly afterwards called to the telephone and, speaking in a voice so hoarse as to be unrecognizable, Milyukov begged him to say nothing about the document and to send it as best he could to the Provisional Government. Bublikov, now responsible for the railways, had sent an emissary to fetch it. Meanwhile Guchkov had had to face a number of angry questions from the railway men, and in fact the doors had been closed to prevent his departure. Shulgin managed to get him out, and another emissary of the new Government brought them with difficulty through the crowd to a motor which was waiting for them. It took them straight to No. 10 on the Millionnaya, where the new Ministers were assembled with the Grand Duke Michael, discussing whether or not he should ascend the throne.

The Grand Duke, a tall youngish man with a pale face, looking, as Shulgin thought, the very picture of fragility, sat in an arm chair in a private drawing room, surrounded by the new Ministers whose authority was so fragile. The question was keenly debated. Both Rodzyanko and Lvov spoke against his acceptance of the throne. On the other side, as Shulgin writes, Milyukov, looking for the time quite worn out, in a voice hoarse from innumerable speeches, almost croaked out the last plea for the monarchy. How strange his words would have sounded to the Liberal leader ten years before. The monarchy was the axle of Russia; there was no Russia without it; the oath to the sovereign was the one thing that bound the country together; it was the people's sanction, its approval, its agreement; the State could not exist without it. It was a passionate plea. Guchkov simply expressed his entire agreement. On the other side was Kerensky. He, like Rodzyanko, expected that if the Grand Duke accepted, his life could not be guaranteed. The Grand Duke asked for half an hour to think it over, and retired. He invited to consult with him Lvov and Rodzyanko. Then he came in and announced that he would only accept if invited by the coming Constituent Assembly; and a second deed of abdication within twenty-four hours, apart from the dismissal of the claim of Alexis, was typed out at one of the desks in the children's school-room next door.

The Russian monarchy, which had stood for over a thousand years, had crumbled to pieces. . . .

2. The Liberal Revolution Reappraised by a Russian Conservative: The Conspiratorial Theory

GEORGE KATKOV

The first act of the drama of the Russian Revolution is usually known as the liberal revolution. It resulted in the overthrow of the autocratic Tsarist regime, and the installation in its place of a liberal, shaky Provisional Government competing for influence and prestige with the Petrograd Soviet of Workers' and Soldiers' Deputies.

Most Western scholars who have dealt with this crucial opening phase of the upheaval usually agree on two points. There is general

SOURCE: George Katkov, *Russia 1917: The February Revolution* (New York: Harper & Row, 1967), pp. 416–30. Copyright © by George Katkov. Reprinted by permission of Harper & Row, Publishers, and Longmans, Green & Co. Limited.

agreement on the rottenness and hopeless inefficiency of the Tsarist regime. It deserved its fate. The regime was actually not overthrown, it collapsed almost by itself. There is also a convergence of opinion on the point that the movement that swept away the dynasty was on the whole a spontaneous affair precipitated by the bread riots of March 8 (February 23). The political parties, including the revolutionary ones, joined only later on. Even some Soviet historians who, as a rule, have presented not only the coup d'etat of October-November, but the whole revolutionary continuum that preceded their triumph as a product of the conscious planning of Communist leadership, are now reconsidering this point. They recently tend to admit, at least tacitly, that spontaneity did play a considerable role in the overthrow of the Tsardom, and that even the Bolshevik Party was caught unawares by the events in the streets of the capital. A good example of this approach is the book by a leading Soviet historian, E. N. Burdzhalov, Vtoraia Russkaia Revoliutsiia (Moscow, 1967), mentioned already in the Introduction.

The dialogue of the liberals and Marxists centering about the issue, spontaneity versus planning, was recently interrupted by the publication of a work by an emigré Russian historian of conservative views, George Katkov of St. Anthony's College, Oxford. His book, Russia 1917: The February Revolution, is a daring and ingenious attempt at re-examining various aspects of the liberal phase of the Revolution. Katkov has challenged the alleged spontaneity of the liberal revolution. According to him the theory of spontaneity is a cover for ignorance. The Revolution, writes Katkov, had been prepared by the conscious, persistent, and largely underground activities of various domestic opponents of the Imperial regime, some of them cooperating consciously or unconsciously with the foreign enemies of Russia. Among the foreign foes he includes, first of all, the German government; Berlin, he argues, had its long range Revolutionierungspolitik which aimed at subverting a regime committed to an alliance with France and Great Britain. They had at their disposal large funds and a host of agents, some of whose activities culminated in the dispatch of Lenin to Russia in April 1917.

By the domestic enemies of the Tsarist regime, Katkov means not only the numerous open opposition parties and groups but also the clandestine Free Masonic lodges. They, according to Katkov, played a crucial role in the political agitation which gradually corroded the prestige and popularity of the Imperial family and regime, and eventually, by means of slanderous and often vitriolic propaganda, discredited the dynasty in the eyes of many people. Quoting the memoirs of Paul Miliukov and other evidence, Katkov suggests that no less than four key members of the Provisional Government were Free Masons. In addition, members of the specifically Russian form of Free Masonry permeated most opposition parties, as well as the various civic auxiliary organizations created ad hoc to help the country's war effort. Everywhere inside them, argues Katkov, the Free Masons and their allies, "carried on revolutionary propaganda and inclined the leadership to action for the overthrow of the Tsarist régime."

Katkov also intimates that there might have been some connections between the Free Masonic lodges and the activities of the German intelligence in Russia. He claims that, despite the previous military setbacks and organizational shortcomings, the strategic situation of Russia was far from desperate. Quite the contrary, by the autumn of 1916 the front was stabilized and the staggering losses of the first two years of fighting replaced. Despite a certain lowering of its morale, so strikingly high in 1914 and at the beginning of 1915, the Russian army, from a logistic and technological point of view was better equipped than any time during the war. The domestic effort, combined with the war materials supplied by the Western allies through Murmansk in the North and Vladivostok in the Far East, provided the Russian soldiers quite well with the weapons and ammunition that were needed for the great offensive planned for the spring of 1917. Thus the overthrow of the Imperial regime came at a most inopportune moment. His explanation of these phenomena is that not the failures but the successes of the regime prompted its opponents to act; they struck in order to prevent Nicholas II and his administration from capitalizing on the impending gains of the coming great spring offensive. The opposition, which had for a long time been accusing the Imperial regime of criminal inefficiency and defeatism, was now so much afraid of being discredited and consequently losing political credit in the country that it made the supreme effort to overthrow the regime by all available means, exactly to prevent it from reaping political benefits from its successful political and military spade work. In balance, argues the author, the mistakes of the Russian regime were not greater than those of the other belligerent powers.

The hero of Katkov's story is the silent, saintly and profoundly wise *statesman, the emperor himself. He was, according to the author, not only a good husband and father but also a statesman-like leader and, in addition, always a perfect gentleman. Although Katkov's thesis is not supported with sufficient evidence, his views, including the conspiratorial factor, have to be taken into account by students of the Revolution, if only as a stimulating contrast to the monotonous unanimity of the traditional condemnations of the Russian Imperial regime.*

Katkov's views are summarized in the closing chapter of his book, given here in its entirety.

★　★　★　★　★

1. 'WAS THERE A REVOLUTION?'

With the renunciation of the throne by Grand Duke Michael and the publication of the document which formed the constitutional basis for the Provisional Government for the next eight months, what is known as the February Revolution in Russia, that is the transition from the autocracy of Nicholas II to the dictatorship of the Provisional Government, was completed. From the point of view of liberals of the type of Milyukov or Maklakov or Nolde,[1] the revolution had taken place and was finished. For revolutionaries of the type of Kerensky, however, it had hardly begun.

The question whether there was a February Revolution in Russia in 1917 is, therefore, not entirely whimsical, except perhaps for people who might think of it as a question of the type: 'Was there a blizzard in Petrograd in February 1917?' This can be answered in the indicative mood, and would express a matter of fact. A simple 'yes' or 'no' to the question: 'Was there a revolution?' is not of the same character as a 'yes' or 'no' to the question: 'Was there a blizzard?' It does not tell us whether certain events took place or not, but rather what the person answering felt

---

[1] Baron B. E. Nolde (1876–1948), international lawyer and historian, chief legal adviser of the ministry of foreign affairs, close to the Kadet Party; together with another Kadet, V. D. Nabokov (1896–1922), drafted the abdication proclamation of Nicholas II.

about them, i.e. whether he believed that his political hopes and aspirations (or perhaps fears and apprehensions) had been fulfilled by what had happened, or not. It expresses a deep-seated emotional attitude towards the surrounding political and social realities of the time rather than the momentary state of jubilation which affected almost everybody at that moment. The almost universal elation which followed the announcement of the two abdications and of the formation of the Provisional Government, and which spread all over Russia (so that the Tsar's ADC Governor-General in Tashkent, Kuropatkin, could describe his feelings in almost the same terms as the SR intellectual Zenzinov[2] in Petrograd) by no means reflected a uniform attitude to the February events. For many it was a sign of relief that the whole business had not ended in massacre; while for others it was an expression of joy at the prospect of things to come. The latter confidently expected that the masses of the people, freed from their age-old shackles, were about to play their part, not only in Russia but also in the political life of humanity at large, in particular in international affairs. It is therefore misleading to say that people accepted or welcomed the February revolution of 1917. What they accepted and welcomed they often had not had the opportunity to formulate or think about articulately. Without an analysis in depth of such emotional attitudes, we cannot understand the peculiar, dreamlike terminology of revolutionary pronouncements concerning the 'defence of the conquests of the revolution,' the appeals for 'a deepening of the revolution,' etc. etc. But this was not part of our task in writing this book. This belongs to the sad and tragic history of the Provisional Government of Russia, which began on 4 [17] March 1917 and ended on 26 October [November 8] with its arrest and the seizure of power by Lenin and his henchmen.

But it must be said that the same emotionalism seriously affected the perception of events by those who were closest to them in the February days. When Prince Lvov, Rodzyanko or Milyukov

---

[2] V. M. Zenzinov (1880–1953), prominent member of the Social Revolutionary Party.

claimed in the announcement which they signed jointly on 2 (15) March that the Provisional Committee of the State Duma had won a victory over the dark forces of the old régime, with the assistance [sic] and the sympathy of the capital's garrison and population, they must have known very well that as a statement of fact this was simply not true. And yet the statement fairly reflects their desire to become the leading factor in the popular rising, which they had neither initiated nor directed until the crowds of workers, soldiers and intelligentsia beleaguered and invaded the Tauride Palace and demanded to be heard, harangued, organised and made use of politically. It took some years for Milyukov to moderate the effects of revolutionary phrase-mongering on his historical analysis. In his *History of the Russian Revolution*, written in the spring and summer of 1918, he still claimed that it was the Duma that had deposed the monarchy. Years later he corrected this statement, but it would obviously have taken him many more years to free his historical thinking of the influence of the political jargon which dominated his mind in February 1917. Possibly this is beyond human powers in general, although another historian of the Russian revolution, S. P. Melgunov,[3] more conscious of the dangers facing an eyewitness who writes history, came very near to freeing himself completely from such influences and to dealing objectively with such pseudo-factual statements as: 'The revolution became victorious in the Petrograd streets late in the evening of 27 February' [March 12]. He has done splendid work in clarifying and exposing the origins of many a legend. But even he clings to one fatal misconception about the revolution which unfortunately has conquered the imagination of Western historians of the revolution as well, and which is particularly important to clear up: this is the notion of the 'spontaneity' of the Russian revolution which has been the point of departure for many histories of it.

[3] S. P. Melgunov (1879–1956), historian and journalist, author of several books on the Revolution: *The Red Terror in Russia* (London, 1931), *Na puti k dvortsvomu perevarotu* [The Way Towards a Palace Revolution] (Paris, 1931), *Kak Bolsheviki zakvatili vlast* [How the Bolsheviks Seized Power] (Paris, 1953).

2. Spontaneity

Paradoxically, those who regarded the February events as the fulfillment of their prophecies of revolution disclaimed both the responsibility and the honour of bringing them about. This applies in particular to the revolutionary parties, including the few Bolsheviks then active underground in Russia. It was their denials on this score which prompted the theory of the *spontaneous* nature of the February revolution. Thus in a passage introducing his account of the events of 1917, in his book *The Bolshevik Revolution 1917–1923*, E. H. Carr writes:

The February Revolution of 1917 which overthrew the Romanov dynasty was the spontaneous outbreak of a multitude exasperated by the privations of the war and by manifest inequality in the distribution of burdens. It was welcomed and utilized by a broad spectrum of the bourgeoisie and of the official class, which had lost confidence in the autocratic system of government and especially in the persons of the Tsar and of his advisers; it was from this section of the population that the first Provisional Government was drawn. The revolutionary parties played no direct part in the making of the revolution. They did not expect it, and were at first somewhat nonplussed by it.

We agree with Carr about the passive attitude of the revolutionary parties in February 1917. But does this justify his assumption of a spontaneous mass movement, i.e. one not instigated from outside?

The Russian word '*stikhiyny*,' of which—in this context—'spontaneous' is the translation, suggests to an even greater degree than its English counterpart that the 'exasperations and privations' suffered by the masses during the war led to the degree of cohesion and purposefulness necessary for effective political action. 'Spontaneous' in Carr's context indicates an inherent tendency—a predisposition—of the masses to react to such grievances as 'a manifest inequality of the distribution of burdens' by organised mass demonstrations on the scale of the Petrograd rising. Had such a disposition for concerted and deliberate action existed, it would have manifested itself in some perceptible way in other parts of Russia, where there was exactly the same inequality in the distribution of burdens. Moreover, had such inherent tendencies really existed among the Petrograd proletariat, they would surely have led to the same purposeful and coordinated action among the workers in the months subsequent to the revolution as well. In fact what we observe during the war, apart from Petrograd and perhaps one or two other industrial centres, is precisely the absence of any disposition among the working masses for sustained and purposeful political action, just as in the months following the revolution we see no sign of any such inherent tendency in the Petrograd population as a whole. The assumption that there was a particular quality of 'spontaneity' which explains the scope and strength of the February demonstrations in Petrograd is wholly gratuitous. The theory of 'spontaneity' only serves to cover up our ignorance.

3. Conspiracies, Real and Imaginary

Several explanations less negative than the notion of 'spontaneity' have been advanced for the success of the rising. We may instance three of these.

According to the first theory, the rising could be attributed largely to a satanic plan of the Tsarist police under Protopopov. He is supposed to have played the same trick as his predecessor Durnovo,[4] who was alleged to have provoked the workers' rebellion of 1905 in order to suppress it by military force. This idea is linked with the legend of the Protopopov machine guns, said to have been mounted on the roofs of Petrograd houses to mow down workers' demonstrations. We have already commented on this tenacious legend. No demonstrators were, of course, mown down by machine gun fire from the house tops during the February days. The number of casualties resulting from what Lenin described as 'a week of bloody battles between workers and the Tsarist police' was

[4] Peter Durnovo (1844–1915), a conservative bureaucrat, head of the Police Department of the Ministry of the Interior (1884–1894) and deputy minister (1905–1906) under Count Segrius Witte, who appointed him member of the State Council, Russia's upper chamber. Durnovo was author of an interesting memorandum, written in February 1914, warning Nicholas to keep out of the war, since the vital interests of Russia and Germany did not clash.

relatively small if one considers the many hundreds of thousands of people involved, and most of these casualties can be put down to the few clashes that took place between the military and the crowd from 26 to 28 February [March 11–13]. The Protopopov machine guns never existed. With them vanishes the whole story of police provocation as a major causative factor in the Petrograd demonstrations.

This is not to say that the police were not equipped for provocation. The various revolutionary committees were penetrated and were kept under observation, and to some extent under control. But the plans of the Minister of the Interior for using the apparatus of police control in workers' circles were quite different from what this theory assumes. Protopopov, through his agents, did encourage among the workers of the WICs (War Industry Committees)[5] extremist, indeed defeatist, ideas on the pattern of the resolutions of the Zimmerwald and Kienthal Conferences.[6] But this he did in order to strike—when the time was ripe—at the WICs themselves. He thought that defeatist propaganda among the workers would reflect on the leadership of the WICs as a whole and discredit it in the eyes of the public. There was no plan to bring the workers out on the streets and the police were not prepared for such an eventuality. On the contrary, the Ministry of the Interior dreaded the thought of casualties on the streets of Petrograd.

Indirectly, however, the action of the Minister of the Interior

[5] War Industries Committees (WICs) were set up in May 1915 under the influence of military defeats. The founders of the WICs tried to bring together prominent members of industry and trade to streamline the supplying of the armed forces. The WICs carried out the mobilization of industries serving the war machine and producing for contracts of the defence agencies. In view of the political conflict between the government and public opinion, the WICs, together with Zemgor, or the Union of Zemstros and Towns, began to assume an increasingly active role in political affairs. In addition to the central WIC, the chairman of which was A. I. Guchkov, its local branches were established in large cities and industrial centers. In the spring of 1916 they numbered 239.

[6] Zimmerwald (September 1915) and Kienthal (April 1916) Conferences were organized by Lenin in Switzerland to mobilize the leftist Socialists against the war and to prepare for a new International. Both meetings failed but Lenin's leadership of the "Zimmerwald Left" or the extreme, defeatist wing of the Left Socialist movement chartered the course of the Bolshevik Party after Lenin's return to Russia in April 1917.

did contribute to the outbreak of these demonstrations. By arresting the leaders of the Labour Group[7] of the WICs he removed the very people who, in February 1916, had succeeded in halting the strike movement in Petrograd. Deprived of the authority and guidance of the Mensheviks in the Labour Group and goaded to further impatience by their arrest, the working masses became even more susceptible to strike propaganda from whatever quarter it might come.

Some students of the February revolution incline to believe that it was brought about by the very circles which pressed for constitutional reform, when they despaired of achieving their aim through legal political means. This school of thought holds that the Petrograd rising was precipitated and facilitated by their wholesale denunciation of the imperial government, and in particular of the Tsar, his family, and his closest advisers. There is little evidence to support this view, although general considerations make it less fantastic than might at first appear. The rivalry between the government and the liberal circles for power had reached its climax. The liberals, whose political aspirations had once been favoured by the fortunes (or rather misfortunes) of war, were beginning to lose ground. Should victory, with Allied help, be won during 1917 all their forecasts would be disproved, and it would be easy for the government to turn the tables on them.

But here again the 'conspiratorial' explanation for the Petrograd rising fails. Not only is there no evidence of any liberal group appealing directly to the workers to strike; but there is proof that they had made preparations for direct political action unconnected with the mass rising in Petrograd, and which were actually

[7] A special role in the activities of the War Industry Committees was played by their Labor Group. Soon after the establishment of the WICs, workers employed in war industries were asked to send delegates to provincial WICs as well as to the Central WIC. Although labor groups functioned consistently only in Petrograd, Moscow, and Kiev, the part they played in the political turmoil preceding the February–March Revolution was considerable. The chairman of the Labor Group in the Central WIC was a Menshevik, K. A. Gvozdov (1883–?), who subsequently became minister of labor in the Provisional Government.

forestalled by it. Guchkov and his friends had worked out a complete plan for a palace coup, which would have put him in power in circumstances far more favourable from his point of view than those in which he became minister after the rising. The coup was planned for the middle of March, but the February events took its organisers by surprise. This project, like others of its kind, was in itself incompatible with a popular rising of the sort that actually took place. But, albeit indirectly and unintentionally, the plotting of the palace coup promoted the success of the mass movement. By stepping up their anti-government propaganda, reinforcing popular rumours of treason in high places, whipping up mass hysteria and directing it against the 'German woman' and the Tsar, liberal circles both in the Duma and the Voluntary Organisations had built up among the newspaper-reading public an atmosphere of such unbearable tension that the fall of the autocratic régime was welcomed like a cleansing thunderstorm.

Guchkov must have contributed in an even more direct way to the success of the popular rising. As we have seen, a military demonstration by units of the Petrograd garrison was part of his plan. This demonstration was to support a new government of 'popular confidence,' and was to neutralise any resistance by the old régime, after the Tsar had been forced to sign the act of abdication, or its equivalent, at some obscure stop on the railway line between Petrograd and Mogilev. The involvement of some of the officers of the Petrograd garrison in the plot may well have undermined the morale of the whole officer corps there. When— on 26–27 February [March 11–12]—the moment came to give, receive and execute battle orders, many of the officers were not quite sure which side they were on. The fall of Nicholas II was about to take place, but under circumstances so different from those expected that the officers were in a quandary as to what to do. The success of the military rising in Petrograd was due in large measure to their vacillation and absence from barracks at the critical juncture. Hence the Guchkov plot did contribute to the *success* of the Petrograd rising, but we cannot on that account regard it as a *cause* of the mass movement.

As for the third 'conspiratorial' theory of the Petrograd rising, we have lent this throughout our unreserved support, more particularly in the chapter on German intervention. The belief that German agents were behind it is as old as the events themselves—indeed older, for the Russian government had suspected and indeed known of the German wartime influence on the labour movement in Russia long before the Petrograd rising. But only in the last ten years or so have certain revelations tended to corroborate these suspicions. We know now for certain that from the very beginning of the war the German government consistently pursued in Russia a *Revolutionierungspolitik*, an essential element of which was the support of an economic strike movement capable, so it was hoped, of gradually escalating into a political revolution. The chief theoretician of this policy, Alexander Helphand [8] thought the country ripe for revolution as early as 1916. We know for certain that the German government expended considerable sums on fostering the strike movement up to the spring of 1916. For most of 1916 and the beginning of 1917, we lack evidence of direct instigation of labour unrest in Russia by the German agencies. It would, however, be foolish to ignore the existence of such agencies as a factor contributing to the revolution of 1917, which took precisely the form predicted by Helphand as early as the spring of 1915. It seems reasonable either to suggest that the successful popular rising of February 1917 was organised by the same agents as instigated the abortive 'trial run' the previous February or to assume that it was a direct sequel to the movement begun in 1916.

A political revolution entailing the fall of the Tsarist régime was the maximum the Germans could hope for in organising and

[8] A. L. Helphand (Gelfand) (1864–1924), better known under his pen name of Parvus, joined the Russian Social Democratic Party in 1890 but soon emigrated to Germany where he became one of the leaders of the left-wing Social Democratic movement. During the war he shifted to the right wing of the German SD Party, which supported the Imperial Government in its war effort. He was a go-between with the Government and Lenin in their secret dealings during the war, and persuaded the German authorities to send Lenin to Russia in a "sealed train" in April 1917. Jointly with L. Trotsky, Helphand-Parvus is the author of the theory known as "permanent revolution."

backing Russian labour unrest during the war. The disruption of the war effort brought about by frequent and prolonged strikes was regarded by them as sufficient justification in itself for the support they gave Helphand and similar agents. The revolution came as a windfall much hoped for by some, but hardly expected by any, and necessitated a radical revision of German policy. The problem was now not so much to weaken Russia as an opponent as to effect a separate peace. Again on Helphand's suggestion, the Germans decided the best way to achieve this result would be to bring to power the Bolshevik Party, which alone among major political groups in the new Russia was prepared to conclude an immediate armistice. The dislocation of production could also safely be left to the Bolsheviks, who would effect it as part of the class war. Military sabotage, which Helphand always linked with his strike propaganda, continued to be organised by special German agents trained for work of this kind. But the tenuous and highly conspiratorial links connecting Helphand with the Russian strike movement could now be safely severed, and all record of them be erased. This explains why so little documentary evidence of these links exists.

4. FOMENTING OR FORESTALLING THE REVOLUTION

The popular rising and the mutiny of the Petrograd garrison resulted in the bloodless collapse of the monarchy only because, as Carr rightly says, liberal circles had decided to exploit them so as to gain their own ends of radical political change. The seditious mass movement originally confined to the capital might by itself have led only to a civil war the outcome of which would have been as questionable as that of the 1905 revolution. Liberal circles, however, did not decide to make use of the popular movement in order to seize power and form a Provisional Government until it became obvious that the Tsarist government could not quell the rising with the troops available in the capital.

For months, indeed for years, by their campaign to denounce and discredit autocracy they had systematically, if unintentionally, paved the way for the success of this rising, and for the country's acquiescence in the fall of the autocracy. There were two aspects to this campaign: one was the historiosophic assumption that autocracy as a form of government was obsolete, and doomed to disappear in Russia, as it had in the other Western countries. The liberals believed that in accordance with some inexorable law of history a modern society, such as Russian society after 1905, would change from an autocracy into a constitutional monarchy, wherein power would first be transferred to the educated and property-owning classes and then, in a process of gradual democratisation, to the people as a whole. Experience of the Soviet régime in the last fifty years has taught us that there was no foundation either for the analogy with West European monarchies or for the belief that autocracy in Russia was obsolete, for autocracy persisted despite the revolution. The very fact that the three men who ruled the country autocratically for many years after 1917 had such totally different characters and backgrounds merely reinforces the view that there are profound reasons why one-man political control could be so easily established and maintained in Russia. The fact that the principle of hereditary succession has been replaced by the elimination of rival successors through political slander and judicial murder in no way effects the issue. To say so is not to give moral sanction to autocracy. It would be paying too great a tribute to nineteenth-century evolutionist optimism to hold that the most viable political form is also the most progressive.

The liberals, as well as making the gratuitous assumption that autocracy was destined to make way for a process of gradual democratisation, justified their demands for an immediate change of régime (war or no war) by levelling at the Tsarist administration countless charges of inertia, ineptitude, inefficacy, arbitrariness and corruption. We have refrained from assessing the degree of justification of these complaints; this does not amount to a denial of the shortcomings of the Tsarist muddles and abuses of wartime administration in other belligerent countries. But they may be discounted as a revolutionising factor, since the liberals' main line of attack on the régime was not to expose its traditional and its newly-acquired vices and weaknesses, but to declare it incapable of coping with wartime problems so long as it remained autocratic. Not only was absolutism, they claimed, leading the country to disaster through inefficiency; it had, so the liberals alleged, no desire or determination to lead it to victory. That treason was being committed in high places and a shameful separate peace prepared—this became a liberal article of faith and a recurrent propaganda theme developed in the press, at congresses of the Voluntary Organisations[9] and in the Duma itself. This conviction was so strong and so ingrained in the minds of those called upon to play a decisive part in the 1917 drama that it outlived many other delusions. In fact, it became a mainstay of those apologists who, horrified at the consequences of their decisions and actions, sought some kind of justification for them. Thus, with reference to the mounting influence of dark irresponsible forces over the will and judgment of the Tsar in the last days of the monarchy, Rodzyanko wrote in 1919:

The influence of Rasputin on the whole circle which surrounded the Empress Alexandra Feodorovna, and through her on the whole policy of the Supreme Power and of the government, increased to unprecedented dimensions. I claim unreservedly that this circle was indubitably under the influence of our enemy and served the interests of Germany. . . . I at least have personally no doubt as to the interconnection of the German Staff and Rasputin: there can be no doubt about it.

There can be no doubt about the sad delusion of the ex-President of the Duma. There never was anything like a Rasputin circle or a concentration of 'dark irresponsible forces' of the type pictured by him. Rasputin's hold over the Empress was certainly not to be underestimated, but neither he nor the Empress herself had any circle of permanent advisers. Instead of the circle in which Rodzyanko asks us to believe there was only a squalid snake

[9] Voluntary Organisations were those bodies which were formed initially to assist the Imperial government in the care of wounded and sick soldiers and civilian refugees. Later on the Voluntary Organisations took on all sorts of duties connected with supplying the Russian armed forces; they were the Union of Zemstros, the Union of Municipalities (often collectively referred to as the Zemgor), and the War Industry Committees (WICs).

pit, in which various reptilian figures tried to devour each other. As far as the German authorities are concerned, they seem to have been oddly slow to exploit the opportunities offered them by the complex intrigues of these creatures.

And yet it was this legend of a powerful clique of pro-German 'dark forces,' and not the many proven and documented short-comings of the government and the High Command, which was used as a lever by the liberals to undermine traditional allegiance to the monarch. It is difficult to believe that people who had access to so much information could in all honesty give credence to the rumours of treason in high places. But such an attitude is quite consistent with the sort of fantasies in which the Russian political opposition had indulged since the turn of the century.

As it became increasingly clear that the attempt of the Pro-gressive Bloc of the Duma and of their allies, the Voluntary Organisations, to seize power by persuading the Tsar to surrender his prerogative to appoint ministers was about to fail, the exasper-ation of liberal circles assumed a hysterical character. It was a question of giving up a political struggle which had been going on for almost a generation, and submitting to the discipline of a society based on personal allegiance to the monarch, or else of breaking this allegiance and giving support to a violent coup d'état. The first alternative was rendered the more difficult because any-one advocating it was immediately denounced as a time-server and a traitor to the cause of progress. The second alternative needed a moral justification difficult to find for a mere struggle for power, which in any case appeared unpatriotic in wartime. The story of treason in high places, with sinister hints at the participation of the Empress in pro-German machinations, provided this justifi-cation and lent a patriotic lustre to what in fact was a struggle for power in home politics. This is why, instead of attacking the real shortcomings of the government, liberal circles concentrated on rumour-mongering. Such articles as V. Maklakov's 'Mad Chauf-feur,' and such speeches as Milyukov's broadside on 1 November 1916 in the State Duma, achieved this end to an extent which the authors possibly did not expect.

Once let loose, rumours are difficult to check, particularly in wartime. The very fact that news and information are controlled only enhances the power and increases the circulation of rumours. A hint in the press at matters which it was supposedly not allowed to mention inflamed popular imagination more than a vivid and circumstantial report. For instance, the fact that Rasputin's name was not allowed to appear in the press in the days after the assassination, so that he had to be referred to as 'the person living in Gorokhovaya Street,' did more to impress the various Rasputin legends on the minds of the people than any actual accounts of his debaucheries. Much of the atmosphere saturated with hatred and slander so typical of the political life of both Russian capitals in 1916 frightened even those who were behind all this rumour-mongering.[10] No wonder that later, when the complete baselessness of most of these rumours became obvious to many, and the hysterical trance in which Russian society was plunged had passed, memoirists (with the few exceptions of those writing in the Soviet Union) tended to soft-pedal these accusations and to go back to the claim that a change of government was necessary not because of the wickedness but because of the ineptitude of the monarch, his counsellors and the régime as a whole.

But how are we to believe that the sense of doom which had hung over the political scene in Russia since the autumn of 1915 was due merely to the tedious wrangle between the government and the Voluntary Organisations, each complaining that the other hampered and impeded its patriotic efforts? The Voluntary Organisations naturally resented the ban on their all-Russian congresses, and claimed that this hampered their work for the front. The government, on the other hand, answered with possibly more factual justification that any activities of the Voluntary Organisations for the front were tolerated and indeed assisted, but that the exploitation of congresses for purely political, if not directly seditious, purposes could not be allowed, especially in wartime.

[10] Here the author gives as an example Prince Lvov's speech in which he said: 'Let us turn away from what is vile and contemptible. Let us not rub salt into the wounded soul of our people.'

The sense of doom was a direct result not of this quarrel but rather of the bitterness it engendered, which led to unwarranted mutual attacks and accusations.

5. 'THE AIDE-DE-CAMP GENERALS' REVOLUTION'

As we have seen, a new element was brought into this struggle between the liberals and the government by the gradual involvement of high military circles, mainly the commanders-in-chief of the fronts. The generals, notably Alekseev, Ruzsky and Brusilov, are often accused of having conspired among themselves and with the representatives of the Voluntary Organisations to overthrow Nicholas II. In support of such allegations a statement is quoted which the Emperor is said to have made to his mother when he met her in Mogilev after the abdication. He complained that Ruzsky had adopted an insolent and threatening attitude towards him when urging him to come to a decision. Alekseev's behaviour on the eve of Nicholas II's departure from Mogilev in the early hours of 28 February roused some suspicion among the courtiers. The ease with which he gave in to pressure from Rodzyanko and appealed to the other commanders-in-chief to support the abdication solution produced the impression of duplicity on the part of the 'cross-eyed friend' of the Emperor. There is some truth in all this, but it does not support the hypothesis of what is sometimes called the 'aide-de-camp generals' revolution.' Throughout the war, the generals adopted a strictly non-political attitude. They resisted being drawn into the struggle between the government and the liberal politicians. The reverses and retreats of 1915 had taught them, however, how precarious the supply machinery of the army was, and how easily it could be brought to a stop if the internal political situation deteriorated further. One can safely assume from the few utterances on this subject of the commanders-in-chief that they were, on the whole, against political and constitutional changes in wartime. At the same time they certainly believed that if any such changes were to become inevitable, everything should be done to ensure that they should come about smoothly, without jeopardising the arms and ammunition production, the food and fodder supplies, and the railway transport on which the fighting capacity of the army depended. If Alekseev did not denounce the Moscow plotters, this must have been not because he identified himself with their views, but because arrests and trials of members of the Voluntary Organisations on charges of sedition would certainly have adversely affected arms production and supplies. There is no definite indication that the Emperor himself knew of the existence of these plots, but the degree of his information on the political ferment in the capitals seems to have been much greater than was believed at the time by those innumerable advisers who persisted in futile attempts 'to open the eyes' of the Tsar to the real situation in Russia. It is therefore highly probable that he at least suspected the existence of some of the plots.[11] But he, like Alekseev, preferred to refrain from counter-measures until victory was assured. The aide-de-camp generals did not consider it their duty to ferret out the plotters of a palace coup. Alekseev could easily have lulled his conscience by believing that he had fully complied with his oath of allegiance when he advised the plotters to desist, without, however, denouncing them. To start a political witch hunt and denounce the plotters to the Minister of the Interior would, it seemed to him, be to take a greater risk from the point of view of the successful prosecution of the war and of national security in general than to let events take their course. Should the palace coup succeed, the Army would have to face the new situation without having undergone a major crisis. Should it fail, those guilty would perish on the spot.

After the unrest in Petrograd had begun it was easy for Rodzyanko to convince the commanders of the fronts that the Golitsyn government could not cope with the situation. But on 1 March he went further and tried all too successfully to make them believe that if they managed to persuade the Tsar to abdicate, the Duma Committee would take matters in hand and restore order

[11] In particular the author points out those hatched in Tiflis in the entourage of Grand Duke Nikolay Nikolaevich.

within a few days. Even so the generals, and in particular Ruzsky, showed a total lack of enthusiasm for the abdication solution to the crisis. Yet Nicholas II's consternation at Ruzsky's behaviour is understandable. As the 'ghost train' approached Pskov, those on it hoped that they were reaching a safe harbour where the magic of the imperial presence would operate. The Emperor was naturally entitled to expect that his Commander-in-Chief of the Northern Front would ask him what his immediate orders and instructions were. Instead an entirely different atmosphere greeted him on his arrival. Ruzsky took the line that the revolution had already taken place, and that there was nothing for it but to give in to the demands of the Duma, and to empower its representatives to form the new government. The personal desires and preferences of the Emperor do not even seem to have been discussed before the abdication. To raise such a question would have been tactless on the part of the generals, for the tone of the conversation was set by the Emperor with the words: 'There is no sacrifice I would not make for the sake of our Mother Russia.'

But even when the abdication had been decided upon the generals still believed that they were taking part in an action to save the monarchy and maintain the dynasty. Not until Rodzyanko raised the matter of withholding publication of the manifesto early on 3 March [16 March] did the generals realise that they had been used to bring about a coup d'état which could not have come at a worse moment from a military point of view. Contrary to his tactics of the previous day, Rodzyanko left Ruzsky and Alekseev completely in the dark as to the negotiations concerning the abdication of Grand Duke Michael. And this with good reason. He knew that if the commanders-in-chief at the fronts had been consulted before the momentous decision to renounce the throne was taken by Michael, they would have supported Michael's candidature. As it was, the generals were faced with a *fait accompli* and found themselves discredited in the new order by having shown readiness to support a political solution which was now considered to be both retrograde and abortive.

3. The Return of Lenin to Petrograd

N. N. SUKHANOV

One of the most brilliant as well as comprehensive single accounts of the Revolution is the seven-volume memoir written by Nikolai Nikolayevich Himmer, better known under his pen name of Sukhanov.

Sukhanov, an expert on agrarian questions and a journalist, was an independent Socialist with roots in the Social Revolutionary movements. He happened to be one of the few Marxist theoreticians of importance present in Petrograd when the Revolution broke out; most others were either abroad, in exile, or in prison. On friendly terms with most leftist figures of the time—he knew both Lenin and Kerensky—an editor of Maxim Gorky's papers, he was an ideal eye-witness to record his personal reminiscences shortly after the events. These recollections are presented on a broad and vividly sketched

SOURCE: N. N. Sukhanov, *The Russian Revolution, 1917: A Personal Record* (New York and London: Oxford University Press, 1955), pp. 269–329.

background of Russian political life. His passion for politics, his refusal to accept active membership in any group, his understanding of the fine points of Marxist doctrine, his awareness of the tactics of all factions, and his aloofness from personal involvement in current politics—all this made for detached analysis. Personally honest and incorruptible, observant and precise, he left a document of great literary as well as scholarly value.

Immediately upon their publication, the memoirs became a first-class source for historians of the great upheaval. For several years they were considered a first-rate historical source and were required reading for the Party, which he himself never joined, although he worked for the Soviet government after 1917. But after 1924, a book which described Stalin as a "sort of grey blur dimly looming up now and then and not leaving any trace" could not remain for a long time on the best seller list, nor its author at liberty. In 1931 Sukhanov was implicated in the so-called "Trial of the Mensheviks," a forerunner of the great purges of the late 1930's. Accused of treason, he confessed to absurd charges (among others, promotion of foreign military intervention to destroy the Soviet State and to restore capitalism). Sukhanov was sentenced to ten years in a concentration camp. Last seen in the late spring of 1931, he disappeared without traces together with so many others.

But his seven volumes of Zapiski o Revolutsii [Notes on the Revolution] remain both a literary and historical monument. Translated by Joel Carmichael and published in an abridged form by Oxford University Press in 1955 under the title The Russian Revolution, 1917: A Personal Record, they are a mine of information to all students of the crucial events. Now a paperback edition is also available.

The excerpts in this anthology include most of Chapter 12 ("Lenin's Arrival") and a segment of Chapter 13 ("The Soviet Conquers the Army and the Government"). Both chapters deal with the effect of the Bolshevik leader's return to Petrograd on April 3 (16), and his indefatigable activities in the days that followed. The return was, undoubtedly, a major turning point of the Revolution. As such it has inspired many colorful accounts and even books, one of which is E. Wilson's brilliant essay, To the Finland Station (New York, 1940). Prior to April 1917, the Provisional Government and the Soviet, both rivals in the struggle for power, did not have strong, determined, charismatic leaders. Both camps had more orators and intellectuals than men of action. Moreover, no political party had either clearcut programs of action or the will to act without a program. With the return of Lenin, one small group (about 10 percent of the Soviet!), which was hitherto not particularly active or even outspoken, underwent a revolutionary change: it was provided with a first-class, determined leader. Judgment on Lenin, as man and statesman, varies in accordance with one's attitude toward the Soviet Union and communism as such. There is, however, a rare unanimity among most historians on one point: Lenin was a revolutionary genius. The proletarian revolution was his element. He was devoted to it body and soul, and had a clear idea how it should be carried out under the conditions then prevailing in Russia. His attitude toward the Revolution was that of a lover, to use the expression of Louis Fischer, a biographer who knew him well.

Thus, Lenin's appearance suddenly provided the Bolsheviks with a leader and a program. Their chances in the struggle for power were considerably enhanced. The leader was a fanatic; the program was demagogic. But as the Jacobin St. Just put it more than a century before: "Wisdom is invariably with moderates, but victory remains mostly with fanatics."

★ ★ ★ ★ ★

The throng in front of the Finland Station blocked the whole square, making movement almost impossible and scarcely letting the trams through. The innumerable red flags were dominated by a magnificent banner embroidered in gold: 'The Central Committee of the R.S.-D.W.P. (Bolsheviks).' Troops with bands were drawn up under the red flags near the side entrance, in the former imperial waiting-rooms.

There was a throbbing of many motor-cars. In two or three places the awe-inspiring outlines of armoured cars thrust up from the crowd. And from one of the side streets there moved out on to the square, startling the mob and cutting through it, a strange monster—a mounted searchlight, which abruptly projected upon the bottomless void of the darkness tremendous strips of the living city, the roofs, many-storeyed houses, columns, wires, tramways, and human figures.

Various delegations that had failed to penetrate into the station had found places on the steps of the main entrance and were vainly trying to retain their composure and keep their places in hand-to-hand struggles with the 'private' public. Lenin's train was expected around 11.

There was a crush inside the station—more delegations, more flags, and sentries at every step demanding special authority for going any further. The title of member of the Executive Committee, however, appeased the most conscientious watchdogs, and through the mass of discontentedly grumbling people tightly packed together I made my way right through the station to a platform, and towards the Tsar's waiting-room, where a dejected Chkheidze[1] sat, weary of the long wait and reacting sluggishly to Skobelev's[2] witticisms. The whole square was clearly visible through the heavily bolted glass doors of the 'imperial' waiting-room; the scene was extraordinarily impressive. 'Delegates' were enviously clinging to the outside of the windows, and discontented women's voices could be heard: 'Party people have to wait in the street, while they let people inside that nobody ever saw before!'

But the indignation was scarcely well founded: I don't recall seeing any 'public,' at all well known in politics, science, or literature, that was not Bolshevik. The parties hadn't sent their official representatives; indeed, of the Soviet people or Executive Committee members, besides the Praesidium, specially detailed to go, I think there was only myself. In any case there weren't more than three or four people in the 'imperial' rooms besides ourselves, since the local Bolshevik commanders had gone to meet Lenin in

[1] N. S. Chkheidze (1864–1926), Menshevik leader of Georgian origin, deputy to the third and fourth Dumas. The first chairman of the Petrograd Soviet in 1917.
[2] M. I. Skobelev (1885–?), Menshevik deputy to the fourth Duma, chairman of the Petrograd Soviet, and later minister of labor in the Provisional Government.

Finland. While we were waiting for Lenin at the station, he in the train was already familiarizing himself thoroughly with the state of affairs from 'immediate sources.'

I passed along the platform. There it was even more festive than in the square. Its whole length was lined with people, mostly soldiers ready to 'present A-a-a-r-m-s!' Banners hung across the platform at every step; triumphal arches had been set up, adorned with red and gold; one's eyes were dazzled by every possible welcoming inscription and revolutionary slogan, while at the end of the platform, where the carriage was expected to stop, there was a band, and a group of representatives of the central Bolshevik organizations stood holding flowers.

The Bolsheviks, who shone at organization, and always aimed at emphasizing externals and putting on a good show, had dispensed with any superfluous modesty and were plainly preparing a real triumphal entry.

This time, however, they had a special reason for making a point of presenting Lenin to the Petersburg masses as a real hero. Lenin was travelling to Russia via Germany, in a sealed train, by the special favour of the enemy Government. Even though this was the only way for Lenin to return to his country, it was clear that the bourgeoisie and all its hangers-on would make appropriate use of it. And something had to be done to counterbalance the repulsive campaign that was already under way.

There is no doubt that without the services of the German Government there was not the slightest possibility of getting back to Russia for all those comrades whom the police of the 'Great Democracies' chose to place in the 'defeatist' category. As early as April 11 [March 24], almost a month before his arrival, Martov[3] informed the Executive Committee that he had exhausted all his means, and that if the most radical steps weren't taken, then he and a group of his followers would be compelled to 'seek special means of entry.' Up to the beginning of May no agreement with

[3] L. Martov (Y. O. Tsederbaum) (1873–1923), originally member of the Jewish Bund; later joined the Russian Social Democratic Workers' Party and led its Menshevik faction.

the Allies had been reached by our revolutionary authorities and the Menshevik group was compelled, like Lenin, to travel in a sealed train.

Everyone understood that in meeting the interests of these Russian citizens half way the Germans were pursuing their own interests exclusively: they were, of course, gambling on the Russian internationalists' undermining the foundations of Russian imperialism, wrenching Russia away from the Allied pirates and pushing her into a separate peace. The Russian *émigré* internationalists were fully aware of the intentions of the German authorities.

First of all, however, the aims of the Russian internationalists had by their nature nothing in common with those of German imperialism; and those of our *émigrés* who had come through Germany later showed this—by the whole character of their propaganda and their attitude towards a separate peace. Since they hadn't a semblance of an agreement with the German authorities and hadn't assumed any moral obligations in advance, the emigrant internationalists had every right to ignore with a clear conscience the speculations of the Berlin régime.

Secondly, when Allied and domestic imperialism resolutely denied Russian citizens their perfectly legitimate rights and restricted the political freedom achieved by the revolution, there was nothing for them to do but resort to the services of German imperialism or else completely renounce their just rights.

The passage through Germany was harmful, since the sealed train was bound to come under the attack of the yellow bourgeois press and incited philistia, but it was less harmful than a refusal by the Socialist party leaders to take any part in world events and their languishing abroad, as in the sombre days of Tsarist reaction.

When the reports about the first emigrant train through Germany reached the Executive Committee, it caused great regret; many thought the step a mistake, but only a few individuals condemned it. In spite of the fact that only Lenin (odious to the majority) was involved for the time being, the Executive Committee, though aware of all the ticklishness of the situation, nevertheless did not hesitate to cover the sealed train with its authority and turn its weapons against the policies of the Government, the bourgeoisie bristling with malice, and the rabble.

These were the themes, among others, that Skobelev, Chkheidze, and myself discussed during the tiresome wait, finding ourselves generally in accord. We waited for a long time. The train was very late.

But at long last it arrived. A thunderous *Marseillaise* boomed forth on the platform, and shouts of welcome rang out. We stayed in the imperial waiting rooms while the Bolshevik generals exchanged greetings. Then we heard them marching along the platform, under the triumphal arches, to the sound of the band, and between the rows of welcoming troops and workers. The gloomy Chkheidze, and the rest of us after him, got up, went to the middle of the room, and prepared for the meeting. And what a meeting it was, worthy of—more than my wretched pen!

Shlyapnikov,[4] acting as master of ceremonies, appeared in the doorway, portentously hurrying, with the air of a faithful old police chief announcing the Governor's arrival. Without any apparent necessity he kept crying out fussily: 'Please, Comrades, please! Make way there! Comrades, make way!'

Behind Shlyapnikov, at the head of a small cluster of people behind whom the door slammed again at once, Lenin came, or rather ran, into the room. He wore a round cap, his face looked frozen, and there was a magnificent bouquet in his hands. Running to the middle of the room, he stopped in front of Chkheidze as though colliding with a completely unexpected obstacle. And Chkheidze, still glum, pronounced the following 'speech of welcome' with not only the spirit and wording but also the tone of a sermon:

'Comrade Lenin, in the name of the Petersburg Soviet and of the whole revolution we welcome you to Russia . . . But—we think that the principal task of the revolutionary democracy is

[4] A. G. Shlyapnikov (1883–193?), since 1915 a member of the Bureau of the Central Committee of the Bolshevik Party, which represented the Party leadership in the Petrograd underground; he was active in the Petrograd Soviet and the October–November Revolution.

now the defence of the revolution from any encroachments either from within or from without. We consider that what this goal requires is not disunion, but the closing of the democratic ranks. We hope you will pursue these goals together with us.'

Chkheidze stopped speaking. I was dumbfounded by surprise: really, what attitude could be taken to this 'welcome' and to that delicious 'But—'?

But Lenin plainly knew exactly how to behave. He stood there as though nothing taking place had the slightest connexion with him—looking about him, examining the persons round him and even the ceiling of the imperial waiting room, adjusting his bouquet (rather out of tune with his whole appearance), and then, turning away from the Executive Committee delegation altogether, he made this 'reply':

'Dear Comrades, soldiers, sailors, and workers! I am happy to greet in your persons the victorious Russian revolution, and greet you as the vanguard of the worldwide proletarian army . . . The piratical imperialist war is the beginning of civil war throughout Europe . . . The hour is not far distant when at the call of our comrade, Karl Liebknecht,[5] the peoples will turn their arms against their own capitalist exploiters . . . The worldwide Socialist revolution has already dawned . . . Germany is seething . . . Any day now the whole of European capitalism may crash. The Russian revolution accomplished by you has prepared the way and opened a new epoch. Long live the worldwide Socialist revolution!'

This was really no reply to Chkheidze's 'welcome,' and it entirely failed to echo the 'context' of the Russian revolution as accepted by everyone, without distinction, of its witnesses and participants.

It was very interesting! Suddenly, before the eyes of all of us, completely swallowed up by the routine drudgery of the revo-

[5] Karl Liebknecht (1871–1919), son of Wilhelm Liebknecht, one of the most eminent German Socialists of the end of the nineteenth century. A pacifist, he played an important role in opposition to the official Social-Democratic Party during the war. Continually arrested and imprisoned, Liebknecht helped to set up the Spartacus League, which became the German Communist Party. He was assassinated, together with Rosa Luxemburg, in 1919 by Rightist elements.

lution, there was presented a bright, blinding, exotic beacon, obliterating everything we 'lived by.' Lenin's voice, heard straight from the train, was a 'voice from outside.' There had broken in upon us in the revolution a note that was not, to be sure, a contradiction, but that was novel, harsh, and somewhat deafening.

Let us admit that essentially Lenin was right a thousand times over. Personally I was convinced that he was quite right, not only in recognizing the beginning of the worldwide Socialist revolution and establishing an unbreakable connexion between the World War and the crash of the imperialist system, but in maintaining that we had to steer towards world revolution and evaluate all contemporary historical events in its light. All this was beyond question.

But it was far from enough. It was not enough to acclaim the worldwide Socialist revolution: we had to understand what practical use to make of this idea in our revolutionary policy. If we didn't, then the proclamation of the worldwide proletarian revolution would not merely be completely abstract, empty, and futile, but would obscure all the real perspectives and be extremely harmful.

In any case it was all *very* interesting!

The official and public part of the welcome was over. The crowd, burning with impatience, envy, and indignation, was already trying to break through the glass doors from the square. It was noisily and insistently demanding that the newly-arrived leader should come out to it in the street. Shlyapnikov again cleared a way for Lenin, shouting: 'Comrades, please! Make way there!'

To another *Marseillaise*, and to the shouts of the throng of thousands, among the red-and-gold banners illuminated by the searchlight, Lenin went out by the main entrance and was about to get into a closed car, but the crowd absolutely refused to allow this. Lenin clambered on to the bonnet of the car and had to make a speech.

'. . . any part in shameful imperialist slaughter . . . lies and frauds . . . capitalist pirates . . .' was what I could hear, squeezed in the doorway and vainly trying to get out on to the square to hear the first speech 'to the people' of this new star of the first magnitude on our revolutionary horizon.

Then I think Lenin had to change to an armoured car and in it, preceded by the searchlight and accompanied by the band, flags, workers' detachments, army units, and an enormous crowd of 'private' people, proceed to the Sampson Bridge and over to the Petersburg Side, to the Bolshevik headquarters—the palace of Kshesinskaya,[6] the ballerina. From the top of the armoured car Lenin 'conducted a service' at practically every street crossing, making new speeches to continually changing audiences. The procession made slow progress. The triumph had come off brilliantly, and even quite symbolically.

On my way home I also followed along quietly at the tail end of the procession, far from its centre, together with a few people, including an old friend of mine, Raskolnikov, at that time a midshipman and later the famous Bolshevik admiral. He was unusually amiable, sincere, and honest, an unwavering revolutionary through and through, and a Bolshevik fanatic.

Raskolnikov[7] was in raptures because of the welcome, Lenin's arrival, Lenin himself, because of everything, indeed, that had been happening before his eyes in his best of all worlds. He talked without ceasing of this leader, his personality, his rôle, his past . . .

It would have been interesting to hear what was being said now about Lenin and his triumphal entry, among 'the people,' especially the soldiers; there were a great many of them both at the station and in the procession. Though I don't remember any officers with them, these soldiers were not there as individuals, but in military units. Hence there could be no question of their being Bolsheviks or Bolshevik sympathizers, or even of their knowing anything definite about Lenin and having voluntarily come

[6] M. Kshesinskaya (Princess Kshesinska-Romanovska) (1872–?), ballerina of the Imperial Marinsky Theater, a former friend of Nicholas II while heir to the throne.
[7] F. F. Raskolnikov (1892–1939), member of the Bolshevik Party, contributor to *Pravda*, and leader of the Kronstadt Soviet.

along to welcome him. They were units that had been ordered out by the organizational talent of Bolshevik party workers. Hasty propaganda speeches had been made in the barracks, and in the absence of any serious objection from anyone, or of any serious reasons for refusing, a few units doubtless passed motions about the welcome without any special difficulty.

But I wondered what these soldiers were thinking and saying. Now that they had time to think, what sort of a parade was this in honour of a man without any rank or title, who was not only not in the Government but was not even a 'Duma member,' not even a member of a Soldiers' and Workers' Soviet and was said, besides, to have travelled via Germany by the special favour of the enemy government? Moreover, now the soldiers had heard some of his speeches too—rather strange speeches, expressed in a way not heard before! During the last few days, to be sure, there had no longer been the former violent reaction on the part of the rank and file to speeches against the war. It could be felt in the air that the Soviet democracy had perhaps passed a turning point, and in the tussle with the bourgeoisie for power and for the army it seemed as though the previous acuteness of the crisis might have passed.

But all this had just barely been accomplished, not only without any guarantees against a relapse but also without the slightest assurance that the turning point had really been passed.

On the other hand, it is true that the very decision to take part in the parade, the very fact of the triumph, must have recommended Lenin to the soldiers honouring him, and made his credit sound enough for anything he felt like saying.

Nevertheless it would have been very interesting to hear what the soldiers marching in the procession were saying.

Until the very end, however, we had no opportunity of listening to the voice of the people. On the Petersburg Side I should have turned right, to the Karpovka, but, drawn along by my agreeable company, I nevertheless went along to the beginning of the Kronvergsky, as far as Kshesinskaya's house, which had all its lights burning and was decked out with red banners.

A crowd was standing in front of the house and from the second-floor balcony Lenin, by now hoarse, was making a speech. I stopped near a detachment of soldiers with rifles, who had accompanied the procession to its very end.

'. . . capitalist pirates,' could be heard from the balcony, 'the extirpation of the nations of Europe for the sake of the profits of a handful of exploiters . . . the defence of the fatherland means the defence of one set of capitalists against another . . .'

'Ought to stick our bayonets into a fellow like that,' a soldier suddenly shouted out, in a lively reaction. 'Eh? The things he says! Eh? If he came down here we'd have to show him! And we'd show him all right! Must be a German . . . Eh, he ought to be . . . !'

I don't know why they hadn't 'shown' him before, when Lenin was making his speeches from a lower platform. I don't think they would have 'shown' him afterwards either, even if he had 'come down.' Nevertheless it was interesting.

And not only interesting: such speeches by Lenin, after all—devoid of the most elementary 'diplomacy,' or any calculation of the concrete background and the soldiers' mentality—were quite risky. Now, after the turning point had been reached, they might rapidly promote the education of the soldiery and their comprehension of the actuality of war; but there was surely a greater chance that the nakedness and clumsiness of such speeches would nullify the effects of the crisis and do great harm to the cause.

After he had got his bearings Lenin grasped this very quickly, adapted himself and took a 'diplomatic' line, generously garnishing his speeches with qualifications and fig leaves. ('We never said we had to stick our bayonets into the ground when the enemy army was ready for battle,' etc.) But now Lenin was speaking straight from the shoulder and uttering obvious truths about the war without any refinements. The reaction of the soldiers showed that this was a very dubious method.

I found myself unexpectedly near the gate, where, among the crowd who were trying to push in, a Bolshevik worker was busy making a strict selection of those who were worthy to penetrate inside the house and take part in an unofficial comradely welcome. Recognizing my face he—again unexpectedly—let me through; he may even have invited me in.

There weren't many people inside—it was clear that people were being let in only after a real screening. But the Bolshevik commanders I knew whom I met inside Kshesinskaya's apartments gave me a hospitable welcome. I am grateful to them for the impressions of that night of April 3 [April 16].

The apartments of the famous ballerina had a rather strange and inappropriate look. The exquisite ceilings and walls were out of all harmony with the unpretentious furnishings, the primitive tables, chairs, and benches set casually about as required by business. There was very little furniture. Kshesinskaya's movable property had been put away somewhere, and it was only here and there that the remains of former grandeur were visible, in the display of flowers and a few examples of artistic furniture and ornaments.

In the dining room upstairs tea and snacks were being prepared, and people were already being called to the table, which was set no better and no worse than our own in the Executive Committee. Triumphant and contented, the Bolshevik elite were strolling about in anticipation of their first banquet with their leader, towards whom they displayed a really extraordinary piety.

But Lenin was not in the dining-room. He had been called out to the balcony again to make more speeches. I was about to follow him, to listen, but met him before arriving at the balcony.

Until then I hadn't known Lenin personally, and had only heard his lectures and speeches in Paris in 1902–1903; at that time I was still fresh from school, while Lenin, an *Iskra*-man, was the companion-in-arms and disciple of Martov and Plekhanov.[8] But not only did I know Lenin quite well by reputation but he knew

[8] G. V. Plekhanov (1856–1918), prominent Marxist theoretician, one of the founders of the Russian Social-Democratic Workers' Party and leader of its Menshevik wing. Plekhanov actively supported the Provisional Government against the Bolsheviks.

me quite well enough too. When I stopped him and mentioned my name, Lenin, excited and lively, greeted me very affably:

'Ah! Himmer-Sukhanov—very happy indeed! You and I have had a lot of disputes on the agrarian question. Why, I followed the way you and your SRs got into a fight. And then you became an internationalist. I got your pamphlets . . .'

Lenin smiled, screwing up his merry eyes, and, wagging his untidy head, took me into the dining-room . . . Afterwards too, at my rare, accidental meetings with him, Lenin for some reason was always very cordial to me, until his disappearance after the July Days. But just then he had forgotten: it was not only on the agrarian question that I'd carried on a polemic with him. In 1914 when Lenin was irritated by my 'little magazine,' the *Sovremennik*, he honoured me with his attention about other things as well ('the bare-faced lying of Messrs. the Martovs and Himmers,' etc.).

We sat down at the table and went on with our talk, now on political themes. Lenin, in his characteristic way, laughed rather coarsely and without mincing words attacked the Executive Committee, the Soviet 'line' and its authors. He kept using the expression 'revolutionary defensism,' which had come into use during the last few days, and attacked the three leaders of this 'revolutionary defensism,' Tsereteli,[9] Chkheidze, and Steklov. This was not quite fair, and I felt bound to defend Steklov, assuring Lenin that during the war Steklov, even though he did not say or do anything, 'thought' in quite a defeatist way, while during the revolution he kept to a definitely Left course and performed the most useful services.

Lenin, however, laughed and shrugged this aside, referring to Steklov as an arch 'Social-lackey.' But our dispute was soon interrupted by the envious disciples of the great teacher.

'Nikolai Nikolayevich!' Kamenev[10] called out from the other

---

[9] I. G. Tsereteli (1882–1960), Georgian and Russian Menshevik leader. A partisan of cooperation with the moderate parties, he participated in the Provisional Government as its minister of communication (May–August) and of the interior (July–August).

[10] L. B. Kamenev (Rosenfeld) (1883–1936), one of the closest of Lenin's coworkers, editor of *Pravda* and leader of the Bolshevik faction in the fourth Duma, member of the Central Committee of the Party.

end of the table, 'That's enough, you can finish later, you're taking Ilyich away from us!'

The meal, however, didn't last long. It was reported that about 200 party workers and others were waiting downstairs in the reception room. We were asked to finish our tea quickly and go on downstairs . . .

I of course very much wanted to be present, and I asked one of those in charge whether it would be all right. After whispering among themselves they told me it would be quite all right.

On the stairs I saw Zinoviev[11] for the first time; I hadn't noticed him at all since his arrival, either at the station or there. Though quite a star himself, he was incapable of shining in the presence of the dazzling Bolshevik sun.

Downstairs, in the fairly large reception room, there were a great many people—workers, 'professional revolutionaries,' and girls. There were not enough chairs, and half the audience stood uncomfortably or sat on the tables. Someone was elected chairman, and welcoming speeches began. In general all this was monotonous and tiresome. But from time to time some characteristic traits of the Bolshevik 'way of life' and of specific methods of Bolshevik party work, all of which I found very curious, slipped out. It became quite obvious that all Bolshevik work was held within the iron framework of a foreign spiritual centre, without which the party workers would have felt themselves to be completely helpless, which at the same time they felt proud of, and of which the best amongst them felt themselves to be the devoted servitors, as knights were of the Holy Grail.

Kamenev also said something rather indefinite, and finally they remembered Zinoviev, whom they applauded a little but who said nothing. At last the welcoming speeches were over.

Then the celebrated master of the order himself rose to reply. I shall never forget that thunder-like speech, which startled and amazed not only me, a heretic who had accidentally dropped in,

[11] G. E. Zinoviev (Radomyslsky) (1883–1936): one of Lenin's oldest and closest collaborators. Member of the Bolshevik Central Committee and the first chairman of the Communist International.

but all the true believers. I am certain that no one had expected anything of the sort. It seemed as though all the elements had risen from their abodes, and the spirit of universal destruction, knowing neither barriers nor doubts, neither human difficulties nor human calculations, was hovering around Kshesinskaya's reception room above the heads of the bewitched disciples.

Lenin was in general a very good orator—not an orator of the consummate, rounded phrase, or of the luminous image, or of absorbing pathos, or of the pointed witticism, but an orator of enormous impact and power, breaking down complicated systems into the simplest and most generally accessible elements, and hammering, hammering, hammering them into the heads of his audience until he took them captive.

Afterwards, about a year and a half later, hearing him as head of the Government, one was bound to regret the former orator, the 'irresponsible' agitator and demagogue. After Lenin had changed from a demagogue and insurrectionary into a statesman, Lenin the orator became flat, faded, and trivial, losing both his power and his originality. His speeches became as like one another as two drops of water.

Lenin spoke probably about two hours. I shall not forget that speech, but I shall make no attempt to reproduce its original words even in a short abstract. For it would be a completely hopeless business to re-create even a feeble reflection of its impression: the dead letter cannot replace the living, tempestuous eloquence; most important of all, it is impossible to bring back the unexpectedness and novelty of its content, that now would not only not be striking, but would sound banal, and wretchedly banal at that.

I don't think Lenin, barely out of his sealed train, expected to expound in his answer his whole credo, and all his programme and tactics in the worldwide Socialist revolution. This speech was probably largely an improvisation, and so lacked any special density or worked-out plan. But each individual part of the speech, each element, each idea, was excellently worked out; it was clear that these ideas had long wholly occupied Lenin and been defended by him more than once. This was shown by the astonishing wealth of vocabulary, the whole dazzling cascade of definitions, nuances, and parallel (explanatory) ideas, which can be attained only through fundamental brainwork.

Lenin began, of course, with the worldwide Socialist revolution, that was ready to explode as a result of the World War. The crisis of imperialism expressed in the war could be resolved only by Socialism. The imperialist war (Lenin said 'imperilist') could not help but turn into a civil war, and could indeed be ended only by a civil war, by a worldwide Socialist revolution.

Lenin jeered at the Soviet's 'peace' policy: no, 'Liaison' Commissions would never liquidate a world war. In general, indeed, the Soviet democracy, led by Tsereteli, Chkheidze, and Steklov, having adopted the point of view of 'revolutionary defensism,' was powerless to do anything for a general peace. Lenin sharply and definitely dissociated himself from the Soviet, and hurled it completely into the enemy camp. In those days this alone, on our terrain, was enough to make his listeners' heads spin!

The worldwide Socialist revolution—that was what the Soviet Manifesto [of March 14, 27] called for. But what petty-bourgeois thinking! No, revolutions are not called for, they are not advised; revolutions arise out of historically established conditions, revolutions mature and grow . . . The Soviet Manifesto bragged to Europe about the successes it had achieved; it spoke of the 'revolutionary force of democracy,' of 'total political liberty.' But what kind of force was this, when the imperialist bourgeoisie was at the head of the country? What kind of political liberty, when the secret diplomatic documents were not published, and we couldn't publish them? What kind of freedom of speech, when all the printing facilities were in the hands of the bourgeoisie and guarded by a bourgeois Government!

'When I was on the way here with my comrades, I thought we should be taken from the station straight to the Peter-Paul. As we see, we turned out to be far from that. But let us not lose hope that we may still not escape it.'

The 'revolutionary-defensist' Soviet led by opportunists and Social-patriots could only be an instrument of the bourgeoisie. For it to serve as an instrument of the worldwide Socialist revolution it must still be conquered and made proletarian instead of petty-bourgeois. Bolshevik strength was inadequate for that now. Well, what of that? They would learn how to be a minority, enlighten, explain, persuade . . .

But with what goals, what programme?

First of all, if the Soviet was bankrupt, what should be said about the bourgeois-imperialist Government at the head of the revolution? As far as I recall Lenin said nothing about whether such a government had been necessary at the moment of the overturn, as the direct successor of Tsarism. But it was quite obvious that now it was unendurable. That, however, was the least of it. In general:

'We don't need a parliamentary republic, we don't need bourgeois democracy, we don't need any Government except the Soviets of Workers', Soldiers' and Farm-labourers' deputies!'

For some reason Lenin didn't use the term Constituent Assembly. This could scarcely have been diplomacy. At this point Lenin was still completely fresh, absolutely free and alien to any diplomatic ideas: he still felt himself abroad, where he was not immersed in any real political work and it was natural to say aloud whatever was in your mind. Diplomacy concerning the Constituent Assembly began later and was carried on with caution until its very dissolution; indeed, for a number of months the struggle against Kerensky and the Soviet petty-bourgeois majority was carried on under the banner of the *defence* of the Constituent Assembly.

But Lenin's constitutional system was a bolt from the blue not only for me. Up to then no one listening to the teacher in Kshesinskaya's room had ever had any inkling of anything like it. And of course every listener with any experience in political theory took Lenin's formula, fired off without any commentaries, for a purely anarchist schema.

For in the first place, the Soviets of Workers' Deputies, those militant class organs historically formed (in 1905) simply out of strike committees—however great their *real power* in the state—had up to then never been thought of as a constitutional agency; they very easily and naturally might be (and already were) the *source* of state power in the revolution; but no one had ever dreamt of them as organs of state power, and unique and enduring ones besides. In any case without the preliminary sociological groundwork of a proletarian dictatorship this whole schema was incomprehensible.

Secondly, between the militant class organs, the Workers' Soviets, there did not exist the slightest stable bond or the most primitive constitution; a 'Government of Soviets' in these circumstances sounded like a *totality of local authority, like the absence of any state in general, like a schema of 'free' (independent) workers' communes.* Moreover, Lenin didn't speak of *Peasant* Soviets, and there were no *farm-labourers'* Soviets, nor could they be formed—as must have been clear to anyone at all equipped for a 'polemic on the agrarian question.'

Later on Lenin's constitutional schema theoretically became quite comprehensible: theoretically it meant a workers' dictatorship, the 'iron broom' called upon to wipe the bourgeoisie off the face of the earth and destroy the whole edifice of capitalism. But the complete bankruptcy of this schema was also revealed as well as its unsuitability for the aims of a proletarian dictatorship—to the mind of Lenin himself; in practice this schema was never introduced [during his régime].

Later on Lenin's system turned out to be futile, but it became understandable—in the general system of Leninist principles. But for a very long time the most erudite Bolsheviks (the proselyte Trotsky most of all) floundered around in it and interpreted the slogan of 'Power to the Soviets' quite chaotically. And even then, on the day of his arrival, having fired off his formula, Lenin, who had been known up to then as a Social-Democrat, caused the more literate of his faithful disciples extreme perplexity.

Continuing his speech, Lenin also touched on agrarian affairs. He kicked aside any agrarian reform on a 'legislative plane' like all the other Soviet policies. 'Organized seizure,' without waiting either for the sanction of any authority, or for any state power—such was the last word of this 'Marxist.' This was the 'approach to Socialism' of the countryside.

As for the towns, there was a vague foreshadowing of a vague new order, in which the only thing definite was that in the absence throughout the country of any Government except the Soviets, the 'armed workers' would stand at the cradle of production, at the factory benches. So much for the towns.

Then the thunderous orator came down on all those who falsely passed themselves off as Socialists. These were not only our Soviet bosses and the majority of European Socialists. He, Lenin, together with Comrade Zinoviev, thank the Lord, had passed through Zimmerwald and Kienthal from the beginning to the end. Only the Zimmerwald Left wing stood guard over proletarian interests and the worldwide revolution. Contemporary Socialism was the enemy of the international proletariat. And the very name of Social-Democracy had been desecrated by treason. It was impossible to have anything in common with it, impossible to purge it: it had to be cast aside as the symbol of the betrayal of the working class.

Lenin was finishing his speech. In two hours he had said a great deal. But his speech lacked one thing—I remember this well and it's quite remarkable: it had no analysis of 'objective premises,' no analysis of the socioeconomic conditions for Socialism in Russia. No economic programme was even referred to. There was the embryo of what Lenin repeated many times later: namely, that the backwardness of our country, the weakness of its productive forces, did not allow it to sustain the desperate tension of the whole organism demanded by the war; this was why Russia had been the first to produce a revolution. But of how this backwardness, this petty-bourgeois, peasant structure, this extreme exhaustion and chaos could be reconciled with a Socialist reorganization independently of the West, before the worldwide Socialist revolution—not a word was said. How the Workers' and Farmlabourers' Soviets, representing a small minority of the country, as bearers of the proletarian dictatorship against the will and the interests of the majority, were to construct Socialism—about this too Lenin was completely silent. Of how, finally, his whole conception was to be reconciled with the elementary foundations of Marxism (the only thing Lenin did not dissociate himself from in his speech)—not a syllable was said. Everything touching on what had hitherto been called scientific Socialism Lenin ignored just as completely as he destroyed the foundations of the current Social-Democratic programme and tactics. Extremely remarkable . . .

Lenin ended his speech. The pupils delightedly, unanimously, lengthily applauded their teacher. On the faces of the majority there was nothing but rapture; not the shadow of a doubt. Happy, innocent souls! But the literate ones, clapping loud and long, seemed to stare strangely in front of them; or else their eyes roved about unseeingly, showing complete confusion: the teacher had given the minds of his Marxist disciples some work to do.

I looked for Kamenev, who, after taking *Pravda* in hand, had been happy three days before to vote for a united front with Tsereteli and all the 'populists.' But in answer to my question as to what he had to say about all this, he merely shrugged his shoulders: 'Wait, just wait!'

As an infidel, I turned to another and then a third of the faithful: after all, I *ought* to understand—what was this really all about? The people I talked to grinned and shook their heads, without the slightest idea of what to say. . . .

A joint session of all the Social-Democrats—Bolsheviks, Mensheviks, and independents—was scheduled the next day in the Tauride Palace. It was organized by a group of people who thought that the most urgent task of the moment was the unification of all tendencies of Social-Democracy into a single party and who did not at the same time think this task utopian. I went to the meeting with great interest.

When I turned up in the Tauride Palace the meeting had long since begun, and Lenin had already occupied the platform for more than an hour. He was no longer amongst his own disciples:

most of the audience was made up of his old ideological adversaries. Accordingly, he had to modify his language. Here Lenin had to emphasize the difference and irreconcilability between his position and the views of the majority: he had to talk about what he would do and call on his fraction to do in *distinction* from the majority of those present.

Thus, at this 'unifying' conference, Lenin was the living incarnation of schism; and the whole point of his speech in the given circumstances boiled down to the interment first of all of the idea of unity.

But both the content and the form of this speech as a whole reproduced the first stupefying debut of the future all-Russian dictator. The Bolshevik devotees present, thinking it indispensable in all circumstances to demonstrate their solidarity and their isolation from the others, the infidels, applauded individual points of Lenin's speech even more than the night before. But the rest of the audience didn't share their feelings at all.

They weren't only stunned: each new word of Lenin's filled them with indignation. Protests and exclamations of outrage began to be heard. It wasn't only a question of the inappropriateness of such a speech at a 'unifying' conference, it was also that together with the idea of unity the foundations of the Social-Democratic programme and of Marxist theory were spat upon . . . I remember Bogdanov,[12] who was sitting opposite me, on the 'Ministerial bench,' two steps away from the platform: 'This is the raving of a madman! It's indecent to applaud this clap-trap!' he cried out, livid with rage and contempt, turning to the audience. 'You ought to be ashamed of yourselves! Marxists!'

Shouts like this of course didn't weaken but intensified the ovation the Bolshevik group gave Lenin when he finished his speech. And the cause of a unified Social-Democracy was already

[12] Probably B. O. Bogdanov, a minor Menshevik leader, not to be mixed up with A. A. Bogdanov (Malinovsky) 1873–1928), Marxist economist and revolutionary, author of several books on economics and philosophy, originally one of the leaders of the Bolshevik Party; broke away from Lenin in 1909 and opposed his views and tactics during the war.

doomed. All speeches after that were completely devoted to Lenin. But I remember only two speeches against him.

Tsereteli constituted himself the 'official Opposition.' I don't think that before Lenin spoke he had had any special hopes of unity with the Bolsheviks or was particularly striving for it. It was clear from what had gone before that such weren't the inclinations of this leader of the Soviet Right. Nevertheless he had thought it his duty to take part in the unifying conference; and Lenin's speech gave him every chance of attacking a policy of schism and demonstrating his piety towards the cause of unity.

Tsereteli was supported by an enormous majority of the meeting, including many Bolsheviks. But the Menshevik leader, while emphasizing the absence of the objective premises for a Socialist overturn in Russia, was still far from summing up the gist of Lenin's position with as much success as a short, brilliant speech by the old Social-Democrat I. P. Goldenberg, the most active of the would-be unifiers, historically a Bolshevik but theoretically a defensist.

'Lenin has now made himself a candidate for one European throne that has been vacant for thirty years—the throne of Bakunin! Lenin's new words echo something old—the superannuated truths of primitive anarchism.'

That was one conclusion stressed by Goldenberg. This was another:

'Lenin has raised the banner of civil war within the democracy. It's ludicrous to talk of unity with those whose watchword is schism and who are placing themselves outside the Social-Democracy of their own accord!'

Further, as I see by the newspaper accounts, the future bard and ideologist of Leninist policy, Steklov, also had his say about the speech of his future commander:

'Lenin's speech,' he said, 'consists of nothing but abstract constructions that prove the Russian Revolution has passed him by. After Lenin becomes acquainted with the state of affairs in Russia he himself will reject all these constructions of his.'

The real Bolsheviks also made no bones—at least in private conversations behind the scenes—about Lenin's 'abstractness.' One even expressed the idea that Lenin's speech had removed the differences within the Social-Democracy, for with respect to Lenin's position there could be no differences between Bolsheviks and Mensheviks. However, at the beginning of his speech Lenin had definitely said and even emphasized that he was speaking for himself personally, without having consulted his party.

The Bolshevik sect was still in a state of bafflement and perplexity. And the support Lenin found may underline more clearly than anything else his complete intellectual isolation, not only among Social-Democrats in general but also among his own disciples. Lenin was supported by no one but Kolontai[13] (a recent Menshevik), who rejected any alliance with those who could not and would not accomplish a social revolution! Her support called forth nothing but mockery, laughter, and hubbub. The meeting dispersed; any chance of serious debate had been destroyed.

Towards evening of this same April 14th the Liaison Commission had to go to the Marian Palace.[14] If I'm not mistaken we were invited this time because the support of the Soviet was being demanded for the new war loan, known by the saccharinely hypocritical name of the Liberty Loan. We had to wait for the arrival of Rodzyanko and his colleagues, and while Skobelev and I strolled about the room, Miliukov came up to us. The conversation turned upon Lenin. Skobelov told Miliukov about his 'lunatic ideas,' appraising him as a completely lost man standing outside the movement. I agreed in general with this estimate of Lenin's ideas and said that in his present guise he was so unacceptable to every one that now he was not at all dangerous for our interlocutor,

[13] A. M. Kolontai (1872–1952), a Menshevik until 1915; during the First World War, she became a Bolshevik. Lived in Western Europe for many years and thanks to her linguistic gifts was active in the continental Social-Democratic parties. Shortly after her return to Russia in 1917, she was elected to the Bolshevik Central Committee.

[14] Marian (*Marinskii* in Russian) Palace was the former seat of the State Council; during the Revolution it served as seat of the Provisional Government.

Miliukov. However, the future of Lenin seemed different to me: I was convinced that after he had escaped from his foreign academic atmosphere and come into an atmosphere of real struggle and wide practical activity, he would acclimatize himself quickly, settle down, stand on firm ground and throw overboard the bulk of his anarchist 'ravings.' What life failed to accomplish with him, the solid pressure of his party comrades would help with. I was convinced that in the near future Lenin would again be converted into a herald of the ideas of revolutionary Marxism and occupy a place in the revolution worthy of him as the most authoritative leader of the Soviet proletarian Left. Then, I said, he would be dangerous to Miliukov. And Miliukov agreed with me.

We refused to admit that Lenin might stick to his abstractions. Still less did we admit that through these abstractions Lenin would be able to conquer not only the revolution, not only all its active masses, not only the whole Soviet—but even his own Bolsheviks.

We were cruelly mistaken . . .

About a week after his arrival, the famous First Theses of Lenin were printed in *Pravda*, in the form of an article. They contained a résumé of the new doctrine expounded in his speeches; they lacked the same thing as his speeches: an economic programme and a Marxist analysis of the objective conditions of our revolution.

The Theses were published in Lenin's name alone: not one Bolshevik organization, or group, or even individual had joined him. And the editors of *Pravda* for their part thought it necessary to emphasize Lenin's isolation and their independence of him. 'As for Lenin's general schema,' wrote *Pravda*, 'it seems to us unacceptable, in so far as it proceeds from the assumption that the bourgeois democratic revolution is finished and counts on the immediate conversion of that revolution into a Socialist revolution.'

It appeared that the Marxist foundations of the Bolshevik Party were firm, that the Bolshevik party mass had taken up arms to defend against Lenin the elementary foundations of scientific Socialism, Bolshevism itself, and the old traditional Lenin.

Alas! Many people, including myself, were vainly deluded:

Lenin compelled his Bolsheviks to accept his 'lunatic ideas' in their entirety. How and why did this happen? I have no intention of investigating this interesting question *au fond*, nevertheless I don't think it superfluous here to note a few undoubted factors in the capitulation of the old Social-Democratic Bolshevism to Lenin's reckless anarcho-seditious system.

First of all—there can be no doubt of it—Lenin is an extraordinary phenomenon, a man of absolutely exceptional intellectual power; he is a first class world magnitude in calibre. For he represents an unusually happy combination of theoretician and popular leader. If still other epithets were needed I shouldn't hesitate to call Lenin a genius, keeping in mind the content of this notion of genius.

A genius, as is well known, is an abnormal person. More concretely, he is very often a man with an extremely limited area of intellectual activity, in which area this activity is carried on with unusual power and productivity. A genius can very often be extremely narrow-minded, with no understanding or grasp of the simplest and most generally accessible things. Such was the generally accepted genius Leo Tolstoy, who (in the brilliant though paradoxical expression of Merezhkovsky)[15] was simply 'not intelligent enough for his own genius.'

Lenin was undoubtedly like this too: many elementary truths were inaccessible to his mind—even in politics. This was the source of an endless series of the most elementary errors—in the period of his dictatorship as well as in the epoch of his agitation and demagogy.

But on the other hand, within a certain realm of ideas—a few 'fixed' ideas—Lenin displayed such amazing force, such superhuman power of attack that his colossal influence over the Socialists and revolutionaries was secure.

In addition to these internal and, so to speak, theoretical qualities of Lenin's, as well as his genius, the following circumstance

[15] D. S. Merezhkovsky (1865–1941), writer and critic, author of several historical novels and series of essays.

also played a primary rôle in his victory over the old Marxist Bolsheviks. In practice Lenin had been historically the exclusive, sole, and unchallenged head of the party for many years, since the day of its emergence. The Bolshevik Party was the work of his hands, and his alone. The very thought of going against Lenin was frightening and odious, and required from the Bolshevik mass what it was incapable of giving.

Lenin the genius was an historic figure—this is one side of the matter. The other is that, except Lenin, there was nothing and no one in the party. The few massive generals without Lenin were *nothing*, like the few immense planets without the sun (for the moment I leave aside Trotsky, who at that time was still outside the ranks of the order, that is, in the camp of the 'enemies of the proletariat, lackeys of the bourgeoisie,' etc.).

In the First International, according to the well-known description, there was Marx high up in the clouds; then for a long, long way there was nothing; then, also at a great height, there was Engels; then again for a long, long way there was nothing, and finally there was Liebknecht sitting there, etc.

But in the Bolshevik Party Lenin the Thunderer sat in the clouds and then—there was absolutely nothing right down to the ground. And on the ground, amongst the party rankers and officers a few generals could be distinguished—and even then I dare say not individually but rather in couples or combinations. There could be no question of *replacing* Lenin by individuals, couples, or combinations. There could be neither independent thinking nor organizational base in the Bolshevik Party without Lenin.

That is how matters stood in the Bolshevik general staff. As for the mass of party officers, they were far from distinguished. Amongst the Bolshevik officers there were many first-rate technicians in party and professional work, and not a few 'romantics,' but extremely few political thinkers and conscious Socialists.

In consequence every form of radicalism and external *Leftism* had an invincible attraction for the Bolshevik mass, while the natural 'line' of work consisted of demagogy. This was very often what all the political wisdom of the Bolshevik committeemen boiled down to.

Thus the 'party public' of course quite lacked the strength or any internal resources to oppose anything whatever to Lenin's onslaught.

Lenin's radicalism, his heedless 'Leftism,' and primitive demagogy, unrestrained either by science or common sense, later secured his success among the broadest proletarian-muzhik masses, who had had no other teaching than that of the Tsarist whip. But the same characteristics of this Leninist propaganda also seduced the more backward, less literate elements of the party itself. Very soon after Lenin's arrival they were faced by an alternative: either keep the old principles of Social-Democracy and Marxist science, but without Lenin, without the masses, and without the party; or stay with Lenin and the party and conquer the masses together in an easy way, having thrown overboard the obscure, unfamiliar Marxist principles. It's understandable that the mass of party Bolsheviks, though after some vacillation, decided on the latter.

But the attitude of this mass could not help but have a decisive influence on the fully-conscious Bolshevik elements too, on the Bolshevik generals, for after Lenin's conquest of the officers of the party, people like Kamenev, for instance, were completely isolated; they had fallen into the position of outlaws and internal traitors. And the implacable Thunderer soon subjected them, together with other infidels, to such abuse that not all of them could endure it. It goes without saying that even the generals, even those who had read Marx and Engels, were incapable of sustaining such an ordeal. And Lenin won one victory after another.

The April Days were a remarkable episode in the revolution. It was not for nothing that Lenin, much later, in a speech on the occasion of the dissolution of the Constituent Assembly, said that it was just these April Days that really opened his eyes for the first time to the true meaning and rôle of a popular uprising.

Lenin learned from the April Days, completed his education,

and steeled his fighting spirit. But in April neither Lenin himself, nor the party he had won over, were yet setting in motion the new Leninist science. Bolshevik elements, to be sure, were forcing the movement against the Provisional Government. At this time Lenin's party had already put forward its programmatic slogan: 'All Power to the Soviets.' But it had no serious intention of realising this programme during the April Days. The position of the Bolsheviks was then neither firm nor effective.

In spite of the enormous temptation, in spite of his overzealous comrades' anticipation of events, Lenin, as we shall see, was projecting all his plans and hopes into the future. But his plans were firmly grounded, and during the April Days his hopes soared. It was not for nothing that he had a good word for these magnificent lessons when he was in power, and thrusting an aspen stake into the Russian democratic republic.

The April Days marked a boundary and a turning point: they infinitely deepened the crack in the Soviet; having broken the petty-bourgeois away from the proletarian groups, they—on the other hand—almost closed the gap between the petty and the big bourgeoisie; they created a hitherto unprecedented contact between them and gave a firm foundation to a united bourgeois front against the proletariat, Zimmerwald, and the revolution.

Just as it was impossible to find a line of demarcation between the 'responsible' and the 'irresponsible' circles of the bourgeoisie, so it was impossible to tell where the bourgeoisie ended and the democracy began. Bourgeois-radical groups passed over directly into Right-Soviet ones. The figure of Kerensky embodied even a personal union. In general the 'Populist' groups—Socialist Populist, Trudoviks, SRs—served as a connecting link. The middle strata—practically speaking, the intelligentsia—were organized around these interstitial groups. And behind them stood the vast Russian peasantry. The peasantry was incontestably and almost exclusively dominated by the SRs from the very beginning. Of course these were the *Right* SRs, who controlled the landholding peasants.

In the very first days of May an All-Russian Peasant Congress was scheduled in Petersburg. Both the bourgeois and the 'Marxist' parties scarcely touched these representatives of the Russian black-lands, amongst whom there was a mass of 'populist' intellectuals, but also quite a few rural kulaks, shopkeepers, and various people from the Co-operative Movement.

But however that may have been, this was where the principal force in Russian society and the revolution was assembling. It was just this petty-bourgeois middle, which had not passed through the furnace of capitalism, that unfortunately was and remains the master of the Russian land and in the last analysis determines the course of events. And now it served as the basic lever of Soviet policy, for the interstitial populist parties were no longer bourgeois but Soviet parties, in the camp not of the Marian but of the Tauride Palace.

In the Soviet, however, by the side of the SR Party itself stood the Right Mensheviks, constituting with it a stable and indivisible bloc. It was this Right Menshevik group, of course, that headed and controlled the SR mass, which lacked enough skilled leaders of its own.

Of the Mensheviks themselves these Soviet leaders had hitherto been quite untypical. Menshevism as a whole was *internationalist* not only before the revolution, under its old leaders—the Zimmer-waldites Martov and Axelrod;[16] at the beginning of the revolution too the Menshevik majority maintained its Zimmerwald position. The Right Mensheviks, defensists and opportunists lording it in the Soviets, represented the minority of the party and did not express its opinion at all.

Now, however, at the end of April, things had changed. The Menshevik opportunists had begun to gain more and more ground within the party. The Petersburg organization was still in the

[16] P. B. Axelrod (1850–1928), began his revolutionary career as a member of populist and anarchist groups. During the emigration at the end of the eighties, together with Plekhanov and Vi. I. Zasulich he founded the Group for the Emancipation of Labour—the first Russian Social-Democratic and Marxist organization. One of the founders and editors of *Iskra* from 1901 on. After the 1903 split between Bolsheviks and Mensheviks he became a Menshevik, which he remained until his death.

hands of the internationalists, but in the provinces the party was entirely taken over by the opportunists.

This was of course aided primarily by the immense activity (throughout Russia) of the Menshevik leaders of the Soviet. It was no wonder that in the eyes of the masses, newcomers in politics, Menshevism came to be identified with the 'line' of Tsereteli, Dan[17] and Chkheidze. No wonder that in such conditions the party began to grow in the provinces and the army precisely amongst petty-bourgeois philistine elements. Headed by a group of talented and authoritative leaders, these *parvenu* March Social-Democrats already made up the *majority* of the party, and had changed the physiognomy of Menshevism.

'Populists' and Right Mensheviks now constituted a stable majority of the Soviet and completely determined its 'line.' These were the 'responsible' elements.

Further to the Left were the 'irresponsible' Soviet groups, parties and tendencies. And in the democratic camp this line of demarcation was drawn much more precisely. All the Left-wing opposition to Tsereteli was called irresponsible. Essentially, however, it was far from homogeneous.

There were, first of all, the Menshevik-Internationalists, whose influence extended over about 20–25 per cent of the advanced proletariat of Petersburg and Moscow. This consistently Marxist Socialist group was, however, very feebly represented in the Petersburg Soviet; and by now it was also getting completely lost in the Executive Committee, where at one time it had constituted, together with associated elements, the central core.

To this period belongs an attempt to organize in the Executive Committee these associated *non*-Menshevik internationalist elements. To increase the striking force of the Opposition, a number of representatives of the Left Centre tried at this time to create from them a group of extra-fractional Social-Democrats. It was joined by people of old Bolshevik origins, who were afraid of the name of Menshevism, but had nothing in common with the

[17] I. F. Dan (Gurvich) (1871–1947), one of the influential Menshevik leaders of the Petrograd Soviet.

present party of Lenin. It was also joined even by some former Mensheviks. In the Executive Committee it had about fifteen to eighteen people, including myself, behind it.

However, no one paid very close attention to this group and, in view of the existence of the Menshevik-Internationalists, it found no support outside the Executive Committee. Indeed, it fairly soon fell apart as an organized unit even within it.

Further to the Left were the Bolsheviks, who made up the most powerful part of the 'irresponsible' Soviet Opposition. Under the influence of various subjective and objective factors this party was growing swiftly and irresistibly. And it was growing almost exclusively amongst the proletariat. It was still far from having a majority of the Petersburg proletariat behind it, but by the first days of May it certainly had already about a third. This was reflected in the composition of the Petersburg Soviet, and even more in its Workers' Section.

Some partial re-elections were taking place in the factories, and giving greater weight to the Bolsheviks, who had begun realizing their programme of conquering the Soviet. The Soviet majority looked somewhat askance at these re-elections. But nevertheless it was not much alarmed: first of all, having concentrated all its attention on a compromise with the bourgeoisie, and having been reassured as to its unshakable strength after the April Days, the Soviet majority was altogether too little concerned about the masses; secondly, Soviet leaders were already accustomed to look for support not to the workers but to the soldiers and the comparatively ignorant country folk that made up (even though illegitimately) the overwhelming majority of the Soviet plenum.

The Bolshevik fraction in the Executive Committee and the Soviet was led by the moderate Kamenev. Lenin and Zinoviev and their assistants were busy with party affairs, *Pravda*, and mass agitation. But Kamenev was by now not very representative of his party's viewpoint, for Lenin had already scored a most decisive victory over his Bolsheviks.

It was just at this time, in the last days of April, that the All-Russian Bolshevik Conference took place in Petersburg, in Kshesinskaya's Palace. Its resolutions, passed almost unanimously by 140 delegates, were nothing but Lenin's famous Theses. They were passed almost without amendment. What Plekhanov had called raving, and what the oldest Bolsheviks a month before had thought wild and absurd, now became the official platform of the party that was hourly capturing more of the Russian proletariat. A very few old party figures could not endure it and left. The rest accepted Lenin's anarchism and shook the dust of Marxism off their feet as though they had never thought anything else, as though their own views of the day before and their own former doctrines had always been in their eyes a bourgeois fraud and Social-traitors' delusion.

I consider this Lenin's most important and fundamental victory, and it was won in the first days of May.

4. The Kornilov Mutiny

W. H. CHAMBERLIN

The setbacks suffered by the Provisional Government in July—the failure of the great offensive on the southwestern front, the barely suppressed Bolshevik uprising in Petrograd, the progressive disintegration of the armed forces, the spread of unrest to the countryside—all this profoundly shook a government which had been weak from its birth. The worsening of the political situation, especially the rapid erosion of the army as an effective fighting force, was watched with apprehension by most Russian military leaders. One of them was General Lavr G. Kornilov who, after the disastrous July offensive, replaced General A. A. Brusilov as commander in chief of all Russian forces. Kornilov anticipated a Bolshevik coup d'etat and believed the

source: William Henry Chamberlin, *The Russian Revolution, 1917–1921,* 2 vols. (New York: The Macmillan Company, 1935)1:192–221. Copyright 1935 by the Macmillan Company and renewed by W. H. Chamberlin. From the chapter originally entitled "Kornilov and the Failure of Counterrevolution."

Provisional Government incapable of resolute action. Anxious to restore discipline at the front, he decided to act on his own. He resolved to seize power by using some of his most reliable troops to suppress the Soviet and to proclaim himself dictator. Assuming that the Prime Minister, Kerensky, was in favor of such a step, Kornilov launched his troops against Petrograd, expecting cooperation on the part of the government against the Soviets. (Any collusion with Kornilov has been emphatically denied by Kerensky in his last book, Russia and History's Turning Point [New York, 1965]). The offensive proved, however, a gamble badly prepared both politically and militarily. The movement of his troops was sabotaged by the railroad workers. The morale of his soldiers was undermined by the agitators dispatched for this purpose by the Soviet. The offensive, paralyzed by the concerted effort of the Provisional Government and the Soviet, collapsed. Kornilov and most of his top assistants were arrested.

The Kornilov mutiny further undermined the prestige of the Provisional Government and strengthened the Bolsheviks, who could from now on invoke, with some credibility, the specter of a right-wing "Bonapartist" dictatorship. Moreover, the emergency created by the advance of the Kornilov troops against the capital allowed the Bolsheviks to form their own armed squads who were provided with weapons by the government. The arms were never returned. These firearms and the experience gained by the Bolshevik agitators who had infiltrated Kornilov's troops, were to be valuable assets in October–November for overthrowing the Provisional Government. Moreover, the government virtually suspended the ban on the Bolshevik Party and released its leaders on bail. This resulted in an upsurge of Bolshevik voting strength, which gave them control of the Petrograd and Moscow Soviets.

The excerpt that follows forms Chapter 9 of the first volume of William Henry Chamberlin's The Russian Revolution (available also in paperback). While Volume 1 ends essentially with the Treaty of Brest-Litovsk, Volume 2 covers the Civil War (1918–1921), until the proclamation of the New Economic Policy (NEP).

Chamberlin's work, a pioneering attempt at historic synthesis, presents a panorama of the four crucial years of Russian history in a dispassionate, detached way. The attitude of the author is reflected in his style: it is essentially descriptive but it avoids emotionalism and aims at dispassion and lucidity above all. Despite the lapse of well over thirty years, it is still a standard work on the subject.

The author was the Christian Science Monitor's correspondent in Russia from 1922 to 1933. In this capacity he had a unique opportunity to investigate research materials that have since been either destroyed on Stalin's order or, at least, made unavailable to foreign scholars. As a newspaperman, the author had an opportunity to meet and interview personally many leaders of the Revolution. Despite the fact that Chamberlin had started his journalistc work sympathetic to the Soviet Union and then underwent an agonized evolution to the right as a result of his Russian experience, his personal views nowhere interfere with his judgment about the great historic drama. It may appear, as he puts it, "heroic, or tragic, or both, according to one's point of view."

★ ★ ★ ★ ★

General Lavr Kornilov, whose mission it was to head the unsuccessful counterrevolutionary movement against the Provisional Government, was a picturesque personality, full of Eastern color. Son of a Siberian Cossack, Kornilov's slanting eyes, slight, erect figure and Mongolian physiognomy suggest that in his veins flowed the blood of some Oriental people. Much of his early military service had been spent in Russian Central Asia and in the Far East; he knew a considerable number of Asiatic tongues and felt himself more at home with Asiatics than with Europeans. His personal bodyguard consisted of Tekintsi, Turcoman warriors from Central Asia, whose devotion to him as their military chief was enhanced by his knowledge of their language.

. Kornilov's career as a soldier revealed him as a man of distinguished personal courage, but not as a very capable commander of large military units. During the retreat of the Russian armies from Galicia in 1915 Kornilov became separated from the division which he was commanding and was. taken prisoner. Subsequently he escaped from an Austrian prison and made his way back to

Russia. After the Revolution he was for a time commander of the Petrograd garrison; but he soon became irked by the low level of order and discipline in this organization and, at his own request, was transferred to the command of the Eighth Army, on the Southwestern Front. Kornilov's troops won the greatest individual measure of success during the short-lived Russian offensive in early July; and, when advance had given way to retreat and rout, Kornilov was promoted to the post of Commander-in-chief of the Southwestern Front. This was followed at the end of July by his appointment as Supreme Commander-in-chief.

Kerensky's decision to place so much potential military power in the hands of a man whom he soon came to distrust and to regard as a dangerous competitor for power may occasion surprise. It must be remembered, however, that Kerensky was of an impulsive nature, quick to make and to withdraw responsible appointments, and a change in the command, after the pitiful failure of the offensive seemed imperative. Brusilov, who of all the old Tsarist Generals had gone farthest in his efforts to adapt himself to revolutionary phraseology, had not succeeded in restoring the army's will or capacity to fight. Perhaps Kornilov, a younger man, with a reputation for great energy and iron will, might be more effective.

Two other factors helped to bring about Kornilov's appointment. On July 29th Kerensky had presided over an important military council at the Stavka, in Moghilev, which was attended by the commanders of European fronts, with the exception of Kornilov, who was detained by military exigencies, and by several other high military authorities. Most of the old-fashioned generals at the conference attacked the revolutionary innovations in the army, lock, stock and barrel; and the outspoken General Denikin,[1] the future leader of the White movement in South Russia, delivered an impassioned speech, in which he did not mince words in attacking the Provisional Government and accused it of "trampling our

[1] A. I. Denikin (1872–1947), lieutenant general, appointed chief of staff by the Provisional Government, later commander in chief of the southern and southwestern front; during the civil war leader of the anti-Bolshevik forces in the South.

banners in filth." By contrast the message which was received from Kornilov, suggesting that commissars and committees in the armies had their functions, but should be placed under definite limitations, sounded to Kerensky liberal and progressive. Furthermore, Kornilov had a valuable political friend and guarantor in the person of Boris Savinkov,[2] Commissar of the Southwestern Front, whom Kerensky was now selecting as the active administrator of the War Department, of which the Premier himself was the nominal head. Savinkov was a veteran member of the Fighting Organization of the Socialist Revolutionaries and had taken an active part in some of the spectacular terrorist plots in Tsarist days. As was the case with many members of his Party, however, Savinkov's "socialism" apparently did not go beyond a tolerably liberal republicanism. A stronger and more resolute character than Kerensky, Savinkov was a fervent believer in the restoration of order and discipline in the army and was convinced that General Kornilov, supplied with proper political guidance, could be a useful instrument in achieving this end.

So the appointment of Kornilov as successor to Brusilov took place; and Savinkov at the War Ministry and Captain Filonenko, who assumed the office of Chief Commissar attached to the Stavka, became the unofficial liaison agents who endeavored to inspire more political discretion in Kornilov and more administrative firmness in Kerensky and, in general, to make it possible for the strongly contrasted and discordant personalities of the Premier and the Commander-in-chief to work in harmony. There was indeed a profound difference and an almost instinctive antagonism between the wordy, gesticulating lawyer-politician, Kerensky, and the stern simple soldier Kornilov, whose political and social ideas were of the vaguest and most limited character, and whose subsequent flowery appeals were written for him by his adjutant, Zavoiko, an expansive landowner with a strong streak of irresponsible adventurism in his make-up, who bears a considerable share

[2] B. V. Savinkov (1879–1925), a leading member of the Social Revolutionary Party. During the war he became an ardent supporter of the Russian war effort; under the Provisional Government he served as assistant minister of war.

of the responsibility for the uncommonly clumsy preparation of the subsequent coup.

Had Kerensky been a revolutionary of the uncompromising type and had Kornilov been an out-and-out monarchist, anxious to replace the Romanovs on the throne, the appointment of the latter would never have taken place, or at least the irrepressible conflict between the two men would have burst out much sooner than it actually did. But as a matter of fact the desires and objectives of the Socialist Revolutionary Premier and of the Cossack General ran along parallel lines to a certain extent. Kerensky, like Kornilov, wished to see an army where the soldiers would obey orders instead of debating them. Kornilov, on his part, a man of humble origin, had no desire to set up a monarchy. The points of difference that proved insuperable and led to the final clash were Kerensky's distrust of Kornilov's ambition and of the methods by which he proposed to create a strong government and to restore discipline in the army and Kornilov's contempt and dislike for Kerensky as an irresolute talker. But much of the confused and contradictory record of the period which immediately preceded Kornilov's open defiance of the Provisional Government is only understandable on the assumption that Kerensky, in his own way and with substantial modifications of emphasis and method, was aiming at goals which were not so very different from those of Kornilov himself. Moreover, Kerensky probably always had at least something of a premonition that by destroying Kornilov he would be simultaneously cutting the ground from beneath his own feet.

Kornilov's first act after being informed of his nomination was a clear indication that politically he was destined to be a more difficult figure to handle than his predecessors, the sick and discouraged Alekseev and the complaisant Brusilov. He dispatched a telegram to the Provisional Government declaring that he could accept the appointment and "bring the people to victory and to a just and honorable peace" only on the following four conditions:

1. Responsibility before his own conscience and before the whole people.

2. Complete noninterference in his operative orders and, therefore, in the appointment of the higher commanding staff.

3. Extension of the measures which had recently been adopted at the front (presumably the reintroduction of the death penalty) to all places in the rear where army reinforcements were stationed.

4. Acceptance of the proposals which he had sent by telegraph to the conference in the Stavka on July 29 [July 16].

Even Kornilov's friend and admirer, Denikin, remarks that the first of these demands would have created "a form of sovereignty of the Supreme Command that would have been very original, from the standpoint of state law." The Government at first took Kornilov's demands rather lightly, attributing the first point, which in strict logic implied the establishment of an independent dictatorship, to his unfamiliarity with political phraseology. However, a second incident followed quickly after the first; Kornilov strenuously objected to the appointment of General Cheremisov as Commander-in-chief of the Southwestern Front and threatened to resign if the nomination were not cancelled. Kerensky on this occasion was inclined to accept Kornilov's resignation; but the influence of Savinkov prevented this and both incidents were quickly settled. Cheremisov, who was one of the generals who endeavored to smooth their careers by keeping up good relations with Soviet circles, was dismissed; and Kornilov accepted the interpretation placed on his first point by Filonenko, who suggested that "responsibility before the whole people" implied responsibility before its authorized organ of representation, the Provisional Government.

Throughout Kornilov's political career one notices these alternations of strongly phrased demands and quick withdrawals and concessions. In all probability this is not attributable to outright hypocrisy, although Kornilov subsequently revealed that he was by no means devoid of guile. It was rather a case of complete inexperience in politics and ready susceptibility to the suggestion of the last adviser. Quite characteristic in this connection was Kornilov's conduct in sending, under Savinkov's influence, a relatively moderate set of demands to the conference in the Stavka and of shortly afterwards assuring Denikin of his agreement with all the latter's demands for the abolition of commissars and committees.

These initial misunderstandings left behind an undercurrent of suspicion that affected all Kerensky's later relations with Kornilov. This suspicion was not dissipated by the two personal meetings of the Premier and the Commander-in-chief which occurred in Petrograd on August 16 and August 23. On the first occasion Kornilov arrived with a memorandum outlining measures which he regarded as necessary for the restoration of fighting capacity at the front and in the rear. His mentors, Savinkov and Filonenko, looking over the memorandum, found it politically unacceptable and suggested that he leave it with them for working over and modification. This he agreed to do; but in the course of his interview with Kerensky he showed the latter the memorandum, which the Premier later characterized as "setting forth a number of measures, the vast majority of which were quite acceptable, but they were set down in such form and with such arguments that the publication of the memorandum would have led to unfavorable results."

Kerensky seized this opportunity of sounding out Kornilov's political sentiments. Hinting vaguely at the possibility of a military dictatorship he warned the General in the following terms: "Suppose I should withdraw, what will happen? You will hang in the air; the railroads will stop; the telegraph will cease to function." To Kerensky's questioning as to whether, in Kornilov's opinion, he should remain at the head of the state the Commander-in-chief gave the somewhat reserved reply that, although Kerensky's influence had declined, nevertheless, as the recognized leader of the democratic party, he should remain at the head of the Government.

Another incident on the occasion of this visit to Petrograd made a strong impression on Kornilov and very possibly predisposed him to listen to the counsels of his more adventurous friends. While he was reporting on the military situation at a session of the Cabinet Kerensky and Savinkov warned him to show discretion in discussing the question of where an offensive might be undertaken. They explained this warning by telling him that some of the Ministers (apparently there was a special insinuation against the Socialist Revolutionary Minister for Agriculture, Chernov)[3] were in close touch with the Executive Committee of the Soviet, among the members of which were German agents. This was calculated to strengthen in Kornilov's politically very primitive mind the conviction that not only the Bolsheviki, but also the members of other parties in the Soviet were traitors and German agents, and that they exercised an impermissible degree of influence upon the Provisional Government. Indeed it is questionable whether Kornilov ever understood that there was any distinction between the Bolsheviki and the more moderate Socialist parties which at that time constituted the majority in almost all the Soviets.

In the words of General Denikin: "Kornilov became a banner. For some of counterrevolution, for others of the salvation of the Motherland."

His visit to Petrograd, followed as it was by rumors about his differences with the Government and about his drastic programme for the restoration of discipline, stirred up the passions both of his sympathizers and his opponents. A campaign was launched against him in the press of the Left and voices were heard to the effect that he should be replaced by General Cheremisov. Conservative and military organizations rallied to his support. So on August 19 the Council of the Union of Cossack Troops flung down the gauntlet to the Provisional Government with the unequivocal declaration that "General Kornilov cannot be removed, because he is the true people's leader and because, in the opinion of the majority of the population, he is the sole general who can re-create the fighting power of the army and bring the country out of its very difficult situation," followed by the undisguised threat: "The

[3] V. M. Chernov (1873–1952), leader of the Social Revolutionary Party and one of its main theoreticians; minister of agriculture in the Provisional Government (May 5 [18]–September 1 [14], 1917); author of the book *The Great Russian Revolution* (New Haven, 1936).

Council regards it as a moral duty to state to the Provisional Government and to the people that it repudiates its responsibility for the behavior of the Cossack troops at the front and in the rear in the event of the replacement of General Kornilov."

The Union of Cavaliers of St. George (holders of the highest Russian military decoration) and the Union of Officers hastened to associate themselves with this militant declaration of the Cossack leaders. A gathering of public men of predominantly conservative sentiments in Moscow dispatched to Kornilov a telegram, under the signature of Rodzyanko, to the following effect:

"In this threatening hour of heavy trial all thinking Russia looks to you with hope and faith."

Not one of these organizations, with the exception of the Cossacks, represented any mass numerical support; and the Cossack leaders, as subsequent developments would show, reflected very imperfectly the sentiments of the rank-and-file Cossack troops. But Kornilov, who, as several witnesses agree, was almost naively susceptible to flattery, very naturally had his head turned to some extent as a result of all these glowing tributes.

Throughout the month of August the air was thick with rumors of plots; and when Kornilov returned to the Stavka from Petrograd Filonenko sent with him his assistant von Vizin with instructions to see to it that Kornilov should not engage in any untoward political activity, under the influence of the Staff. It is impossible to know precisely at what moment Kornilov began to consider seriously the advisability of placing himself at the head of an attempt at a forcible change in the existing regime. But his first overt act seems to have occurred on the nineteenth or the twentieth of August, when his Chief of Staff, General Lukomsky, was surprised to receive an order to concentrate the Third Cavalry Corps (made up of Cossack units) and the so-called Savage Division (cavalry recruited from the mountain tribes of the Caucasus) in the neighborhood of the towns Nevel, Novi Sokolniki and Veliki Luki, within convenient railroad striking distance of Petrograd and Moscow. Lukomsky suggested to Kornilov that such a region of concentration was of little value as a means of strengthening the

Northern Front, but was quite convenient for the eventuality of a blow at Petrograd or Moscow and asked the Commander-in-chief to tell him frankly what was in his mind. This Kornilov promised to do. The circumstances of Kornilov's second visit to the capital were even more strained than those of his first visit. Some of his friends strongly advised him not to leave Moghilev, suggesting that Kerensky might arrest him. It required all the pleadings of Savinkov and Filonenko, accompanied by reminders that they had defended Kornilov against his enemies and critics in Petrograd, to persuade the Commander-in-chief to make the second visit. And when Kornilov finally set out he took along a bodyguard of Tekintsi with two machine-guns. When he went to pay his official call on Kerensky in the Winter Palace he took his fierce Central Asian warriors along; and passers-by in the corridors of the Palace could witness the piquant spectacle of the Turco-mans with the two machine-guns waiting in the vestibule and ready to rush to the assistance of the General at his first call for help.

The main occasion for the interview which took place with this extraordinary background was the consideration of Kornilov's military program. It had been revised and softened in its phrasing by Filonenko; but the latter simultaneously added proposals for the militarization of the railroads and of the War industries. Kornilov handed this memorandum to Kerensky; and the latter, seeing the new demands for the militarization of the railroads and War industries, asked time for further consideration, simultaneously expressing dissatisfaction that his assistant, Savinkov, should have signed such a document without his consent. At the close of the interview Kornilov told Kerensky that he had heard rumors about his impending removal from his post and bluntly advised the Premier, assuming there were any basis for these rumors, not to carry out any such intention.

The memorandum was further discussed with Kornilov at a session of the familiar "inner circle" of the Government, consisting of Kerensky, Nekrasov and Tereschenko; and in the end Kornilov's original memorandum was found preferable to Filonenko's edited and amplified version. Kornilov, however, received only vague assurances about the precise time of carrying out his recommendations; and even after Kornilov's memorandum, as a result of the insistence of the Cadet Minister Kokoshkin,[4] had been formally discussed at a regular Cabinet session, the decision, adopted after hot debate, remained decidedly indefinite:

"To recognize in principle the possibility of applying various measures, including the death penalty in the rear, but to carry them out only after the discussion in legislative order of each concrete measure, according to the circumstances of time and place."

Kornilov returned to the Stavka thoroughly disgusted with what he regarded as the weak temporizing of Kerensky and frankly outlined to Lukomsky the real purpose of the cavalry concentration which had excited the latter's suspicion.

"It's time to hang the German supporters and spies, with Lenin at their head," Kornilov burst out in conversation with Lukomsky, "and to disperse the Soviet of Workers' and Soldiers' Deputies so that it would never reassemble. You are right. I am shifting the cavalry corps mainly so as to bring it up to Petrograd by the end of August and, if a demonstration of the Bolsheviki takes place, to deal with these traitors as they deserve. I want to commit the leadership of this operation to General Krimov. I am convinced that he will not hesitate, in case of necessity, to hang every member of the Soviet."

This was plain soldierly speaking. Kornilov intended to make short work of the Bolsheviki and of the Soviet. But as regards the political side of his projected move he was more uncertain. He told Lukomsky that he did not intend to come out against the Provisional Government and hoped to come to an agreement with it, although he was prepared to strike at the Bolsheviki on his own account, if he did not reach an agreement with Kerensky and Savinkov.

[4] F. F. Kokoshkin (1871–1918), one of the founders of the Kadet Party, professor of law at the Moscow University, state controller under the Provisional Government.

"I want nothing for myself," Kornilov concluded. "I only want to save Russia and I will obey unconditionally a cleansed and strengthened Provisional Government."

Here was the main outline of the Kornilov plot. The political side had been sketchily filled in; and here a good deal depended upon the expansive Zavoiko, whose favorite diversion was shuffling and reshuffling the ministerial portfolios in the Cabinet which would emerge after the coup.

A striking interlude in the development of the Kornilov affair was the Moscow State Conference, which was held from the twenty-fifth until the twenty-eighth of August. The idea of such an assembly of the "live forces of the country," to use a phrase much in vogue at the time, had commended itself to the Provisional Government shortly after the resignation of Prince Lvov as Premier.[5] A noteworthy weakness of the Provisional Government throughout the whole course of its career was the absence of any generally recognized national assembly on which it could lean. The Vtsik (All-Russian Central Executive Committee of the Soviets) could not serve as such a body, because only the Bolsheviki had favored the assumption of power by the Soviets and the non-Socialist part of the population would not have acknowledged the Soviets as representative bodies.

The Moscow State Conference was not conceived in any way as a legislative assembly; it was rather designed to be a large-scale consultative body, where representatives of every class and profession could find expression. Among the 2,414 delegates who took part in the sessions of the Conference the largest delegations were from members of the four Dumas (488), from the cooperatives (313), from the trade unions (176), from commercial and industrial organizations and banks (150), from municipalities (147), from the Executive Committee of the United Soviets of Workers', Soldiers' and Peasants' Deputies (129), from the Army and Navy (117) and from the Soviets of Workers' and Soldiers' and of Peasants' Deputies, each of which received 100 places. There was an effort to balance the Conference carefully between

[5] In July 1917.

the Right and the Left; and it was a symptom of the post-July reaction that the organizations of the propertied classes were granted representation out of all proportion to their numerical weight in the population.

The Bolsheviki denounced the State Conference as a counter-revolutionary gathering from the beginning and took no part in it. They had some representatives in the delegation of the Vtsik; but Chkheidze, the President of the delegation, refused to permit them to carry out their intention of reading a declaration denouncing the Conference and then walking out of the place of assembly as a demonstration; and as a result of this the Bolshevik delegates absented themselves altogether. On the day of the opening of the Conference, however, the delegates received convincing proof that Bolshevism was very much alive, even if its voice was not heard in the ornate opera-house where the Conference was held. A one-day general strike of protest, initiated by the Bolsheviki and effectively carried out by the workers, despite the fact that the Moscow Soviet had voted against it by a narrow majority, was in full swing. The delegates could not ride on the streetcars or take tea in the restaurants.

This was regarded as an annoying interlude; but the tendency at the time was to underestimate the strength of the Bolsheviki. Popular attention was concentrated on what was felt to be the inevitable impending clash between Kerensky and Kornilov. So great was the apprehension that the large Conference in historic and ancient Moscow might be utilized by the conservative forces for the proclamation of a change of government that the Moscow Soviet, with its Menshevik-Socialist Revolutionary majority, decided to give Bolshevik agitators free access to the barracks where the soldiers of the garrison were quartered for a period of three days. Reacting nervously to the rumor of a monarchist plot the authorities placed the Grand Dukes Paul and Michael Alexandro-vitch under house arrest and arrested some other persons. This was apparently a completely false scent; the prisoners were soon released for lack of evidence against them; and Kerensky later expressed the opinion that an imaginary plot had been deliberately conjured up to divert attention from the actual plot in the Stavka. The Moscow Bolshevik newspaper offered the following comment: "To arrest a pair of brainless puppets from the Romanov family and leave at liberty the military clique of the army commanders with Kornilov at the head—that is to deceive the people."

The State Conference was conceived as a rallying point of national unity. Its failure in this respect was dismal and complete. Not only were the considerable masses of workers and soldiers who were already following the banner of Bolshevism outside its pale; but from the very moment of its opening the participants split into two hostile and irreconcilable camps. Indeed the spectacle which was represented by the sessions of the Conference in the operahouse that had often witnessed performances of "Boris Godunov" and other epic operas of Russia's past had many elements of historical drama.

On the right side of the auditorium sat representatives of the old propertied and military classes, assembled for what was destined to be their last dress-parade. There one could see bemedalled generals and officers, some in picturesque Caucasian uniforms, solid representatives of the business and financial world, professors and publicists of Cadet sympathies, many of whom had been regarded as dangerously advanced in Tsarist days, but who instinctively found themselves on the side of the Right in a country that was experiencing the first tossings of social revolution. On the Left side there were, to be sure, no typical figures of the July Days, no Kronstadt sailors, eager to wipe out the bourgeoisie, no grimy workers from the Putilov Factory Red Guard, nervously fingering their unfamiliar rifles. But there sat the flower of the self-styled "democratic forces" of the country: leaders of the moderate Socialist parties, trade-union organizers, radical lawyers and journalists and, last but not least a fair sprinkling of the lieutenants, sergeants, corporals and private soldiers who represented the rank-and-file of the Army.

A stranger quite ignorant of the Russian language would have had little difficulty in sensing the spirit of the Moscow Conference; when the Left burst into applause the Right was stonily silent, and vice versa. There was something at once pathetic and futile in the clashing of these two groups, both of which within three months would be thoroughly submerged by the rising tide of Bolshevism.

Kerensky sat symbolically in the precise center of the stage and throughout the Conference pursued his increasingly difficult task of political tightrope walking, endeavoring to balance himself between the Right and the Left. On this occasion he was undoubtedly the favorite of the Left side of the Conference, as the representatives of the Right saw their hero in Kornilov.

Kerensky's speech at the opening of the Conference on the afternoon of August 25 [August 12] was mainly directed against the suspected conspirators of the Right, although, for the sake of balance, there was also a threat against the Bolsheviki.

"Let all those who already once attempted to raise armed hands against the people's power [a clear reference to the July Days][6] know that such an attempt will be crushed with iron and blood. Still more let those plotters beware who think the time has come to overthrow the revolutionary government, relying on bayonets [an even clearer hint to his enemies on the Right] . . . Here, in attempts at open attack or hidden plots is the limit of our patience. And anyone who transgresses that limit will meet a power which in its repressive measures will make the criminals remember what was under the old autocracy."

The rest of Kerensky's speech conformed to a familiar pattern: loud phrases which covered up feeble and irresolute actions and an almost painful effort to placate both sides of his audience which could scarcely have satisfied either. So he paid a tribute to the courage of the Russian officers and recalled that he had proposed to the Provisional Government a partial restoration of the death penalty, but dampened the welcome which the latter statement evoked on the Right by sounding a warning that "no one should dare to present to us any unconditioned demands on this point." A gloomy note pervaded the speech; one finds such phrases as "The state lives through an hour of mortal danger . . . Hungry cities,

[6] The abortive Bolshevik uprising in Petrograd of July 3 (16)–July 5 (18), 1917.

ever more disorganized transport." The speech was full of carefully balanced reproaches: so he simultaneously denounced the fall in the productivity of the workers and the refusal of the propertied classes to support the Government.

On the following day Kornilov arrived in Moscow and was greeted by his sympathizers with a maximum of pomp and ceremony. A guard of honor, recruited from the military schools of the city, was drawn up at the station and met the Commander-in-chief with bands playing and banners flying; deputations from a number of conservative groups and military organizations were waiting to welcome Kornilov as he stepped out of his car and passed through the double line of his Turcoman guards. The well-known Cadet orator Rodichev[7] pronounced a speech of welcome, ending: "We believe that at the head of the revived Russian army you will lead Russia to victory over the enemy and that the slogan, 'Long live General Kornilov'—now a slogan of hope—will become a cry of people's triumph. Save Russia and the grateful people will crown you." There were loud hurrahs and Kornilov was showered with flowers. Later he proceeded to the Chapel of the Iberian Virgin, the most famous shrine in Moscow, which Tsars habitually visited before their coronation, and prayed before its reputedly wonder-working ikon.

In the evening there was an acrid interchange of opinion between Kerensky and Kornilov about the contents of the speech which the General was to pronounce on the following day. Kerensky insisted that Kornilov should restrict himself to military and strategic questions, while Kornilov retorted that he would speak as he wished. Actually, however, the speech which had been prepared for the General was not so uncompromising or defiant as to provoke a breach with the Government. It had been written by Commissar Filonenko and, while it hinted broadly at the necessity for applying drastic measures in the rear as well as at the front, it did not directly attack the Government and Kornilov even

---

[7] F. I. Rodichev (1856–1933), one of the founders of the Kadet Party, member of its Central Committee, commissioner on Finnish affairs under the Provisional Government.

declared that he was not an opponent of the army committees, merely demanding that they should not interfere in operative orders. Kornilov's appearance on the platform at the session of August 27 [August 14] was the signal for a storm of ovation from the Right, during which the Left remained demonstratively silent. It was significant for the fate of the future attempted coup that the soldiers' representatives remained sullenly seated, which made them a target for taunts and abuse from the conservatives. Kornilov emphasized such points as the tremendous fall of productivity in munition factories and hinted that further military reverses would be the inevitable consequence of a continuation of the Government's lax policies, remarking: "We must not permit that order in the rear should be the consequence of our loss of Riga and that order on the railroads would be reëstablished at the price of yielding Moldavia and Bessarabia to the enemy."

A more outspoken champion of the conservative viewpoint was General Kaledin,[8] Ataman (elected governor) of the territory inhabited by the Don Cossacks. He aroused loud cheers from the seats of the Right when he boasted that the Cossacks, just because they had never known serfdom, were not intoxicated by the new liberty and that the Cossack regiments had no deserters; and a chorus of approval from the Right, mingled with hisses and protests from the Left, greeted his sweeping proposal that "all Soviets and committees must be abolished, both in the army and in the rear."

Kaledin found his opponent later in the course of the Conference when a young Cossack officer, Nagaev, elected as a delegate from the Caucasian Front, contested Kaledin's right to speak in the name of "twelve Cossack territories" and urged the General "not to tear off the Cossacks from the people." Nagaev's declarations that the rank-and-file Cossacks would not follow Kaledin's anti-Soviet slogan elicited lively applause on the Left and much indignation on the part of a group of officers who were sitting in

[8] A. M. Kaledin (1861–1918), general of Cossack origin, headed the anti-Bolshevik forces at the beginning of the civil war.

a box. Someone in the box called out "German marks," and the auditorium was filled with cries of protest. Kerensky intervened; and, when no one responded to the demand that the man who uttered this insinuation should give his name, declared: "Lieutenant Nagaev and all the Russian people who are present here are quite satisfied with the silence of a coward."

As the Conference dragged on, with scores of orators expressing the varied views of political parties, nationalities, social classes and religious organizations, it became increasingly evident that no united concrete decisions would be taken as a result of its labors. The few conciliatory gestures which marked the Conference, such as the public handshaking of the Soviet moderate leader, Tseretelli, and the prominent industrialist, Bublikov, could not obliterate the dominant impression that the country was divided into two irreconcilably hostile camps. And there was something at once tragic and futile in this continual sniping between the two camps, one consisting of representatives of the propertied classes, the other of moderate Socialists, because both the contending groups were predestined to speedy obliteration at the hands of Bolshevism. If most of the participants in the Conference felt that the issue of power lay between Kerensky and Kornilov events would soon show that the real victor in the struggle for power would be Lenin.

A curious sense of impending collapse seems to have pervaded the last scene before the curtain fell on the deliberations of the State Conference. In Kerensky's last speech banalities alternated with flights of hysterical rodomontade.

"Let my heart become stone; let all the strings of faith in man perish, let all the flowers and wreaths of man dry up . . . I shall throw far away the keys of my heart, which loves men, I will think only about the state."

The atmosphere of sentimental bathos was intensified when a woman's voice cried: "You cannot do that; your heart will not permit it."

So great was the Premier's nervous exhaustion and loss of self-possession that he had to be applauded into stopping his rambling speech; and when he absentmindedly started to walk off the stage he had to be recalled to bring the Conference to a formal conclusion.

The Moscow Conference was only an interlude in the development of Kornilov's plot. It certainly did not bring the General any closer to Kerensky; and the homage which the conservative classes paid him was calculated still further to turn the head of the unsophisticated Kornilov and to strengthen his belief that he was the man of destiny whose mission was to save his country by instituting a strong government. How far such veteran Duma political leaders as Rodzyanko and Milyukov directly encouraged Kornilov in his adventurous scheme is difficult to say. There is certainly reason to suspect that they looked not unkindly on a military dictatorship as a temporary remedy for the country's difficulties. Kornilov was much more directly under the influence of his adjutant Zavoiko, who played the role of publicity agent for the General, issuing in a large edition a short popular biography of Kornilov; and after the Moscow Conference two other men, Aladin, a former Laborite Duma Deputy who had lost all trace of radicalism, and Dobrinsky, a Red Cross official, who made a doubtful claim to great influence among the Caucasian mountaineers, began to play subsidiary roles in the General's circle of intimate counsellors.

By the beginning of September the military side of the plot was fully worked out. Quartermaster-General Romanovsky, one of the main participants, on September 3 signed an order to distribute hand grenades among the three cavalry units with which it was proposed to envelop and seize Petrograd from the south: the Savage Division, concentrated near Dno, the First Don Cavalry Division, near Pskov, and the Ussuri Division, near Veleiki Luki. This order was a clear indication that these units were designed not for service on the front, against the Germans, but for street fighting in Petrograd. About the same time orders were given to insure a ten days' reserve of food and forage for these divisions. While these three divisions were to move from the south, the Fifth Caucasian Cavalry Division, concentrated between Viborg and Byeloostrov, was to move in a southeastern direction and close in on the capital from the north. The capital was to be subjected to a regular military occupation, the river Neva being the line of division between the sections to be taken over by the troops arriving from the south and those coming in from the north. A definite date for this operation was fixed: "as soon as news is received about the beginning of disorders in Petrograd and not later than the morning of September 14."

There was special significance in this alert anticipation of disorders in Petrograd. It was believed that the stricter measures for restoring discipline in the army which the Government would soon proclaim would provoke some demonstration of protest on the part of the Bolsheviki, and very probably on the part of the Soviet as well. Moreover the fact that September 9 [August 27] marked the lapse of six months since the occurrence of the Revolution, which took place on February 27, Old Style, aroused the belief in the ranks of Kornilov's sympathizers that some sort of Bolshevik outbreak would occur on this day and would serve as a pretext for decisive repressive measures.

In Petrograd itself two patriotic conservative organizations, "The Union of Military Duty" and "The Republican Centre," were ready to give Kornilov active support; in the Stavka it was understood that two thousand armed men could be counted on in the city; and Kornilov gave orders that officers should be sent from Petrograd to the front, under various pretexts, in order to give these auxiliaries training and instruction. While the members of these organizations in Petrograd took their strength very seriously and were prepared to provoke and simulate Bolshevik outbursts, in case no real disorder occurred, and subsequently "to seize armored automobiles, to arrest the Provisional Government, to arrest and execute the more prominent and influential members of the Soviet, etc.," their actual capacity for action, as subsequent events proved, was practically non-existent.

While a coup d'état, under the thin pretext of protecting the Provisional Government against a hypothetical attack from the side of the Left, was thus being prepared in the Stavka, Kerensky, in his eternal wavering between Right and Left policies, had veered rather definitely toward the Right. A series of explosions in munitions factories in Petrograd and Kazan during the last week of August suggested that German agents were at work and that discipline and watchfulness at these strategic enterprises were badly relaxed. Riga was on the verge of surrender; it actually fell on the night of September 2; and these events, combined with the impressions which he had brought away from the Moscow State Conference, had apparently convinced the Premier that he could hold his slipping power only by adopting a firmer line of policy in military affairs. So, on August 30, he informed Savinkov, whom he left in charge of the War Ministry, despite their former differences of opinion, that he was prepared to accept Kornilov's memorandum of August 23 as the basis for new military legislation. This concession, which Savinkov promptly communicated to the Stavka, did not, however, retard the military preparations which were being made there. Kerensky was cordially distrusted and despised by conservative officers of the old school, and his expressed willingness to accept Kornilov's recommendations was probably interpreted as a sign of weakness.

Immediately after the fall of Riga [September 2] Kornilov telegraphed to Kerensky a request that all troops in the Petrograd district should be directly subordinated to him. (Hitherto the Petrograd district had been under a general directly responsible to the Provisional Government.) Kerensky, however, refused to agree to this, insisting that the city of Petrograd and its environs should remain in direct subordination to the Government. Kerensky cherished a lively apprehension that, if the Petrograd garrison were turned over to Kornilov, "we could have been eaten up at any time."

The development of the plot now took an extremely curious turn; and Kerensky was very nearly placed in the anomalous position of a conspirator against himself. On September 5 Savinkov, always an advocate of rapprochement between Kerensky and Kornilov, arrived in the Stavka and laid before Kornilov the following requests of Kerensky:

1. To liquidate the Union of Officers, because some of its members were reported to be involved in a plot.

2. To liquidate the political department attached to the Stavka, for the same reasons.

3. To convince Kornilov that the city of Petrograd should be excepted from the status of direct subordination to the Commander-in-chief which was to apply to the Petrograd district.

4. *To ask Kornilov for a cavalry corps, which was to enforce martial law in Petrograd and to defend the Provisional Government against any attacks, especially from •the side of the Bolsheviki.* (Italics are Chamberlin's—Ed.)

Kornilov and his associates must have been pleasantly surprised indeed by this last request, which amounted to a legal sanction of the very operation which they had been planning to carry out conspiratively. Kerensky himself, when the whole Kornilov affair was subsequently a matter of judicial investigation, was decidedly vague in his testimony as to why he wanted a cavalry corps. Apparently he was convinced, on the basis of the reports of some foreign intelligence service, that there was danger of a repetition of the July Days, possibly in combination with a German landing in Finland. Moreover, he probably wanted to be prepared for any opposition on the part of the Soviet to his programme. Of course he did not realize that he was playing into the hands of conspirators who, if their plans succeeded, would certainly not leave him at the head of the Government.

Kornilov, overjoyed at finding his scheme promoted from such an unexpected source, agreed with Kerensky's other requests and did not raise any objection when Savinkov asked him not to appoint General Krimov, who bore the reputation of being a monarchist, as head of the cavalry corps and not to send the Savage Division, the officers of which were considered politically unreliable, to Petrograd. Actually Kornilov made no change in his dispositions, which contemplated both the employment of Krimov as Commander of the expedition and the utilization of the Savage Division. Savinkov, if we may trust Lukomsky's testimony, employed as strong language as Kornilov himself might have used about the necessity for smashing the Bolsheviki and the Soviet also, if it should solidarize itself with them. Lukomsky, who was by far the ablest man among Kornilov's immediate associates, distrusted the intentions of the Government; but Kornilov himself seems to have derived from his talk with Savinkov a comforting conviction that the more energetic members of the Government were on his side and that Kerensky himself could easily be won over or swept aside, as circumstances might require.

The Kornilov affair might well have taken a much more serious turn if the movement of cavalry on Petrograd had proceeded with the Government's full sanction and authorization. But, almost immediately after Savinkov had departed for Petrograd, Kornilov received another visitor, Prince V. N. Lvov (not to be confused with the Prince G. Lvov who was the first Premier in the Provisional Government), who was destined to play the role of evil genius of his conspiracy.

V. N. Lvov, who for a time had filled the post of Procurator of the Holy Synod in the Provisional Government, was a good-hearted, somewhat weakheaded man, of moderate conservative views, whose bustling, officious character made him prone to undertake commissions which a more discreet and experienced politician would have hesitated to accept. After the Moscow State Conference, Lvov came to the conclusion that the position of the Provisional Government, in its present form, was untenable, because it had lost the support of so large a part of the propertied and educated classes. And when his friend, Dobrinsky, who belonged to the circle of "advisers" who fluttered about Kornilov, let slip some hints that plans were brewing in the Stavka for a change in the composition of the Provisional Government, Lvov felt it was a duty of patriotism and friendship to go to Kerensky and expound the situation to him. The first of three interviews in which Lvov, quite unconsciously, was to tear up the threads of a conspiracy which he by no means fully understood occurred on the evening of September 4 [August 22] in Kerensky's office in the Winter Palace. Lvov spoke at some length of the weak position of the Government and suggested that it should be reorganized along broader lines, through the inclusion of representatives of the more conservative political groups. This sort of advice was familiar enough; but what excited Kerensky's interest and suspicion was that Lvov mysteriously gave himself out as the representative of "important social groups," "possessing real strength."

There is a good deal of discrepancy in the subsequent testimony of Kerensky and Lvov as to the precise reply of the Premier to the hints and proposals of Lvov. Kerensky stated that he "did not consider it possible to refrain from further discussions with Lvov, expecting from him a more exact explanation of what was in his mind." Lvov, on the other hand, asserted that he had obtained from Kerensky permission to turn to various political groups with suggestions for the reorganization of the Government on broader lines. It seems most probable that Kerensky encouraged Lvov to sound out the groups which he professed to represent, hoping in this way to learn more of what might prove to be a formidable plot, and that Lvov considerably exaggerated and overstepped the bounds of his commission.

The second of the three fateful interviews occurred in Moghilev. Received by Kornilov late on the evening of the sixth [August 24], Lvov told the Commander-in-chief that he had Kerensky's authorization to learn Kornilov's demands. The arrival of a man of Lvov's political standing, representing himself as Kerensky's personal envoy, so soon after the visit of Savinkov, convinced Kornilov that Kerensky was ready to capitulate and that conspirative methods were no longer necessary. So when Lvov, at Kornilov's request, called on him again on the morning of the seventh [August 25] the General put forward the two following requests: declaration of martial law in Petrograd and the handing over of all military and civil authority to the Commander-in-chief, whoever he might be. Kornilov added that he could not vouch for the lives of Kerensky and Savinkov anywhere in Russia and invited them to come to the Stavka, simultaneously suggesting that Kerensky might be Minister for Justice and Savinkov Minister for War. A further talk with the boastful and garrulous Zavoiko, Kornilov's adjutant and political adviser-in-chief, left Lvov in no doubt that it was proposed not only to remove Kerensky from power, but also to assassinate him at the first convenient moment. The personnel of the new Cabinet was being freely discussed in the Stavka.

Hurrying back to Petrograd Lvov had his second talk with Kerensky in the Winter Palace on the evening of the eighth [August 26]. The Premier was amazed as Lvov set forth Kornilov's demands. Kerensky urged that these be put in writing. This Lvov did, outlining as the three demands: the declaration of martial law in Petrograd, the transfer of all power to the Commander-in-chief and the resignation of all members of the Cabinet. At the same time he communicated to Kerensky Kornilov's invitation to come to Moghilev, but added a warning that it would be dangerous to accept this invitation.

A thousand lurking suspicions must have found sudden confirmation in Kerensky's mind as he heard Lvov's communication, which was all the more surprising because Savinkov had just reported optimistically about Kornilov's readiness to coöperate with the Government. The possibly fatal mistake which he had made in ordering a concentration of reactionary cavalry units in Petrograd loomed large before his eyes. His first lawyer's instinct was to obtain proof, with witnesses, of the correctness of Lvov's words.

In the presence of a companion, Virubov, Kerensky got into direct touch with Kornilov from the War Ministry. Lvov was supposed to be present at this interview, but was late, and Kerensky impersonated him in the conversation, which was carried on by means of the Hughes telegraphic apparatus. Kerensky first asked whether he should act "according to the information given him by Lvov," and when he received an affirmative answer he assumed the role of Lvov and asked whether "it is necessary to carry out that definite decision about which you asked me to inform Kerensky personally," to which Kornilov replied that he desired Lvov to convey to Kerensky his "urgent request to come to Moghilev." Kerensky, revelling in the web of mystification, assured Kornilov that he hoped to leave Petrograd for Moghilev on the following day and ended the interview with the words: "Goodbye, we shall soon see each other." It is significant that Kerensky avoided any direct reference to the demands which Kornilov had communicated to him through Lvov. He was interested now not in explanations or in possibilities of reconciliation, but only in destroying his rival as quickly as possible.

Still playing his part of an examining lawyer, Kerensky took Lvov (who had arrived just when the conversation with Kornilov had ended) with him to the Winter Palace, where Assistant Police Chief Balavinsky was concealed as a witness. Kerensky made the unsuspecting Lvov repeat the whole story and at the end of it dramatically placed him under arrest. The unfortunate Lvov was not only compelled to go to bed with two guards posted in the neighborhood; but found his sleep hopelessly disturbed because Kerensky, pacing up and down in an adjoining room, sang snatches from operatic airs without intermission.

After describing the situation which had arisen to Nekrasov[9] and Savinkov, rejecting the plea of the latter for direct negotiations with Kornilov and asking the advice of military experts about the technical possibilities of resisting Kornilov's troops, Kerensky, about four A.M. on the ninth, convoked a Cabinet session. The Ministers, astounded at the news, conferred on Kerensky unlimited powers of action in dealing with the emergency and proffered their resignations. The Cadet Ministers, who, if they did not directly sympathize with Kornilov's undertaking, were certainly opposed to a decisive and uncompromising deposition of the General on whom they had placed such great hopes, followed up their resignations by staying away from their offices for the duration of the crisis. The others, after Kerensky had refused to accept their resignations, continued to carry on their functions. After this session of the Cabinet Kerensky addressed to Kornilov the decisive telegram, which announced the final breach:

I order you immediately to turn over your office to General Lukomsky, who is to take over temporarily the duties of Commander-in-chief,

[9] N. V. Nekrasov (1879–?), member of the third and fourth Dumas, leader of the Kadet Party, minister of communications of the Provisional Government (March–June), minister without portfolio (July) and minister of finance (from July 26, August 6); one of the closest coworkers of Kerensky.

until the arrival of the new Commander-in-chief. You are instructed immediately to come to Petrograd.

Some reflection of the flurry in the mind of the Premier may be seen in the fact that the telegram bore no number and was signed simply "Kerensky," although the dismissal of the Commander-in-chief was supposed to require a decree of the Provisional Government.

Kornilov, after his talk with Kerensky, retired on the night of the eighth [August 26] confident that his plans would meet no further opposition. He was correspondingly surprised, on the following morning, to receive Kerensky's curt telegram of dismissal and immediately decided to remain at his post. His Chief of Staff, Lukomsky, refused to obey Kerensky's instructions to take over the command, and dispatched a message to the Premier in which he declared that "for the sake of Russia's salvation you must go with General Kornilov, and not against him." Lukomsky refused to assume responsibility for the army, even for a short time, and informed the commanders of the various fronts of his decision and of the general situation.

Kerensky sent out an order to stop all troop movements toward Petrograd; Kornilov countermanded this order and instructed the cavalry units to proceed toward the capital according to plan. So the issue of civil war was fairly joined. In the first days the prevalent mood in the Stavka was one of confidence. General Krasnov, who was to command the Fifth Caucasian Cavalry Division, one of the units involved in the expedition, was assured before he left Moghilev that "No one will defend Kerensky. This is only a promenade." And Prince Trubetzkoy, chief of the diplomatic department attached to the Stavka, summed up as follows in a telegram to Foreign Minister Tereschenko on September 10 what he regarded as the points in favor of Kornilov's success: "The whole commanding staff, the overwhelming majority of the officers and the best fighting units of the army are for Kornilov. On his side in the rear are all the Cossacks, the majority of the military training schools and also the best fighting units." Along with this

Prince Trubetzkoy characterized as the mood of the masses "indifference that submits to the blow of the whip."

Had it been merely a question of defending Kerensky, Kornilov might have encountered little resistance. But Prince Trubetzkoy, living in the secluded atmosphere of the Stavka, most fundamentally misjudged the mood of the masses when he anticipated from them an attitude of passive indifference. Among the city workers, and the poorer classes generally, among the soldiers there was still a large residue of the mood of fierce discontent that had boiled over in the July Days. Kornilov's challenge to the Provisional Government, his effort to set up a military dictatorship was just the stimulus that was needed to turn this mood into one of vigorous, active resistance. From the very beginning the attempted coup was doomed by the cloud of sabotage and propaganda which enveloped it. Railroad workers refused to operate or delayed the dispatch of the trains which carried the Kornilov troops. Telegraph operators declined to transmit the messages of Kornilov's generals. At every station the Kornilov troops found themselves surrounded by impromptu propagandists, workers and soldiers of the local garrisons, who rapidly undermined their morale by pointing out that they were being sent against the legal Government and urging them not to fight: an uncommonly popular appeal to the staunchest Russian troops in 1917. As Milyukov says: "The issue was decided not so much by the troop movements, by the strategic or tactical successes of the Government or Kornilov detachments as by the sentiment of the troops. . . . Bloodshed did not take place, for the simple reason that no one wanted to shed blood and sacrifice himself, on either side."

A lively war of words between Kerensky and Kornilov developed on the 9th [August 27]. Savinkov, who was naturally one of the most active advocates of agreement, vainly endeavored to persuade Kornilov to give up his post as a means of paving the way to further discussion and removal of misunderstanding. Kerensky issued a rather temperately worded manifesto (its mildness probably reflected the influence of some of his counsellors, such as

Tereschenko, who were still hoping for a compromise solution) in which he declared that Kornilov had despatched Lvov to him with the demand for the handing over of all military and civil power, ordered Kornilov to turn over his command to General Klembovsky, Commander of the northern front, proclaimed a state of martial law in Petrograd and urged all citizens to maintain order and tranquillity.

Kornilov responded with a much more violently worded telegram, characterizing the first part of Kerensky's manifesto as "a complete falsehood," inasmuch as he had not sent Lvov to Kerensky, but Lvov had come to him as Kerensky's spokesman. "So," Kornilov continued, "a great provocation, which placed the fate of the fatherland at stake, was carried out." Kornilov's declaration, written in a style of old-fashioned sentimentality by his literary aide, Zavoiko, urged all Russians "to pray the Lord God for the greatest miracle, the salvation of the native land" and ended:

I, General Kornilov, son of a Cossack peasant, say to everyone that personally I desire nothing, except the preservation of Great Russia, and I vow to bring the people, by means of victory over the enemy, up to the Constituent Assembly, at which it will itself decide its fate and choose the form of its new state life. I cannot betray Russia into the hands of its ancestral enemy, the German race, and make the Russian people slaves of the Germans and I prefer to die on the field of honor and battle, so as not to see the shame and destruction of the Russian land.

Russian people, the life of your motherland is in your hands.

While such an appeal was calculated to strike a responsive chord in the heart of an old-fashioned officer, landowner or priest, its propagandist effect among the masses could scarcely have been great, even if it could have been widely distributed. War and victory were not popular slogans in Russia at that time; and the workers and soldiers were inclined to see the enemy in the "bourgeoisie" and not in the Germans.

Kornilov received the unanimous support of the commanders of the four European fronts. General Klembovsky declined the offered post of Commander-in-chief with the observation that he "considered any change in the higher command extremely dangerous." From the southwestern front the blunt, outspoken General Denikin, the future outstanding leader of the White cause in the civil war, sent to Kerensky a telegram with the following sharp and unambiguous phrases: "Seeing in Kornilov's removal a return of the Government to the method of systematic destruction of the army and, consequently, of destruction of the country, I consider it my duty to inform the Provisional Government that on this road I will not go with it." Denikin took this occasion to remind the Premier that he had already accused the Government of having "destroyed the army and trampled our fighting banners in the mud." General Baluev, on the western front, and General Sherbatchev, on the Rumanian front, also expressed solidarity with Kornilov.

This support by the highest Generals was, of course, infinitely less significant than it would have been in a country where ordinary army discipline prevailed. Not one of these commanders of fronts was in a position to send to Kornilov's aid a company, to say nothing of a corps or division of troops. Denikin, the most active and energetic of them, could do no more than place a guard at the telegraph station in Berditchev, where his headquarters were located; and by September 11 [August 29] the committee of the southwestern front felt itself strong enough to place Denikin, his Chief of Staff, Markov, and some of his other associates under arrest.

In Petrograd Government circles, however, the weakness of Kornilov's position was not immediately grasped; and the representations of the Generals, combined with exaggerated rumors about the progress of Kornilov's military units strengthened the hands of the advocates of some sort of face-saving compromise. The tenth was a day of nervous conferences of the Ministers. The Cadet leader, Paul Milyukov, was especially active in endeavoring to find a solution which would not permit Kornilov to be crushed. As late as the evening of the tenth [August 28] Milyukov was urging, in a conference at the Winter Palace, that Kerensky should resign his office in favor of General Alekseev, to whom Kornilov might be expected to submit. Such a "compromise" would have been a victory for Kornilovism, if not for Kornilov, because Alekseev, while a much more cautious and discreet man, certainly shared Kornilov's views as to the necessity for a drastic restoration of discipline and for a generally more conservative turn of governmental policy. Even Kerensky's closest political friends were wavering: Tereschenko suggested that "both Kerensky and Kornilov should obtain satisfaction at the price of mutual sacrifices," and Nekrasov, who seems to have considerably overestimated Kornilov's chances of military success, also advised Kerensky to retire.

At this moment, however, according to Milyukov's account, Kerensky received a sudden access of moral reinforcement. A delegation from the Soviet appeared, demanding the uncompromising suppressing of Kornilov's movement. The idea of a compromise Premiership of Alekseev vanished. Another effort at mediation failed when Tereschenko, on the eleventh [August 29], politely declined a tender of good offices as mediators in the conflict which the British Ambassador, Sir George Buchanan, made on behalf of the representatives of all the Allied powers and the United States on the evening of the tenth. Sir George accompanied the offer with the statement that it was made "with the sole object of averting civil war and serving the interests of Russia and her allies." Tereschenko replied that Kornilov's attitude made it impossible for the Government to make terms with him. By the eleventh the balance of forces had visibly changed to Kornilov's disadvantage.

The effect of Kornilov's move on the Petrograd Soviet was that of an electric shock, awakening that organization to new life and to a unanimous will to resistance. The Mensheviki and the Socialist Revolutionaries were quick to forget the unpleasant memories of the July Days in facing the immediate menace of an occupation of the revolutionary capital by Krimov and his Caucasian and Cossack cavalry. There was a general feeling that the Kornilov officers would make small distinction between members of the various revolutionary parties when the hangings began. And it was a Menshevik, Weinstein, who proposed formal cooperation with the Bolsheviki at the session of the Vtsik on the evening of September 9.

According to Weinstein's proposal, which was accepted, a "Committee for Struggle with Counterrevolution," consisting of three Bolsheviki, three Mensheviki, three Socialist Revolutionaries, five representatives of the Vtsik and the Executive Committee of Peasants' Deputies and two representatives each from the trade unions and from the Petrograd Soviet, was created. The Bolshevik spokesman, Sokolnikov, promised the cooperation of his Party; its influence on the soldiers and workers was indeed indispensable to the successful organization of the masses.

The Bolshevik tactics at this important turn of events (summed up by Lenin in the phrase: "We will fight with Kornilov, but we will not support Kerensky") revealed a high measure of finesse and flexibility. Exploiting to the utmost the opportunity for winning the masses away from the more moderate Socialist parties, they made all possible use of the possibilities for legal action which were extended to them and did not compromise themselves by any premature and ill-judged effort to overthrow the shadowy Provisional Government, which, with tongue in cheek, they were defending.

Their greatest success, perhaps, was in securing the approval of the Committee for Struggle with Counterrevolution for the creation of an armed workers' militia. This was little more than a legalization and rearming of the Red Guard which had been to some extent repressed and driven underground after the July Days. Within a few days some 25,000 recruits were enlisted in this organization, and the Bolshevik Military Organization succeeded in supplying them not only with rifles, but also with machine guns.

While the Bolsheviki were the main driving force in organizing the masses, Kerensky, with his usual instinct for balancing between Right and Left, entrusted the defense of Petrograd to two men who had only recently been earnest advocates of Kornilov's military programme, Savinkov, who was appointed military governor, and his assistant, Filonenko. Savinkov took measures to assure the food supply and the railroad communication of the capital and simultaneously kept an eye on the Bolsheviki, sending back to Kronstadt 2,000 sailors who had arrived on their own initiative and who impressed him as undesirable champions of the Provisional Government.

The Committee for Struggle with Counterrevolution inaugurated a nationwide campaign for resistance to Kornilov, encouraging the creation of similar local committees in all important towns, sending instructions to the garrisons of the neighboring towns and to the strategically important railroad and post and telegraph workers. The outskirts of Petrograd were an armed camp. True, the military quality of the Petrograd troops, if one may credit the testimony of Filonenko and of the Commander of the Moscow garrison, Verkhovsky, who had preserved his loyalty to the Provisional Government, was very low; the chances of resistance to a powerful, well organized attack of disciplined troops would have been slight.

But the whole political and social background simply excluded the possibility of any such attack. Kornilov's warriors, so formidable in the imagination of nervous Ministers, simply melted away, like their predecessors, the force which Nicholas II dispatched against Petrograd under General Ivanov.

From a purely military standpoint the preparation of the coup was very incompetent and reflects little credit on the capacity of many of Kornilov's officers who were responsible for making the plans. The Savage Division, one of the main units involved, consisted of only 1,350 horsemen and was short of 600 rifles, 1,000 lances and 500 spears. The units were not provided with field telegraph apparatus, and were consequently exposed to loss of communication both with the Stavka and among themselves. Kornilov himself, instead of taking the field with his troops, remained in Moghilev.

The fate of the units which took part in the affair was much the same, with minor variations. The Savage Division, under the command of Prince Bagration, reached the railroad station Viritsa, about twenty-four miles from Tsarskoe Syelo, on the evening of the tenth [August 28]. Here its progress was checked because the railroad line was torn up. On the following day a Mohammedan delegation, organized by the Soviet, arrived in Viritsa. It included among its members a grandson of the national hero of the mountaineers of the East Caucasus, Shamil. The exhortations and arguments of this delegation, voiced in the varied guttural tongues of the Caucasian tribesmen, quickly shook the confidence of the troops in their officers; on the twelfth Prince Bagration ordered the cessation of any hostile activity of his soldiers against the troops of the Provisional Government (actually no bloodshed had occurred). And on the thirteenth [August 31] a delegation of the Caucasian warriors in their picturesque native costumes appeared in Petrograd with vows of loyalty to the Provisional Government and expressions of regret for having been misled.

The Cossack regiments which were to cooperate with the Savage Division had much the same experience. Wherever they moved they were surrounded by zealous propagandists, who slipped in among them, despite the efforts of the officers to prevent this and used such arguments as:

"Comrades, Kerensky freed you from the officer's stick, gave you freedom; and do you want to crawl before the officer again? . . . Kerensky is for freedom and the happiness of the people. Kornilov is for discipline and the death penalty. Are you really for Kornilov? . . . Kornilov is a traitor to Russia and goes to lead you to battle in defense of foreign capital. He got much money for this, and Kerensky wants peace." There was no lack of agencies of propaganda: the Soviets, the station committees, the garrisons which were stationed in towns like Yamburg, Narva and Luga. Moreover, partly as a result of the poor technical preparation of the whole affair, partly because of the vigorous and deliberate sabotage of the railroad workers, the cavalry force by September 12 [August 30] was in a hopelessly scattered and disorganized state, dispersed along eight railroad lines and poorly supplied with food and forage. The authority of the officers had almost disappeared; the actual power was in the hands of the soldiers' committees, which hastened to offer assurances of submission to the Provisional Government. The generals and higher officers had no alternative except to follow their example.

The collapse of the enterprise was so evident that General Krimov himself went to Petrograd; and after an interview with Kerensky, who accused him of deliberate mutiny, withdrew to the apartment of one of his officers and shot himself through the heart.

The other forces which were supposed to cooperate in making the coup successful proved quite impotent. The leaders of the Petrograd patriotic societies proved to be charlatans and adventurers. When the time for action came they either disappeared altogether, in some cases taking with them the funds of the organizations, or were found carousing in restaurants. The Committee for Struggle with Counterrevolution raided the Astoria Hotel, a favorite rendezvous of officers, and made fourteen arrests; but the precaution was almost superfluous.

The Don Cossack Ataman Kaledin, on whose support Kornilov had relied, and to whom he addressed a personal appeal, was threatened with arrest by the Soviet of Voronezh, a town lying near the frontier of the Don Territory and hastened back to his capital, Novo-Cherkassk, by a circuitous route, avoiding the larger railroad centres. The loyalty of the majority of the Cossacks was a sufficient guaranty for Kaledin's safety in Novo-Cherkassk; but he was in no position to exert any influence outside the frontiers of the Don Territory.

It now only remained to clear up the centre of the frustrated coup, Moghilev. On September 12 [August 30], Kerensky himself assumed the office of Commander-in-chief, appointing as his Chief of Staff General Alekseev. The latter's assumption of office under Kerensky is explained by his desire to make the liquidation of the abortive coup as painless as possible for its participants. After some long distance conversations with Kornilov and Lukomsky, Alekseev proceeded to Moghilev and on September 14 [September 1] after being insistently prodded by Kerensky, who himself was being urged by the Soviet to show no leniency toward the conspirators, he formally arrested Kornilov, Lukomsky, Romanovsky and Colonel Pluschevsky-Pluschik. Members of an investigating commission arrived on the following day and carried out further arrests. This commission, which consisted of representatives of various public organizations, headed by a judicial investigator, Shablovsky, was decidedly indulgent in its attitude toward the arrested prisoners; as Lukomsky testifies: "After the first examinations which the members of the commission carried out it was evident that they were all very well disposed toward us." Instead of pressing on the investigation with a view to a speedy trial the commission carried on its work in very leisurely fashion. Meanwhile the prisoners were transferred from Moghilev to a monastery in the neighboring town of Bikhov, where they were joined by Denikin, Markov and other persons arrested in Berditchev, who narrowly escaped being lynched by the enraged mob. After the Bolshevik Revolution the Generals were able to flee from Bikhov, and played a prominent part in the civil war in South Russia.

The Kornilov plot collapsed without the firing of a shot and without bloodshed—except for such local excesses as the drowning of ten officers suspected of sympathy with Kornilov in Viborg and the shooting of four naval officers of the warship *Petropavlovsk* by sailors who were infuriated by the refusal of the officers to sign a pledge of loyalty to the Provisional Government. But its significance was far-reaching in the extreme. Quite probably an ultimate victory of Bolshevism was predetermined by the entire political, economic and social condition of Russia in 1917. But Kornilov's futile, clumsy thrust for power facilitated and expedited this victory. It was no accident that the two most important Soviets in the country cast their first Bolshevik majorities immediately after the Kornilov affair: Petrograd on September 13 [September 1], and Moscow on September 18 [September 5].

5. The Capture of the Winter Palace

LEON TROTSKY

Trotsky's three-volume History of the Russian Revolution occupies a truly exceptional place in the vast bibliography on the subject. In many ways the qualifications of the author are unique. He was not only a major leader and spokesman of the Bolshevik Party and the second most important protagonist of the victorious coup, but also an ubiquitous, mercurial reporter of many of the events described in his work. His literary gifts, his dazzling brilliance of imagery, his ability to analyze and summarize a situation, to characterize a personality in a few epigrammatic words, are hardly matched among his contemporaries. Moreover, his work was obviously based on a respectable amount of research. Its scope is impressive. It reminds us of a broad panorama, not unlike the murals of his Mexican friend Diego Rivera.

SOURCE: Leon Trotsky, The History of the Russian Revolution, 3 vols. (New York: Simon & Schuster, 1936) 3:247–275. Reprinted by permission of the publisher.

Yet, the shortcomings of his work are also striking. As he proudly puts it in the preface, he scornfully rejected the scholarly concept of impartiality and refused to assume the position of an observer who can stand "on the wall of a threatened city and behold at the same time the besiegers and the besieged." This, he argued, would amount to practicing "conciliatory justice," contrary to the position of a fighter morally and politically engaged in the struggle to the hilt. He never hides his hostility and scorn for his Party's enemies. As B. D. Wolff pointed out, Trotsky is never satisfied with cutting his opponent's heart; he insists on showing that it is empty. The Marxist notion that individuals are mere instruments, slaves of historical process, specks of dust on the wheel of history, is strikingly absent from Trotsky's work. He ascribes, for example, the decisive role in the Revolution to Lenin. He asserts that "had Lenin not managed to come to Petrograd in April, 1917, the October Revolution would not have taken place." Trotsky stresses that the Revolution took place in 1917 not because of any basic change in the country's socioeconomic structure, which was essentially stationary since 1905/7, but because of the changes in the attitudes of the masses, and because in 1917 she was provided with the superior leadership of Lenin.

Volume 1 of the trilogy covers the overthrow of the Tsarist regime and the establishment of the Provisional Government. Volume 2 deals with the attempts of that government to deal with the opposition on the Left (the Bolshevik July uprising) and the Right (the Kornilov affair). Volume 3 is devoted to the Bolshevik action which preceded the October–November coup and its execution; it is entitled, The Triumph of the Soviets. The first draft of the History of the Russian Revolution was started soon after the October upheaval. During the subsequent years, Trotsky went on working at his major historical work but he completed it only in 1930 while in exile on Prinkipo Island, in Turkey. As his main biographer, Isaac Deutscher, put it, Trotsky "defended the revolution against its enemies; and he defended his own place in it." These circumstances, as Deutscher has admitted, were "designed to inflame his passion, to rob him of every calm thought, and to distort his vision." Consequently he produced a most impressive but frankly partisan work, a weapon in his life-and-death struggle against his political rival, Stalin.

The capture of the Winter Palace, the seat and symbol of the Provisional Government, described in the passage that follows, consummated the Bolshevik seizure of power in Petrograd (October 25, November 7, 1917). The seizure of the palace was followed by the proclamation by Lenin of the triumph of the Bolsheviks and the formation of the Soviet of People's Commissars, or the Soviet Government.

Whether the operation was a carefully planned, dramatic offensive, or merely a series of chaotic, erratic, rather anticlimactic and rather accidental operations, has been the subject of many debates among historians. The fragments of a chapter of Leon Trotsky's History of the Revolution (translated by Max Eastman) included in the present anthology give an early Bolshevik version of the event. They are fully in accordance with the "heroic/inevitable" line consistently followed by the Communist historiography from the beginning to the present day.

★   ★   ★   ★   ★

It had been proposed in the preliminary calculations to occupy the Winter Palace on the night of the twenty-fifth [November 7], at the same time with the other commanding high points of the capital. A special trio had been formed already as early as the twenty-third [November 5] to take the lead in seizing the palace, Podvoisky[1] and Antonov[2] being the central figures. The engineer Sadovsky, a man in military service, was included as a third, but soon fell away, being preoccupied with the affairs of the garrison. He was replaced by Chudnovsky, who had come with Trotsky in May from the concentration camp in Canada, and had spent three months at the front as a soldier. Lashevich also took an important part in the operations—an old Bolshevik who had done enough service in the army to become a non-commissioned officer. Three years later Sadovsky remembered how Podvoisky and Chudnovsky quarrelled furiously in his little room in Smolny over the

[1] N. I. Podvoisky (1880–1948), a leader of the Bolshevik military organization, and one of the organizers of the Red Guards.
[2] V. A. Antonov-Ovseyenko (1884–1938), a professional officer who joined the Bolshevik Party in May 1917. In October–November he was secretary of the Petrograd Soviet's Military-Revolutionary Committee.

map of Petrograd and the best form of action against the palace. It was finally decided to surround the region of the palace with an uninterrupted oval, the longer axis of which should be the quay of the Neva. On the river side the circle should be closed up by the Peter and Paul fortress, the [cruiser] *Aurora,* and other ships summoned from Kronstadt and the navy. In order to prevent or paralyze attempts to strike at the rear with Cossacks and junker detachments, it was decided to establish imposing flank defenses composed of revolutionary detachments.

The plan as a whole was too heavy and complicated for the problem it aimed to solve. The time allotted for preparation proved inadequate. Small incoordinations and omissions came to light at every step, as might be expected. In one place the direction was incorrectly indicated; in another the leader came late, having misread the instructions; in a third they had to wait for a rescuing armored car. To call out the military units, unite them with the Red Guards, occupy the fighting positions, make sure of communications among them all and with headquarters—all this demanded a good many hours more than had been imagined by the leaders quarrelling over their map of Petrograd.

When the Military Revolutionary Committee announced at about ten o'clock in the morning that the government was overthrown, the extent of this delay was not yet clear even to those in direct command of the operation. Podvoisky had promised the fall of the palace "not later than twelve o'clock." Up to that time everything had run so smoothly on the military side that nobody had any reason to question the hour. But at noon it turned out that the besieging force was still not filled out, the Kronstadters had not arrived, and that meanwhile the defense of the palace had been reinforced. This loss of time, as almost always happens, made new delays necessary. Under urgent pressure from the Committee the seizure of the palace was now set for three o'clock—and this time "conclusively." Counting on this new decision, the spokesman of the Military Revolutionary Committee expressed to the afternoon session of the Soviet the hope that the fall of the Winter Palace would be a matter of the next few minutes. But another hour passed and brought no decision. Podvoisky, himself in a state of white heat, asserted over the telephone that by six o'clock the palace would be taken no matter what it cost. His former confidence, however, was lacking. And indeed the hour of six did strike and the denouement had not begun. Beside themselves with the urgings of Smolny,[3] Podvoisky and Antonov now refused to set any hour at all. That caused serious anxiety. Politically it was considered necessary that at the moment of the opening of the Congress[4] the whole capital should be in the hands of the Military Revolutionary Committee. That was to simplify the task of dealing with the opposition at the Congress, placing them before an accomplished fact. Meanwhile the hour appointed for opening the Congress had arrived, had been postponed, and arrived again, and the Winter Palace was still holding out. Thus the siege of the palace, thanks to its delay, became for no less than twelve hours the central problem of the insurrection.

The main staff of the operation remained in Smolny, where Lashevich held the threads in his hands. The field headquarters was in the Peter and Paul fortress, where Blagonravov[5] was the responsible man. There were three subordinate headquarters, one on the *Aurora*, another in the barracks of the Pavlovsky regiment, another in the barracks of the sailors. In the field of action the leaders were Podvoisky and Antonov—apparently without any clear order of priority.

In the quarters of the general staff a trio was also bending over the map: the commander of the district Colonel Polkovnikov, the chief of his staff General Bagratuni, and General Alexeiev, especially invited in as a high authority. Notwithstanding this so well qualified commanding staff, the plans of the defense were in-

[3] Smolny Institute, formerly a fashionable girls' boarding school, was headquarters of the Military Revolutionary Committee; it became Lenin's headquarters after midnight October 25 (November 7).
[4] The Second Congress of Soviets was to meet in Petrograd at the end of October (Old Style). The Military Revolutionary Committee was called for in a resolution of the Executive Committee of the Petrograd Soviet on October 12 (25) and actually convoked on October 20 (November 2).
[5] A. A. Blagonravov (1894–?), then a junior officer of artillery, later on a Soviet lieutenant general.

comparably less definite than those of the attack. It is true that the inexperienced marshals of the insurrection did not know how to concentrate their forces rapidly and deal a punctual blow. But the forces were there. The marshals of the defense had cloudy hopes in place of forces: maybe the Cossacks will make up their minds; maybe loyal units will be found in the neighboring garrison; maybe Kerensky will bring troops from the front. The feelings of Polkovnikov are known from his night telegrams to headquarters: he thought that the game was up. Alexeiev, still less inclined to optimism, soon abandoned the rotten ship.

Delegates from the military schools were brought into headquarters for the purpose of keeping in touch, and an attempt was made to raise their spirits with assurances that troops would soon arrive from Gatchina, Tsarskoe[6] and the front. However, they did not much believe in these misty promises, and a depressing rumor began to creep through the schools: "There is a panic in headquarters, nobody is doing anything." And it was so. Cossack officers coming to headquarters to propose that they seize the armored cars in the Mikailovsky Riding Academy found Polkovnikov sitting on the window seat in a condition of complete prostration. Seize the riding academy? "Seize it. I have nobody. I can't do anything alone."

While this languid mobilization of the schools for the defense of the Winter Palace was going on, the ministers assembled at a meeting. The square before the palace and its adjacent streets were still free from insurrectionists. On the corner of Morskaia[7] they were absorbed in carrying out their too complicated plan. Military units, workers' detachments, armored cars, are still assembling for this wide encirclement. The palace district begins to look like a plague spot which is being encircled far away to avoid direct contact with the infection.

The court of the palace opening on the square is piled up with logs of wood like the court of Smolny. Black three-inch field guns

[6] Gatchina and Tsarskoe Selo, both summer residences of the tsars.
[7] Morskaia, a side street of the Nevsky Prospect, one of the main thoroughfares of Petrograd; Nevsky Prospect runs from the Admiralty and the Winter Palace, both at the Neva, through most of the central part of the city.

are set up to left and right. Rifles are stacked up in several different places. The small guard of the palace clings close to the building. In the court and the first story, two schools of ensigns from Oranienbaum and Peterhoff [8] are quartered—not the whole schools by any means—and a squad from the Constantinovsky Artillery School with six cannon.

During the afternoon a battalion of junkers from the engineering school arrived, having lost half a company on the road. The picture presented when they arrived could in no wise have increased the fighting spirit of the junkers which, according to Stankevich, was inadequate even before. Inside the palace they found a lack of provisions. Even of this nobody had thought in time. A truckload of bread had been seized, it turned out, by patrols of the Committee. Some of the junkers did sentry duty; the rest lay around inactive, uncertain and hungry. No leadership whatever made itself felt. In the square before the palace, and on the quay on the other side, little groups of apparently peaceful passers-by began to appear, and they would snatch the rifles from the junker sentries, threatening them with revolvers.

"Agitators" also began to appear among the junkers. Had they gotten in from the outside? No, these were still evidently internal troublemakers. They succeeded in starting a ferment among the Oranienbaum and Peterhoff students. The committees of the school called a conference in the White Hall, and demanded that representatives of the government come in and make an explanation. All the ministers came in, with Konovalov at their head. The argument lasted a whole hour. Konovalov was heckled and stopped talking. The Minister of Agriculture, Maslov,[9] made a speech as an old revolutionist. Kishkin[10] explained to the junkers that the government had decided to stand firm as long as possible.

[8] Oranienbaum and Peterhoff (since 1944 Petrodvorets), both Imperial summer residences as well as seats of military schools situated near Petrograd.
[9] S. L. Maslov, member of the Right faction of the Social Revolutionary Party and minister of agriculture (October 1917).
[10] N. M. Kishkin, member of the Kadet Party, commissar of the Provisional Government in Moscow (March–August 1917), minister of welfare (September–October), appointed to command Petrograd on the very last day of the existence of the Provisional Government (October 25–November 7).

According to Stankevich one of the junkers was about to express his readiness to die for the government, but "the obvious coolness of the rest of his comrades held him back." The speech of the other ministers produced actual irritation among the junkers, who interrupted, shouted and even, it seems, whistled. The bluebloods explained the conduct of the majority of the junkers by their low social origin: "They were all from the plow, half-illiterate, ignorant beasts, cattle . . ."

The meeting in the besieged palace ended nevertheless in conciliation. The junkers,[11] after they had been promised active leadership and correct information about what was happening, agreed to stay. The chief of the engineering school, appointed commander of the defense, ran his pencil over the plan of the palace, writing in the names of the units. The forces on hand were distributed in fighting positions. The majority of the junkers were stationed on the first floor where they could train their guns on Winter Palace Square through the windows. But they were forbidden to fire first. A battalion of the Engineering School was brought out into the courtyard to cover the artillery. Squads were appointed for barricade work. A communication squad was formed with four men from each unit. The artillery squad was directed to defend the gate in case of a breach. Fortifications of firewood were laid up in the court and before the gates. Something like order was established. The sentries felt more confident.

A civil war in its first steps, before real armies have been formed and before they are tempered, is a war of naked nerves. As soon as a little activity developed on the side of the junkers,—their clearing of the square with gunfire from behind the barricades—the forces and equipment of the defense were enormously overestimated in the attacking camp. In spite of the dissatisfaction of the Red Guard and the soldiers, the leaders now decided to postpone the assault until they had concentrated their reserves; they were chiefly awaiting the arrival of the sailors from Kronstadt.

The delay of a few hours thus created brought some small reinforcements to the besieged. After Kerensky's promise of infantry

[11] Junkers—officer cadets.

to the Cossack delegation, the Council of the Cossack Troops had gone into session, the regimental committees had gone into session, and the general assembly of the regiments had gone into session. Decision: Two squadrons and the machine gun crew of the Uralsky regiment, brought in from the front in July to crush the Bolsheviks, should immediately enter the Winter Palace, the rest not until the promise was actually fulfilled—that is, not until after the arrival of infantry reinforcements. But even with the two squadrons this was not accomplished without argument. The Cossack youth objected. The "old men" even had to lock the young ones up in the stable, where they could not hinder them from equipping themselves for the march. Only at twilight, when they were no longer expected, did these bearded Uraltsi appear in the palace. They were met like saviors. They themselves, however, looked sulky. They were not accustomed to fight about palaces. Yes, and it was not quite clear which side was right.

Sometime later there arrived unexpectedly forty of the Cavaliers of St. George under command of a staff captain on a cork leg. Patriotic cripples acting as the last reserves of democracy. . . . But even so they felt better. Soon came also a shock company of the Woman's Battalion. What encouraged them most of all was that these reinforcements had made their way through without fighting. The cordon of the besieging forces could not, or did not dare, deny them access to the palace. Quite obviously, therefore, the enemy was weak. "Glory be to God, the thing is beginning to pull itself together," said the officers, comforting themselves and the junkers. The new arrivals received their military allotments, replacing those who were tired. However, the Uraltsi glanced with no great approval upon those "wenches" with rifles. Where is the real infantry?

The besiegers were obviously losing time. The Kronstadters were late—not, to be sure, through their own fault. They had been summoned too late. After a tense night of preparation they had begun to embark at dawn. The destroyer *Amur* and the cruiser *Yastreb* had made straight for Petrograd. The old armored cruiser *Zaria Svobodi*, after landing marines at Oranienbaum, where it was proposed to disarm the junkers, was to anchor at the entrance to the Morskoy Canal, in order in case of need to bombard the Baltic railroad. Five thousand sailors and soldiers disembarked early in the morning from the Island of Kotlin in order to embark on the social revolution. In the officers' cabin a solemn silence reigns. These officers are being taken along to fight for a cause which they hate. The commissar of the detachment, the Bolshevik, Flerovsky, announces to them: "We do not count upon your sympathy, but we demand that you be at your posts. . . . We will spare you any unnecessary unpleasantness." He received the brief naval answer: "Aye, Aye, sir!" All took their places. The commander ascended the bridge.

Upon arriving in the Neva a triumphal hurrah: the sailors are greeting their own. A band strikes up on the *Aurora*, anchored in midstream. Antonov addresses the new arrivals with a brief greeting: "There is the Winter Palace . . . We must take it." In the Kronstadt detachment the most resolute and bold choose themselves out automatically. These sailors in black blouses with rifles and cartridge belts will go all the way. The disembarkation on Konnogvardeisky Boulevard takes but a few moments. Only a military watch remains on the ship.

The forces are now more than adequate on the Nevsky. There are strong outposts on the bridge of the Ekaterininsky Canal and on the bridge of the Moika armored automobiles and Zenith guns aimed at the Winter Palace. On this side of the Moika the workers have set up machine guns behind screens. An armored car is on duty on Morskaia. The Neva and its crossings are in the hands of the attackers. Chudnovsky and ensign Dashkevich are ordered to send troops from the Guard regiments to hold Mars Field. Blagonravov from the fortress, after crossing the bridge, is to get into contact with the troops on Mars Field. The sailors just arrived are to keep in contact with the fortress and the crew of the *Aurora*. After artillery fire the storm is to begin.

At the same time five ships of war arrive from the Baltic battle fleet: a cruiser, two destroyers, and two smaller vessels. "However sure we may have been of winning with the forces on hand," writes Flerovsky, "this gift from the navy raised everybody's spirits." Admiral Verderovsky, looking from the windows of the Malachite Hall [of the Winter Palace], could probably see an imposing mutinous flotilla, dominating not only the palace and the surrounding district but also the principal approaches to Petrograd.

About four o'clock in the afternoon Konovalov summoned to the palace by telephone the political leaders standing close to the government. The besieged ministers had need at least of moral support. Of all those invited only Nabokov appeared. The rest preferred to express their sympathy by telephone. Minister Tretiakov complained against Kerensky and against fate: The head of the ministry has fled leaving his colleagues without defense. But perhaps reinforcements will come? Perhaps. However, why aren't they here? Nabokov expressed his sympathy, glancing stealthily at his watch, and hastened to take his farewell. He got out just in time. Shortly after six the Winter Palace was at last solidly surrounded by the troops of the Military Revolutionary Committee. There was no longer any passage either for reinforcements or for individuals.

From the direction of Konnogvardeisky Boulevard, the Admiralty Quay, Morskaia Street, Nevsky Prospect, Mars Field, Milliony Street and Dvortsovy Quay, the oval of the besiegers thickened and contracted. Imposing cordons extended from the iron fences of the Winter Palace garden, still in the hands of the besieged, from the arch between Palace Square and Morskaia Street, from the canal by the Hermitage, from the corners of the Admiralty, and the Nevsky nearby the palace. Peter and Paul fortress frowned threateningly from the other side of the river. The *Aurora* looked in from the Neva with her six-inch guns. Destroyers steamed back and forth patrolling the river. The insurrection looked at that moment like a military maneuver in the grand style.

On Palace Square, cleared by the junkers three hours before, armored automobiles now appeared and occupied the entrances and exits. Their old patriotic names were still visible on the armor under the new designations painted hastily in red. Under the protection of these steel monsters the attackers felt more and more confident on the square. One of the armored cars approached the main entrance of the palace, disarmed the junkers guarding it, and withdrew unhindered.

In spite of the complete blockade now at last established, the besieged still kept in touch with the outside world by telephone. To be sure, as early as five o'clock a company of the Keksgolmsky regiment had already occupied the War Ministry, through which the Winter Palace had kept in touch with headquarters. But even after that an officer still remained apparently for some hours at the apparatus of the southwestern front, located in an attic chamber of the ministry where the captors never thought of looking. However, as before, this contact was of no help. The answers from the northern front had become more and more evasive. The reinforcements had not turned up. The mysterious bicycle battalion never arrived. Kerensky himself seemed to have disappeared like a diver. The city friends confined themselves to brief and briefer expressions of sympathy. The ministers were sick at heart. There was nothing to talk about, nothing to hope for. The ministers disagreed with each other and with themselves. Some sat still in a kind of stupor, others automatically paced up and down the floor. Those inclined to generalization looked back into the past, seeking a culprit. He was not hard to find: the democracy! It was the democracy which had sent them into the government, laid a mighty burden on them, and at the moment of danger left them without support. For this once the Kadets were fully at one with the socialists. Yes, the democracy was to blame! To be sure, in forming the Coalition both groups had turned their back on an institution as near to them as the Democratic Conference.[12] Independence of the democracy had indeed been the chief idea of the Coalition. But never mind: what does a democracy exist for, if not to rescue a bourgeois government when it gets into trouble? The Minister of Agriculture Maslov, a Right Social Revolutionary, made a note which he himself described as a dying utterance. He solemnly promised to die with a curse to the democracy upon his

[12] Democratic Conference, a consultative body convoked at the insistence of the Central Executive Committee of the Soviets.

lips. His colleagues hastened to communicate this fateful intention to the Duma by telephone. His death, to be sure, remained only a project, but there was no lack of curses right on hand.

Up above near the chambers of the commandant there was a dining room where the court servants served the officer gentlemen a "divine dinner and wine." One could forget unpleasantnesses for a time. The officers figured out seniorities, made envious comparisons, and cursed the new power for its slow promotions. They gave it to Kerensky especially: yesterday at the Pre-Parliament[13] he was vowing to die at his post, and today he beats it out of town dressed up as a sister of mercy. Certain of the officers demonstrated to the members of the government the folly of any further resistance. The energetic Palchinsky declared such officers Bolsheviks, and tried even to arrest them.

The junkers wanted to know what was going to happen next, and demanded from the government explanations which it was not in a position to give. During this new conference between the junkers and the ministers, Kishkin arrived from staff headquarters, bringing an ultimatum signed by Antonov and delivered from the Peter and Paul fortress to the Quartermaster-General, Poravelov, by a bicycle man: Surrender and disarm the garrison of the Winter Palace; otherwise fire will be opened from the guns of the fortress and the ships of war; twenty minutes for reflection. This period had seemed small. Poravelov had managed to extract another ten minutes. The military members of the government, Manikovsky[14] and Verderevsky,[15] approached the matter simply. Since it is impossible to fight, they said, we must think of surrendering—that

[13] Pre-Parliament or Provisional Council of the Republic, a deliberative consultative body, set up by the Democratic Conference, was to serve as a temporary representation of the people until the convocation of the National Assembly. Most of the Pre-Parliament's 350 delegates were appointed from among the members of the Democratic Conference, another consultative body summoned by Kerensky after the failure of Kornilov's mutiny. The 53 Bolshevik delegates to the Pre-Parliament walked out at its first session of November 2 (October 20) after having read a sharply-worded declaration protesting its "bourgeois" character.
[14] A. A. Manikovsky, general and assistant minister of war.
[15] D. V. Verderevsky, rear admiral, commander of the Baltic Fleet from May–June, and minister of the navy, August–October 1917.

is, accept the ultimatum. But the civilian ministers remained obstinate. In the end they decided to make no answer to the ultimatum, and to appeal to the city duma as the only legal body existing in the capital. This appeal to the duma was the last attempt to wake up the drowsy conscience of the democracy.

Poravelov, considering it necessary to end the resistance, asked for his discharge: he lacked "confidence in the correctness of the course chosen by the Provisional Government." The hesitations of the officer were put an end to before his resignation could be accepted. In about half an hour a detachment of Red Guards, sailors and soldiers, commanded by an ensign of the Pavlovsky regiment, occupied the staff headquarters without resistance, and arrested the faint-hearted Quartermaster-General. This seizure of the headquarters might have been carried out some time before since the building was completely undefended from within. But until the arrival of armored cars on the Square, the besiegers feared a sortie of junkers from the palace which might cut them off.

After the loss of headquarters the Winter Palace felt still more orphaned. From the Malachite Room, whose windows opened on the Neva, and seemed, as it were, to invite a few shells from the *Aurora*, the ministers removed themselves to one of the innumerable apartments of the palace with windows on the court. The lights were put out. Only one lonely lamp burned on the table, its light shut off from the windows by newspapers.

What will happen to the palace if the *Aurora* opens fire? asked the ministers of their naval colleague. It will be a pile of ruins, exclaimed the admiral readily, and not without a feeling of pride in his naval artillery. Verderevsky preferred a surrender, and was not unwilling to frighten these civilians out of their untimely bravery. But the *Aurora* did not shoot. The fortress also remained silent. Maybe the Bolsheviks after all will not dare carry out their threat?

General Bagratuni,[16] appointed in place of the insufficiently

---

[16] General Bagratuni, chief of staff of the Petrograd Military District, commanded by Colonel Polkovnikov.

steadfast Polkovnikov, considered this the appropriate moment to announce that he refused any longer to occupy the post of commander of the district. At Kishkin's order the general was demoted "as unworthy," and was requested immediately to leave the palace. On emerging from the gates the former commander fell into the hands of the sailors, who took him to the barracks of the Baltic crew. It might have gone badly with the general, but that Podvoisky, making the rounds of his front before the final attack, took the unhappy warrior under his wing.

From the adjacent streets and quays many noticed how the palace which had just been glimmering with hundreds of electric lights was suddenly drowned in darkness. Among these observers were friends of the government. One of the colleagues of Kerensky, Redemeister, has written: "The darkness in which the palace was drowned presented an alarming enigma." The friends did not take any measures toward solving this enigma. We must confess, however, that the possibilities were not great.

Hiding behind their piles of firewood the junkers followed tensely the cordon forming on Palace Square, meeting every movement of the enemy with rifle and machine gun fire. They were answered in kind. Towards night the firing became hotter. The first casualties occurred. The victims, however, were only a few individuals. On the square, on the quays, on Milliony, the besiegers accommodated themselves to the situation, hid behind projections, concealed themselves in hollows, clung along the walls. Among the reserves the soldiers and Red Guards warmed themselves around campfires which they had kindled at nightfall, abusing the leaders for going too slow.

In the palace the junkers were taking up positions in the corridors, on the stairway, at the entrances, and in the court. The outside Sentries clung along the fence and walls. The building would hold thousands, but it held hundreds. The vast quarters behind the sphere of defense seemed dead. Most of the servants had scattered, or were hiding. Many of the officers took refuge in the buffet, where they compelled those servants who had not yet made their getaway to set out continual batteries of wines. This drunken debauch of the officers in the agonizing palace could not remain a secret to the junkers, Cossacks, cripples and women soldiers. The denouement was preparing not only from without but from within.

An officer of the artillery squad suddenly reported to the commandant of the defense: The junkers have left their weapons in the entrance and are going home, in obedience to orders received from the commandant of the Constantinovsky school. That was a treacherous blow! The commandant tried to object: nobody but he could give orders here. The junkers understood this, but nevertheless preferred to obey the commandant of the school, who in his turn was acting under pressure from the commissar of the Military Revolutionary Committee. A majority of the artillery men, with four of the six guns, abandoned the palace. Held up on the Nevsky by a soldier patrol, they attempted to resist, but a patrol of the Pavlovsky regiment, arriving just in time with an armored car, disarmed them and sent them to its barracks with two of the guns. The other two were set up on the Nevsky and the bridge over the Moika and aimed at the Winter Palace.

The two squadrons of the Uraltsi were waiting in vain for the arrival of their comrades. Savinkov, who was closely associated with the Council of the Cossack Troops, and had even been sent by it as a delegate to the Pre-parliament, attempted with the co-operation of General Alexeiev to get the Cossacks in motion. But the chiefs of the Cossack Council, as Miliukov justly observes "could as little control the Cossack regiment as the staff could the troops of the garrison." Having considered the question from all sides, the Cossack regiment finally announced that they would not come out without infantry, and offered their services to the Military Revolutionary Committee for the purpose of guarding the government property. At the same time the Uralsky regiment decided to send delegates to the Winter Palace to call its two squadrons back to the barracks. This suggestion fell in admirably with the now quite well-defined mood of the Uralsky's "old men." There was nobody but strangers around: junkers—among them a number of Jews—invalid officers—yes, and then these female shock troops. With angry and frowning faces the Cossacks gathered up their saddle bags. No further arguments could move them. Who remained to defend Nerensky? "Yids and wenches . . . but the Russian people have stayed over there with Lenin." It turned out that the Cossacks were in touch with the besiegers, and they got free passes through an exit till then unknown to the defenders. It was about nine o'clock in the evening when the Uraltsi left the palace. Only their machine guns they agreed to leave for the defense of a hopeless cause.

By this same entrance too, coming from the direction of Milliony Street, Bolsheviks had before this got into the palace for the purpose of demoralizing the enemy. Oftener and oftener mysterious figures began to appear in the corridors beside the junkers. It is useless to resist; the insurrectionists have captured the city and the railroad stations; there are no reinforcements; in the palace they "only keep on lying through inertia." . . . What are we to do next? asked the junkers. The government refused to issue any direct commands. The ministers themselves would stand by their old decision; the rest could do as they pleased. That meant free egress from the palace for those who wanted it. The government had neither will nor idea left; the ministers passively awaited their fate. Maliantovich subsequently related: "We wandered through the gigantic mousetrap, meeting occasionally, either all together or in small groups, for brief conversations—condemned people, lonely, abandoned by all. . . . Around us vacancy, within us vacancy, and in this grew up the soulless courage of placid indifference."

Antonov-Ovseënko had agreed with Blagonravov that after the encirclement of the palace was completed, a red lantern should be raised on the flagpole of the fortress. At this signal the *Aurora* would fire a blank volley in order to frighten the palace. In case the besieged were stubborn, the fortress should begin to bombard the palace with real shells from the light guns. If the palace did not surrender even then, the *Aurora* would open a real fire from its six-inch guns. The object of this gradation was to reduce to a minimum the victims and the damage, supposing they could not be altogether avoided. But the too complicated solution of a simple problem threatened to lead to an opposite result. The difficulty of carrying this plan out is too obvious. They are to start off with a red lantern. It turns out that they have none on hand. They lose time hunting for it, and finally find it. However, it is not so simple to tie a lantern to a flagpole in such a way that it will be visible in all directions. Efforts are renewed and twice renewed with a dubious result, and meanwhile the precious time is slipping away.

The chief difficulty developed, however, in connection with the artillery. According to a report made by Blagonravov the bombardment of the capital had been possible on a moment's notice ever since noon. In reality it was quite otherwise. Since there was no permanent artillery in the fortress, except for that rusty-muzzled cannon which announces the noon hour, it was necessary to lift field guns up to the fortress walls. That part of the program had actually been carried out by noon. But a difficulty arose about finding gunners. It had been known in advance that the artillery company—one of those which had not come out on the side of the Bolsheviks in July—was hardly to be relied on. Only the day before it had meekly guarded a bridge under orders from headquarters. A blow in the back was not to be expected from it, but the company had no intention of going through fire for the soviets. When the time came for action the ensign reported: The guns are rusty; there is no oil in the compressors; it is impossible to shoot. Very likely the guns really were not in shape, but that was not the essence of it. The artillerists were simply dodging the responsibility, and leading the inexperienced commissars by the nose. Antonov dashes up on a cutter in a state of fury. Who is sabotaging the plan? Blagonravov tells him about the lantern, about the oil, about the ensign. They both start to go up to the cannon. Night, darkness, puddles in the court from the recent rains. From the other side of the river comes hot rifle fire and the rattle of machine guns. In the darkness Blagonravov loses the road. Splashing through the puddles, burning with impatience, stumbling and falling in the mud, Antonov blunders after the commissar through the dark court. "Beside one of the weakly glimmering lanterns," relates Blagonravov . . . "Antonov suddenly stopped and peered inquiringly at me over his spectacles, almost touching my face. I read in his eyes a hidden alarm." Antonov had for a second suspected treachery where there was only carelessness.

The position of the guns was finally found. The artillery men were stubborn: Rust . . . compressors . . . oil. Antonov gave orders to bring gunners from the naval polygon and also to fire a signal from the antique cannon which announced the noon hour. But the artillery men were suspiciously long monkeying with the signal cannon. They obviously felt that the commanders too, when not far off at the telephone but right beside them, had no firm will to resort to heavy artillery. Even under the very clumsiness of this plan for artillery fire the same thought is to be felt lurking: Maybe we can get along without it.

Somebody is rushing through the darkness of the court. As he comes near he stumbles and falls in the mud, swears a little but not angrily, and then joyfully and in a choking voice cries out: "The palace has surrendered and our men are there." Rapturous embraces. How lucky there was a delay! "Just what we thought!" The compressors are immediately forgotten. But why haven't they stopped shooting on the other side of the river? Maybe some individual groups of junkers are stubborn about surrendering. Maybe there is a misunderstanding? The misunderstanding turned out to be good news: not the Winter Palace was captured but only headquarters. The siege of the palace continued.

By secret agreement with a group of junkers of the Oranienbaum school, the irrepressible Chudnovsky[17] gets into the palace for negotiations: this opponent of the insurrection never misses a chance to dash into the firing line. Palchinsky arrests the daredevil, but under pressure from the Oranienbaum students is compelled to release both Chudnovsky and a number of the junkers. They take away with them a few of the Cavaliers of St. George. The unexpected appearance of these junkers on the square throws the

[17] G. I. Chudnovsky, a member of the Bolshevik Party, commissar of the Preobrazhensky regiment.

cordons into confusion. But there is no end of joyful shouting, when the besiegers know that these are surrendering troops. However, only a small minority surrenders. The remainder continue to fire from behind their cover. The shooting of the attackers has increased. The bright electric light in the court makes a good mark of the junkers. With difficulty they succeed in putting out the light. Some unseen hand again switched on the light. The junkers shoot at the light, and then find the electrician and make him switch off the current.

The Woman's Battalion suddenly announce their intention to make a sortie. According to their information the clerks in General Headquarters have gone over to Lenin, and after disarming some of the officers have arrested General Alexseiev—the sole man who can save Russia. He must be rescued at any cost. The commandant is powerless to restrain them from this hysterical undertaking. At the moment of their sortie the lights again suddenly flare up in the high electric lanterns on each side of the gate. Seeking an electrician the officer jumps furiously upon the palace servants: in these former lackeys of the tzar he sees agents of revolution. He puts still less trust in the court electrician; "I would have sent you to the next world long ago if I hadn't needed you." In spite of revolver threats, the electrician is powerless to help. His switchboard is disconnected. Sailors have occupied the electric station and are controlling the light. The women soldiers do not stand up under fire and the greater part of them surrender. The commandant of the defense sends a corporal to report to the government that the sortie of the Woman's Battalion has "led to their destruction," and that the palace is swarming with agitators. The failure of the sortie causes a lull lasting approximately from ten to eleven. The besiegers are busied with the preparation of artillery fire.

The unexpected lull awakens some hopes in the besieged. The ministers again try to encourage their partisans in the city and throughout the country: "The government in full attendance, with the exception of Prokopovich, is at its post. The situation is considered favorable. . . . The palace is under fire, but only rifle fire and without results. It is clear that the enemy is weak." In reality the enemy is all-powerful but cannot make up his mind to use his power. The government sends out through the country communications about the ultimatum, about the *Aurora*, about how it, the government, can only transfer the power to the Constituent Assembly, and how the first assault on the Winter Palace has been repulsed. "Let the army and the people answer!" But just how they are to answer the ministers do not suggest.

Lashevich meantime has sent two sailor gunners to the fortress. To be sure, they are none too experienced, but they are at least Bolsheviks, and quite ready to shoot from rusty guns without oil in the compressors. That is all that is demanded of them. A noise of artillery is more important at the moment than a well-aimed blow. Antonov gives the order to begin. The gradations indicated in advance are completely followed out. "After a signal shot from the fortress," relates Flerovsky, "the *Aurora* thundered out. The boom and flash of blank fire are much bigger than from a loaded gun. The curious onlookers jumped back from the granite parapet of the quay, fell down and crawled away . . ." Chudnovsky promptly raises the question: How about proposing to the besieged to surrender. Antonov as promptly agrees with him. Again an interruption. Some group of women and junkers are surrendering. Chudnovsky wants to leave them their arms, but Antonov revolts in time against this too beautiful magnanimity. Laying the rifles on the sidewalk the prisoners go out under convoy along Milliony Street.

The palace still holds out. It is time to have an end. The order is given. Firing begins—not frequent and still less effectual. Out of thirty-five shots fired in the course of an hour and a half or two hours, only two hit the mark, and they only injure the plaster. The other shells go high, fortunately not doing any damage in the city. Is lack of skill the real cause? They were shooting across the Neva with a direct aim at a target as impressive as the Winter Palace: that does not demand a great deal of artistry. Would it not be truer to assume that even Lashevich's artillerymen intentionally aimed high in the hope that things would be settled without destruction and death? It is very difficult now to hunt out any trace of the motive which guided the two nameless sailors. They themselves have spoken no word. Have they dissolved in the immeasurable Russian land, or, like so many of the October fighters, did they lay down their heads in the civil wars of the coming months and years?

Shortly after the first shots, Palchinsky brought the ministers a fragment of shell. Admiral Verderevsky recognized the shell as his own—from a naval gun, from the *Aurora*. But they were shooting blank from the cruiser. It had been thus agreed, was thus testified by Flerovsky, and thus reported to the Congress of Soviets later by a sailor. Was the admiral mistaken? Was the sailor mistaken? Who can ascertain the truth about a cannon shot fired in the thick of night from a mutinous ship at a tzar's palace where the last government of the possessing classes is going out like an oil-less lamp?

The garrison of the palace was greatly reduced in number. If at the moment of the arrival of the Uraltsi, the cripples and the woman's battalion, it rose to a thousand and a half, or perhaps even two thousand, it was now reduced to a thousand, and perhaps considerably less. Nothing can save the day now but a miracle. And suddenly into the despairing atmosphere of the Winter Palace there bursts—not, to be sure, a miracle, but the news of its approach. Palchinsky announces: They have just telephoned from the City Duma that the citizens are getting ready to march from there for the rescue of the government. "Tell everybody," he gives orders to Sinegub, "that the people are coming." The officer runs up and down stairs and through the corridors with the joyful news. On the way he stumbles upon some drunken officers fighting each other with rapiers—shedding no blood, however. The junkers lift up their heads. Passing from mouth to mouth the news becomes more colorful and impressive. The public men, the merchantry, the people, with the clergy at their head, are marching this way to free the beleaguered palace. The people with the clergy! "That will be strikingly beautiful!" A last remnant of energy flares up: "Hurrah! Long live Russia!" The Oranienbaum junkers, who by that time had quite decided to leave, changed their minds and stayed.

But the people with the clergy come very slowly. The number of agitators in the palace is growing. In a minute the *Aurora* will open fire. There is a whispering in the corridors. And this whisper passes from lip to lip. Suddenly two explosions. Sailors have got into the palace and either thrown or dropped from the gallery two hand grenades, lightly wounding two junkers. The sailors are arrested and the wounded bound up by Kishkin, a physician by profession.

The inner resolution of the workers and sailors is great, but it has not yet become bitter. Lest they call it down on their heads, the besieged, being the incomparably weaker side, dare not deal severely with these agents of the enemy who have penetrated the palace. There are no executions. Uninvited guests now begin to appear no longer one by one, but in groups. The palace is getting more and more like a sieve. When the junkers fall upon these intruders, the latter permit themselves to be disarmed. "What cowardly scoundrels!" says Palchinsky[18] scornfully. No, these men were not cowardly. It required a high courage to make one's way into that palace crowded with officers and junkers. In the labyrinth of an unknown building, in dark corridors, among innumerable doors leading nobody knew where, and threatening nobody knew what, the daredevils had nothing to do but surrender. The number of captives grows. New groups break in. It is no longer quite clear who is surrendering to whom, who is disarming whom. The artillery continues to boom.

With the exception of the district immediately adjoining the Winter Palace, the life of the streets did not cease until late at night. The theaters and moving-picture houses were open. To the respectable and educated strata of the capital it was of no consequence apparently that their government was under fire. Redemeister on the Troitsky Bridge saw quietly approaching pedestrians whom the sailors stopped. "There was nothing unusual to be

[18] P. Palchinsky, governor general of Petrograd after the Kornilov mutiny and president, Special Council of Defense.

seen." From acquaintances coming from the direction of the People's House Redemeister learned, to the tune of a cannonade, that Chaliapin had been incomparable in *Don Carlos*. The ministers continued to tramp the floors of their mousetrap.

"It is clear that the attackers are weak"; maybe if we hold out an extra hour reinforcements will still arrive. Late at night Kishkin summoned Assistant-Minister of Finance Khrushchev, also a Kadet, to the telephone, and asked him to tell the leaders of the party that the government needed at least a little bit of help in order to hold out until the morning hours, when Kerensky ought finally to arrive with the troops. "What kind of a party is this," shouts Kishkin indignantly, "that can't send us three hundred armed men!" And he is right. What kind of a party is it? These Kadets who had assembled tens of thousands of votes at the elections in Petrograd could not put out three hundred fighters at the moment of mortal danger to the bourgeois regime. If the ministers had only thought to hunt up in the palace library the books of the materialist Hobbes, they could have read in his dialogues about civil war that there is no use expecting or demanding courage from store-keepers who have gotten rich, "since they see nothing but their own momentary advantage . . . and completely lose their heads at the mere thought of the possibility of being robbed." But after all Hobbes was hardly to be found in the tzar's library. The ministers, too, were hardly up to the philosophy of history. Kishkin's telephone call was the last ring from the Winter Palace.

Smolny was categorically demanding an end. We must not drag out the siege till morning, keep the city in a tension, rasp the nerves of the Congress, put a question mark against the whole victory. Lenin sends angry notes. Call follows call from the Military Revolutionary Committee. Podvoisky talks back. It is possible to throw the masses against the palace. Plenty are eager to go. But how many victims will there be, and what will be left of the ministers and the junkers? However, the necessity of carrying the thing through is too imperious. Nothing remains but to make the naval artillery speak. A sailor from Peter and Paul takes a slip of paper to the *Aurora*. Open fire on the palace immediately. Now, it seems, all will be clear. The gunners on the *Aurora* are ready for business, but the leaders still lack resolution. There is a new attempt at evasion. "We decided to wait just another quarter of an hour," writes Flerovsky, "sensing by instinct the possibility of a change of circumstances." By "instinct" here it is necessary to understand a stubborn hope that the thing would be settled by mere demonstrative methods. And this time "instinct" did not deceive. Towards the end of that quarter of an hour a new courier arrived straight from the Winter Palace. The palace is taken!

The Palace did not surrender but was taken by storm—this, however, at a moment when the power of resistance of the besieged had already completely evaporated. Hundreds of enemies broke into the corridor—not by the secret entrance this time but through the defended door—and they were taken by the demoralized defenders for the Duma deputation. Even so they were successfully disarmed. A considerable group of junkers got away in the confusion. The rest—at least a number of them—still continued to stand guard. But the barrier of bayonets and rifle fire between the attackers and defenders was finally broken down.

That part of the palace adjoining the Hermitage is already filled with the enemy. The junkers make an attempt to come at them from the rear. In the corridors phantasmagoric meetings and clashes take place. All are armed to the teeth. Lifted hands hold revolvers. Hand grenades hang from belts. But nobody shoots and nobody throws a grenade. For they and their enemy are so mixed together that they cannot drag themselves apart. Never mind: the fate of the palace is already decided.

Workers, sailors, soldiers are pushing up from outside in chains and groups, flinging the junkers from the barricades, bursting through the court, stumbling into the junkers on the staircase, crowding them back, toppling them over, driving them upstairs. Another wave comes on behind. The square pours into the court. The court pours into the palace, and floods up and down stairways and through corridors. On the befouled parquets, among mattresses and chunks of bread, people, rifles, hand grenades are wallowing.

The conquerors find out that Kerensky is not there, and a momentary pang of disappointment interrupts their furious joy. Antonov and Chudnovsky are now in the palace. Where is the government? That is the door—there where the junkers stand frozen in the last pose of resistance. The head sentry rushes to the ministers with a question: Are we commanded to resist to the end? No, no, the ministers do not command that. After all, the palace is taken. There is no need of bloodshed. We must yield to force. The ministers desire to surrender with dignity, and sit at the table in imitation of a session of the government. The commandant has already surrendered the palace, negotiating for the lives of the junkers, against which in any case nobody had made the slightest attempt. As to the fate of the government, Antonov refuses to enter into any negotiations whatever.

The junkers at the last guarded doors were disarmed. The victors burst into the room of the ministers. "In front of the crowd and trying to hold back the onpressing ranks strode a rather small, unimpressive man. His clothes were in disorder, a wide-brimmed hat askew on his head, eyeglasses balanced uncertainly on his nose, but his little eyes gleamed with the joy of victory and spite against the conquered." In these annihilating strokes the conquered have described Antonov. It is not hard to believe that his clothes and his hat were in disorder: It is sufficient to remember the nocturnal journey through the puddles of the Peter and Paul fortress. The joy of victory might also doubtless have been read in his eyes; but hardly any spite against the conquered in those eyes. I announce to you, members of the Provisional Government, that you are under arrest—exclaimed Antonov in the name of the Military Revolutionary Committee. The clock then pointed to 2:10 in the morning of October 26 [November 8]. The members of the Provisional Government submit to force and surrender in order to avoid bloodshed—answered Konovalov. The most important part of the ritual was thus observed.

Antonov summoned twenty-five armed men, choosing them from the first detachments to break into the palace, and turned over to them the defense of the ministry. After drawing up a minute of the proceeding, the arrestees were led out into the square. In the crowd, which had made its sacrifice of dead and wounded, there was in truth a flare up of spite against the conquered. "Death to them! Shoot them!" Individual soldiers tried to strike the ministers. The Red Guards quieted the intemperate ones: Do not stain the proletarian victory! Armed workers surrounded the prisoners and their convoy in a solid ring. "Forward!" They had not far to go—through Milliony and across the Troitsky Bridge. But the excitement of the crowd made that short journey long and full of danger. Minister Nikitin[19] wrote later very truly that but for the energetic intercession of Antonov the consequences might have been "very serious." To conclude their misadventure, the procession while on the bridge was fired on by accident, and the arrestees and their convoy had to lie down on the pavement. But here too nobody was injured. Somebody was evidently shooting in the air as a warning.

In the narrow quarters of the garrison club of the fortress, lighted with a smoky kerosene lamp because the electricity had refused to function that day, forty or fifty men were crowded. Antonov, in the presence of the commissar of the fortress, calls the roll of the ministers. There are eighteen of them, including the highest assistants. The last formalities are concluded; the prisoners are distributed in the rooms of the historic Trubetskoy Bastion. None of the defenders had been arrested: the officers and junkers were paroled on their word of honor that they would not take any action against the soviet power. Only a few of them kept their word.

Immediately after the capture of the Winter Palace rumors went round in bourgeois circles about the execution of junkers, the raping of the Woman's Battalion, the looting of the riches of the palace. All these fables had long ago been refuted when Miliukov wrote this in his History: "Those of the Woman's Battalion who had not died under fire were seized by the Bolsheviks, subjected

[19] A. M. Nikitin, a Menshevik, minister of postal telegraphs (July–August) and of the interior (September–October 1917).

during that evening and night to the frightful attentions of the soldiers, to violence and execution." As a matter of fact there were no shootings and, the mood of both sides being what it was at that period, there could not have been any shootings. Still less thinkable were acts of violence, especially within the palace where alongside of various accidental elements from the streets, hundreds of revolutionary workers came in with rifles in their hands.

Attempts at looting were actually made, but it was just these attempts which revealed the discipline of the victors. John Reed,[20] who did not miss one of the dramatic episodes of the revolution, and who entered the palace on the heels of the first cordons, tells how in the basement stores a group of soldiers were prying drawers open with the butts of their guns and dragging out carpets, linen, china, glassware. It is possible that regular robbers were working in the disguise of soldiers, as they did invariably during the last years of the war, concealing their identity in trenchcoats and *papakhi* [fur hats]. The looting had just begun when somebody shouted: "Comrades, keep your hands off, that is the property of the people." A soldier sat down at a table by the entrance with pen and paper: two Red Guards with revolvers stood behind him. Everyone going out was searched, and every object stolen was taken back and listed. In this way they recovered little statues, bottles of ink, daggers, cakes of soap, ostrich feathers. The junkers were also subjected to a careful search, and their pockets turned out to be full of stolen bric-a-brac. The junkers were abused and threatened by the soldiers, but that was as far as it went. Meanwhile a palace guard was formed with the sailor Prikhodko at the head. Sentries were posted everywhere. The palace was cleared of outsiders. In a few hours Chudnovsky was appointed commandant of the Winter Palace.

But what had become of the people advancing with the clergy at their head to liberate the palace? It is necessary to tell about this heroic attempt, the news of which had for a moment so touched the hearts of the junkers. The City Duma was the center of the

---

[20] John Reed (1892–1920), author of *Ten Days that Shook the World* (New York: International Publishers, 1919).

anti-Bolshevik forces; its building on the Nevsky was boiling like a cauldron. Parties, factions, sub-factions, groups, remnants and mere influential individuals were there discussing this criminal adventure of the Bolsheviks. From time to time they would call up the ministry languishing in the palace, and tell them that under the weight of universal condemnation the insurrection must inevitably expire. Hours were devoted to dissertations on the moral isolation of the Bolsheviks. Meanwhile the artillery began to speak. The minister Prokopovich,[21] arrested in the morning but soon released, complained to the Duma with a weeping voice that he had been deprived of the possibility of sharing the fate of his comrades. He aroused warm sympathy, but the expression of this sympathy used up time.

From the general confusion of ideas and speeches a practical plan is at last produced, and wins stormy applause from the whole meeting. The Duma must march in a body to the Winter Palace in order to die there, if necessary, with the government. The Social Revolutionaries, Mensheviks and Cooperators[22] are all alike seized with a willingness either to save the ministers or fall by their sides. The Kadets, not generally inclined to risky undertakings, this time decide to lay down their heads with the rest. Some provincials accidentally turning up in the hall, the Duma journalists, and one man from the general public, request permission in more or less eloquent language to share the fate of the Duma. The permission is granted.

The Bolshevik faction tries to offer a prosaic piece of advice: Why wander through the streets in the dark seeking death? Better call up the ministers and persuade them to surrender before blood is shed. But the democrats are indignant: These agents of insurrection want to tear from our hands not only the power, but our right to a heroic death. Meanwhile the members decided, in

[21] S. N. Prokopovich, economist and publicist, moderate Social Democrat, minister of trade and industry (July–September), minister of food (September–October 1917).
[22] In 1917 there were over 30 thousand credit, consumers', and agricultural cooperatives with nearly 20 million members. The Democratic Conference included their representatives into the Pre-Parliament.

the interest of history, to take a vote by roll call. After all, one cannot die too late—even though the death be glorious. Sixty-two members of the Duma ratify the decision: yes, they are actually going to die under the ruins of the Winter Palace. To this the fourteen Bolsheviks answer that it is better to conquer with Smolny than to die in the Winter Palace, and immediately set off for the meeting of the Soviet Congress. Only three Menshevik-Internationalists decide to remain within the walls of the Duma: they have nowhere to go and nothing to die for.

The members of the Duma are just on the point of setting out on their last journey when the telephone rings and news comes that the whole of the Executive Committee of the Peasants' Deputies is coming to join them. Unending applause. Now the picture is complete and clear: The representatives of one hundred million peasants, together with the representatives of all classes of the city population are going out to die at the hands of an insignificant gang of thugs. There is no lack of speeches and applause.

After the arrival of the Peasants' Deputies the column finally sets out along the Nevsky. At the head of the column march the burgomaster, Schreider, and the minister Prokopovich. Among the marchers John Reed noticed the Social Revolutionary, Avksentiev,[23] president of the Peasant Executive Committee, and the Menshevik leaders, Khinchuk[24] and Abramovich,[25] the first of whom was considered Right, the second Left. Prokopovich and Schreider each carried a lantern: it had been so agreed by telephone with the ministers, in order that the junkers should not take friends for enemies. Prokopovich carried beside this an umbrella, as did many others. The clergy were not present. The clergy had been created out of misty fragments of the history of the fatherland by the none too opulent imagination of the junkers.

[23] N. D. Avksentiev (1878–1943), prominent member of the Social Revolutionary Party, chairman of the Democratic Conference and the Pre-Parliament, minister of the interior (August–September 1917).
[24] L. V. Khinchuk (1868–?), a Menshevik, one of the organizers of the Petrograd Soviet.
[25] R. A. Abramovich (Rein) (1880–?), a prominent leader of the Bund and the Menshevik Party; a leading member of the Petrograd Soviet.

But the people also were absent. Their absence determined the character of the whole scheme. Three or four hundred "representatives" and not one man of those whom they represented! "It was a dark night," remembers the Social Revolutionary, Zenzinov, "and the lights on the Nevsky were not burning. We marched in a regular procession and only our singing of the Marseillaise was to be heard. Cannon shots resounded in the distance. That was the Bolsheviks continuing to bombard the Winter Palace."

At the Ekaterininsky Canal a patrol of armed sailors was stretched out across the Nevsky, blocking the way for this column of the democracy. "We are going forward," declared the condemned, "what can you do to us?" The sailors answered frankly that they would use force: "Go home and leave us alone." Someone of the marchers suggested that they die right there on the spot. But in the decision adopted by a roll call vote in the Duma this variant had not been foreseen. The minister Prokopovich clambered up on some sort of elevation and "waving his umbrella"—rains are frequent in the autumn in Petrograd—urged the demonstrators not to lead into temptation those dark and deceived people who might actually resort to arms. "Let us return to the duma and talk over methods of saving the country and the revolution."

This was truly a wise proposal. To be sure, the original plan would then remain unfulfilled. But what can you do with armed ruffians who will not permit the leaders of the democracy to die a heroic death? "They stood around for a while, got chilly and decided to go back," writes Stankevich mournfully. He too was a marcher in this procession. Without the Marseillaise now—on the contrary in a glum silence—the procession moved back along the Nevsky to the Duma building. There at last it would surely find "methods of saving the country and the revolution."

With the capture of the Winter Palace the Military Revolutionary Committee came into full possession of the capital. But just as the nails and hair continue to grow on a corpse, so the overthrown government continued to show signs of life through its official press. The "Herald of the Provisional Government," which on the twenty-fourth [November 6] had announced the retirement of the Party Councillors with right to uniform and pension, had suddenly disappeared on the twenty-fifth [November 7]—an event which, to be sure, nobody noticed. But on the twenty-sixth it appeared again as if nothing had happened. On the first page it carried a rubric: "In consequence of the shutting off of the electric current the issue of October 25 did not appear." In all other respects except only the electric current, the governmental life was going on in due order, and the "Herald" of a government now located in the Trubetskoy Bastion announced the appointment of a dozen new senators. In its column of "administrative information" a circular of the Minister of the Interior, Nikitin, advised the commissars of the provinces "not to be influenced by false rumors of events in Petrograd where all is tranquil." The minister was not after all so far wrong. The days of the revolution went by peacefully enough, but for the cannonading, whose effect was only acoustic. But just the same the historian will make no mistake if he says that on October 25 not only was the electric current shut off in the government printing plant, but an important page was turned in the history of mankind.

6. The Bolshevik Gamble

ROBERT V. DANIELS

The seizure of power in Russia by the Bolsheviks, one of the decisive events of the twentieth century, despite the fact that hundreds of books have been written on the subject, is still surrounded by many riddles, puzzles and obscurities. More, perhaps, than any other phase of the Revolution it contains a host of controversial problems of fact as well as interpretation. No wonder, therefore, that "the ten days that shook the world" have been the subject of innumerable debates among scholars.

The official Soviet writing on the Revolution has always maintained that the capture of power had been planned far ahead by the Party, acting under the guidance of the omniscient, infallible Lenin. Communist historians have insisted that Bolshevik triumph was the in-

SOURCE: Robert V. Daniels, "The Bolshevik Gamble," *The Russian Review* 26 (October 1967): 331–340. This article was derived from the work that appeared in book form as *Red October*. Reprinted by permission of the author.

evitable consequence of the Russian domestic conditions and of the international struggle of proletariat against bourgeoisie; the Communists were victorious first in Russia because in Russia they dealt a timely, masterful, powerful blow at the weakest link in the "chain of capitalism." Anti-Communist historians, however they may deplore the Bolshevik triumph, are inclined to see the coup as the inevitable result of circumstances in which the weak, helpless Provisional Government found itself victim of its own faults as well as of cold-blooded determination and superior planning by Lenin. As a French historian put it: "On a l'histoire qu'on merite." ("One has the history one deserves.")

One of the most recent as well as most thorough and brilliant works on the subject is the monograph of Robert V. Daniels, Red October (New York, 1967). Daniels has scrupulously reexamined the day-by-day, hour-by-hour, events of October 1917, sifted the existing evidence, and raised a host of pertinent questions. Did the Bolsheviks actually set any date for their coup? And if so, what date? When did the Bolshevik action of November 6 (October 24), which began as a riposte to the Provisional Government's seizure of the Party press, actually become an armed uprising? Contrary to the official Soviet view, Daniels shows that one day before the convening of the All-Russian Congress of the Soviets, the Party had not yet set a time for the insurrection, although Lenin had insisted that it come before the first session of the Congress, repeating over and over again that "delay is death." Thus, Daniels rejects the "myth that the insurrection was timed and executed according to a deliberate Bolshevik plan." He views the coup as an extraordinary series of accidents that, despite the Party's miscalculations and mistakes, gave them victory. Daniels asserts that neither Russia's cultural heritage nor her inexperience in democracy, neither the socioeconomic conditions nor the mechanics of the revolution, neither the weakness of the Provisional Government nor "Lenin's genius and trickery in propaganda" were primarily responsible for the startling Bolshevik success. All these factors did play their part, he admits. But even all of them combined did not make the triumph of communism inevitable or even likely.

As we see, Daniels emphatically repudiates most existing interpretations of the mechanics of the Bolshevik coup, liberal or Communist, and puts forward his own. It is based on an impressive body of research and is presented with logic and clarity. He sums up his thesis in one key sentence of the concluding chapter of his Red October: "The stark truth about the Bolshevik Revolution is that it succeeded against incredible odds in defiance of any rational calculation that could have been made in the fall of 1917."

The passage that follows is an article by Professor Daniels, published in The Russian Review of October 1967, devoted to the anniversary of the crucial event. This article, entitled "The Bolshevik Gamble," is a masterly condensation of his book. As such the article gives, perhaps, a better idea of the work as a whole than any single chapter or selection of excerpts would.

★   ★   ★   ★   ★

There are two main explanations of the Bolshevik overthrow of the provisional Russian democracy. According to one, the October Revolution was the product of the deepest historical trends in the Russian past. The other maintains that it was a willful imposition on those trends, arbitrarily reversing them. Marxist historiography naturally holds to the first view, though Soviet historians have always contended at the price of a certain inconsistency that Lenin's personal genius had to be present to make the inevitable revolution happen. It is also possible to see the Bolshevik Revolution as something natural if not inevitable, without being a Marxist and without even approving the outcome. However, most non-Communist historiography represents the Bolshevik coup as a deliberate and untoward reversal of what is presumed to be Russia's natural evolution toward constitutional democracy. The Bolshevik success, in this view, has to be explained by the singular qualities of monolithic organization, brilliant chicanery, and unabashed will-to-power which presumably characterized V. I. Lenin and his "instrument," the Bolshevik Party. But neither this personal will theory nor the inevitability theories is particularly convincing if evaluated critically in the light of the historical record. There is another range of considerations which needs more stress, in the often neglected realm of contingency and default.

There are at least four distinct interpretations of the October

Revolution as the natural course of Russian history: one, of course, is the official theory of the proletarian revolution; another is the theory of the revolutionary wave; a third is the theory of the modernizing dictatorship; a fourth is the notion that Russian cultural traditions made a democratic solution impossible. All of these theories, however, suffer from serious weaknesses.

The Marxist theory of the proletarian revolution to which the Bolshevik victors dogmatically subscribed holds that the development of the productive forces and class structure of a society inevitably propels it, sooner or later, from the feudal social system into capitalism, and then (when the latter has come into contradiction with the maturing forces of large-scale industry) into proletarian socialism and the classless society. Applied to Russia, the scheme immediately runs into difficulties which the Communists have resolved only by fiat. One is the obvious paradox that the so-called proletarian revolution came not, as expected (even by Lenin as late as 1916), in the most advanced countries, but in Russia. The other, associated problem is the ridiculously short duration—eight months—assigned to a "bourgeois" regime in Russia. The Russian revolution was premature and telescoped. From the theoretical standpoint these are serious aberrations which call into question either the truth of Marxism or the Marxist legitimacy of Communist power.

There were various Marxist attempts to resolve this problem. The simplest was the Menshevik view that Russia was in fact only ripe for a bourgeois regime to which they would be the loyal opposition. In the vain attempt to make this theory stand up in 1917 the Mensheviks threw away their chance to lead a truly popular revolution.

The most sophisticated adjustment of Marxism to Russia was Trotsky's "theory of permanent revolution," his proposition of 1905 that the "uneven development" of Russia would cause the bourgeois revolution to swing directly into a workers' take-over, which, in turn, would inspire the international proletarian revolution and assure the foreign support required for the survival of the Russian revolution. This messianic hope was practically official Bolshevik doctrine in 1917, and it predicted events in Russia remarkably well, though the international side fell through.

Apart from Trotsky, Marxist thought is very shallow on the actual process of revolutions. Much more light has been shed by the comparative historical and sociological analysis of revolutions, the best known of which is Crane Brinton's *Anatomy of Revolution*. According to this model of a revolutionary "wave" or "fever" following a crisis in the old order, an initial moderate revolution is naturally succeeded by an extremist phase and then a reaction. The moderate phase is, of course, represented by the February Revolution in Russia, while the Bolsheviks, as the extremists, were the Russian equivalent of the French Jacobins and the regime of Oliver Cromwell.[1] But after this point the Russian Revolution deviated from the pattern set by its predecessors. In Russia the extremists have remained indefinitely in power instead of being overthrown by a "Thermidorean reaction" or "Restoration." Russia deviates all the more if the model of revolution is adjusted to square with the vast majority of revolutions from 1848 to the present. The outcome in most cases has been the suppression or overthrow of the extremists, and the resolution of the revolutionary crisis by a nationalist or militarist dictatorship—*vide* Louis Napoleon, Mussolini, Hitler, Franco and Afro-Asian states too numerous to mention.

Was there a force in Russia in 1917 which represented the more typical, "rightist" solution? Obviously there was, in the conservative and military elements sympathetic to the abortive Kornilov coup in August. Kornilov's failure did not put an end to such sentiment; the upsurge of Bolshevik strength that followed in the fall of 1917 convinced most of the conservatives, some even in the cabinet, that the Provisional Government would have to yield to a force more resolutely prepared to reckon with the Bolsheviks and the Soviet. Kerensky has written bitterly of the tacit cooperation between the "Bolsheviks of the Right" and those of the Left, equally determined to get rid of him.

[1] Oliver Cromwell (1599–1658), Puritan leader in the British civil war and lord protector (1848–1858).

In the chaotic circumstances of 1917 it is not surprising that the Bolsheviks, as the most radical force in the country, could capitalize on the hopes and fears of the masses and strike for power while their rivals were divided. In the perspective of comparative revolutions, the uniqueness of Lenin's movement was its ability to hold power afterwards, against the forces of a prospective military dictatorship. No one in the whole political spectrum from the far Right to the Zinoviev-Kamenev faction of Bolsheviks expected Lenin's party to be able to hold out alone.

It may be argued, in explanation of the unexpected Bolshevik success, that they were historically necessary in a sense different from the Marxian. This is the view that the Bolshevik dictatorship was a national requirement, to deal with just those problems of backwardness that made the dictatorship of the proletariat so anomalous from the Marxian standpoint. Modernization, as Cyril Black has recently pointed out in *The Dynamics of Modernization*, has confronted practically every country in the world with the hurdle of violent change. The Bolsheviks had the qualities of discipline and determination to hold power under the difficult circumstances of a country in transition, and eventually they undertook the systematic modernization of Russia by dictatorial measures of state socialism. But this is not to say, because the Communists did modernize Russia, or at least bring it a long way, that theirs was the only alternative. A military dictatorship with a paternalistic state-promoted capitalism—perhaps something like Japan before World War II—could have done as well; Japan in fact has achieved in this century just about the same per capita economic growth as Russia, by very different methods. In any case, the modernization role has nothing to do with the Bolshevik victory in 1917 and little to do with their successful tenure of power in the early years. In their doctrine and program the Bolsheviks were completely unprepared for the modernizing role. They were counting on the world revolution to bail them out. The industrializing function of the socialist dictatorship had to be worked out more or less blindly and very painfully in the course of the intra-party struggles of the twenties and early thirties.

The last of the main necessitarian theories suggests that because of the limitations of Russian tradition and the Russian psycho-cultural pattern nothing but a dictatorship could successfully keep power in the country. The record of Russia's experiment with every sort of democracy in 1917—political, industrial, even military—certainly supports the notion that Russians swing from passive submission to an altogether unworkable anarchism. The history of the Russian revolutionary movement is full of examples of impatience with democratic procedures and the conviction that the masses need the tutelage of their leaders to reshape them into the Good Society. It can well be argued, given the circumstances of 1917—the weak foundation for democracy, the head of the revolutionary fever, the facts of class conflict, the challenge of modernization—that no democratic regime could have held out in Russia against a resolute dictatorial movement. On the other hand, while the Communists constituted such a movement, they were not the only alternative. Once again, a military dictatorship would have answered to the situation much more directly and quickly.

While circumstances made the Bolshevik success possible, it was neither inevitable nor, except on a temporary basis, likely. The obvious alternative explanation to fill the gap is the theory of the willful imposition of Bolshevik power on an unwilling and un-natural victim, in other words, the theory of the personal role of Lenin in shaping the future of Russia. That he was alone responsible for nipping in the bud a presumably natural development of Russian democracy is implausible, in the light of the conditions described above. He was more instrumental, certainly, in keeping Russia out of the pattern of counterrevolutionary military dictatorships.

The success of the Bolsheviks in taking power by armed insurrection and holding it as a one-party dictatorship is inconceivable without the personal force of Lenin, his truly Nietzschean will-to-power. From the moment he returned to Russia in April 1917, Lenin sensed the chance to take power and rule alone, and from then on he contemplated no serious alternative. He was determined to seize power by force and violence, *even if they were not necessary*, to baptize his revolution in blood and drive encumbering and equivocal allies into opposition where he could destroy them. Without Lenin the Bolsheviks would have been another left-wing debating society, if they kept any identity separate from the left-wing Mensheviks.

Lenin's will alone, of course, was not enough to change the course of history. He had to have some point of application, and some instrument to apply his will. The ways he met these needs give rise to two particular lines of interpretation of his success: the propagandistic and the organizational.

Lenin was a brilliant propagandist and sloganeer, even if Trotsky and Lunarcharsky were more enthralling speakers. Lenin was able to sense the mood of the masses and play upon it adroitly with promises of bread, land, peace, and power to the soviets. He was able to exploit momentary issues and misunderstandings to great effect—for example, the rumors early in October that there was a right-wing plot afoot to surrender Petrograd to the Germans and thus stifle the revolution. This is not to say that Lenin's line was a cynical deception; there was no reason for him to disbelieve such rumors. The point is the adroit use he made of his opportunities.

Even more commonly stressed, by both Communist and anti-Communist historians, is the role of the Bolshevik Party as the monolithic instrument that transmitted Lenin's will to the masses and made his intentions a reality. In fact the Bolshevik Party is probably the most overrated factor in the entire history of the revolution. The party had burgeoned almost overnight from a sect into a mass movement; its membership rose nearly ten-fold between February and August. The Secretariat consisted of Sverdlov[2] and half-a-dozen women: it was all they could do to maintain the correspondence with the provincial party organizations, let alone discipline anyone. It even took a couple of months to disabuse some of the provincial Bolsheviks of the notion of reuniting with the Mensheviks. The party maintained a large press, but was

[2] Y. M. Sverdlov (1885–1919), a leading Bolshevik.

chronically short of funds; the documents published by Z. A. B. Zeman[3] show no evidence of German money reaching the Bolsheviks after the July Days. The dissension in the top Bolshevik leadership is of course well known—the resistance of Lenin's closest aides, Zinoviev and Kamenev, to the whole idea of an armed insurrection. What is less widely realized is the tacit opposition among many more Bolshevik leaders, such that until the last minute very little was being done to implement Lenin's insurrectionary demands. The party was at best a dull and loose-jointed instrument, except as compared with the other political movements in Russia.

It may be argued with some plausibility that Lenin, with his will-to-power, his sense of timing and slogans, a few steadfast lieutenants (Sverdlov, Dzerzhinsky,[4] Smilga[5] in Finland), and the Bolshevik Military Organization with its toe-hold in the Petrograd garrison, was able to engineer a deliberate conspiracy in the best Blanquist tradition. (Lenin's denials of Blanquism protested too much.) It is sometimes held that he tried such a conspiracy in the July Days. But in fact there is very little evidence of a careful conspiracy either in July or in October. The specialists of the Bolshevik Military Organization, aware of the cowardice and unreliability of the reservists in the Petrograd garrison, were among the most emphatic *opponents* of an attempt to seize power prior to the Second Congress of Soviets, as Lenin demanded. The Bolshevik preparations for the uprising were last-minute improvisations; the Military-Revolutionary Committee, usually dated October 9 [22] or 12 [25] when the Petrograd Soviet adopted the idea, did not meet and begin work until the twentieth [November 2], only four days before the final clash began. Two regiments, some sailors, and a couple of thousand untrained Red Guards were all

[3] Z. A. B. Zeman, author of *Germany and the Revolution in Russia 1915–1918. Documents from the Archives of the German Foreign Ministry* (London, 1958).
[4] F. E. Dzerzhinsky (Dzierzynski) (1877–1926), a leading Bolshevik, future head of the Soviet Secret Police (CHEKA).
[5] I. T. Smilga (1892–?), a leading Bolshevik from Latvia; from April 1917 member of the Central Committee.

the Bolsheviks could count on when the crisis came, and if the rest of the Russian army had not been neutral or paralyzed, Lenin would never have had a chance.

From any rational contemporary standpoint, the Bolshevik Revolution was a desperate gamble, unlikely to succeed and still less likely to hold out. This is what everyone believed, from the rightists who hoped the Bolsheviks would get rid of Kerensky, through moderates like Dan and Tseretelli who feared the same thing, to the Bolsheviks who worried with Zinoviev and Kamenev that recourse to arms might mean the destruction of the Bolshevik Party. Everyone in this whole range of opinion judged—with good reason—that if Russia's tenuous democratic equilibrium were disrupted, a military dictatorship was the most likely outcome.

Why, then, did Lenin take the chance he did? Because, for him, this slim opportunity at the peak of the revolutionary wave was the *only* possibility for the personal dictatorship to which he aspired. Lenin had his own theory of the willful reversal of the trend of history: "The fate of the Russian and world revolutions depends on two or three days of fighting. . . . To delay is death." In other words, Marxism or no, history gave Lenin this one opportunity which might never be repeated.

This explains why Lenin tried, but not how his long-shot gamble actually succeeded. It was, as it turned out, a victory partly by default, partly by a series of lucky developments that no one could have counted on. Most of the mass grievances that Lenin capitalized on were the consequences of default—particularly the failure of the Provisional Government to do anything meaningful about the war or the land. Lenin captured the emotional appeal of the soviets because the Mensheviks and Socialist Revolutionaries, nominal socialists, were unwilling to lead a revolution against the interests of property. Finally, Lenin made telling use of the fear of the Right, a fear made real and acute by the Kornilov movement. In October 1917 Russia was in a state of panic over invasion and counter-revolution resembling France in August 1792. In both cases, it was this fear that galvanized the insurrectionists into action, and paralyzed the moderates.

The circumstances of the moment, though not of the long term, did give Lenin a plausible chance. But his control over the party was weak, and his own followers, including Trotsky, were about to let the moment slip by. They were in fact waiting for the Congress of Soviets to be convened, just the course that Lenin condemned as a "constitutional illusion," fatal to the sort of revolution he wanted. There would have been no one-party armed insurrection at all, but for another stroke of historical accident: Kerensky's ill-conceived effort to silence the Bolshevik press on the morning of the twenty-fourth of October [November 6].

The events of October 24, distorted through the prisms of Communist and anti-Communist mythologies, can hardly be disentangled in a short essay. (The reader may be referred to my book, Red October, for a full account of how the Bolsheviks stumbled into power.) Essentially the facts are these: The Bolsheviks had failed, after their resolutions endorsing insurrection in principle, to make any concrete plans for the uprising. When the government's move came on the morning of the twenty-fourth, the Bolsheviks saw it as the first blow in a campaign to suppress the Congress of Soviets. They called out their few reliable men for what they thought was a desperate holding action. To the surprise of both sides, the government found that it could command no effective force, and Petrograd fell by default into the hands of the Bolsheviks. It remained only for Lenin to make his way from his hideout to Smolny and take command in the early hours of October 25 [November 7] for the affair to take on the appearance of a planned insurrection.

Chance put Lenin in power, and chance kept him there during the dizzying days that followed. No one could have counted on the Cossacks' refusing to defend the Provisional Government. No one could have anticipated that General Cheremisov, commander of the Northern Front, would stop the orders to the troops who were to relieve the Winter Palace. No one could have foreseen the collapse of General Krasnov's offensive at Pulkovo nor the premature rising and defeat of the officer cadets in Petrograd. No one could have bet with assurance on Bolshevik victory in the

Civil War. The accession and survival of the Soviet regime in its early days were little short of a historical miracle.

This conclusion may be difficult to accept, frequent though such decisive accidents are in history. Human reason rebels at the thought that any great development, good or bad, could depend on the random play of contingency. Yet there are critical points in the history of nations where two or more divergent alternatives lie open and where the accidents of politics, the words of a negotiator, the path of a few shots, can decide the fate of generations. It was a series of such unpredictable events that diverted Russia from the customary course of modern revolutions and paved the way for the unique phenomenon of twentieth-century Communism.

7. The Bolsheviks in Power: The First Day

JOHN REED

The short life of John Reed was full of tension and drama. Born in 1887, son of a United States marshal, Charles J. Reed, a Roosevelt liberal from Portland, Oregon, John went to Harvard in 1905 at the age of eighteen. There he joined a dozen activities. He played water polo, was on the staff of Monthly and Lampoon, and was president of the Cosmopolitan Club. Eager to learn and open minded, he soon turned to political issues of the day and became an active spokesman for social reform; from February 1913 he contributed articles to Masses and took part in various manifestations protesting exploitation of labor. Late in 1913 he went to Mexico for Metropolitan Magazine. Fascination with Villa deepened his early interest in the cause of social justice which he give expression to in his enthusiastic book

SOURCE: John Reed, *Ten Days That Shook the World* (London: Boni & Liveright, 1919), pp. 112–139. Reprinted in 1934 and 1935 by International Publishers. By courtesy of Random House.

Insurgent Mexico. The idea of the proletarian revolution fired his imagination. He drew closer to socialism.

When World War I broke out, Metropolitan Magazine sent its capable reporter first to the western, then to the eastern front. From the very beginning he opposed the war, which he ascribed to intrigues of munition manufacturers and their henchmen. In 1916 he voted for Woodrow Wilson "because Wall Street was against him." Already armed with a certificate describing him as a "Socialist comrade," in September 1917 John Reed returned to Russia. Immediately he plunged into revolutionary activities, attending meetings of all parties and talking with whomever he could reach. He interviewed members of the Provisional Government, as well as those of the Petrograd Soviet, and visited troops at the northern front. For him, the Revolution was an exciting adventure which he enjoyed with a boyish gusto.

While doing his duty as a newspaper correspondent, he was gathering material for a book that would interpret the Revolution for the workers of America. In the fall of 1919, after a brief visit to the United States, he was attached to the bureau of the Communist International founded earlier that year. He participated in the Second Congress of the Comintern and was a member of its Executive Committee. In September 1920 he went to Baku where he made a roaring speech to the Congress of Oriental Nationalities. There he ate unwashed fruit, caught typhus, and died on October 17, 1920, at the age of 32. He was buried in Moscow in the Kremlin wall with great fanfare. Leading Bolsheviks made glowing speeches at the grave of their American comrade.

John Reed described his book, Ten Days That Shook the World, as "a chronicle of those events which I myself observed and experienced and those supported by reliable evidence." There is, however, no doubt that he saw largely through Bolshevik eyes, and that while collecting supporting evidence he applied Communist criteria. As he said in his Preface, "In the struggle my sympathies were not neutral." Neither is the resulting account—palpitating, thrilling, but politically naive.

For John Reed the second phase of the Revolution was the story of the Bolshevik struggle against the conspiracy of "the propertied classes." They were the villains, the aggressors. To their attacks the Bolsheviks "retorted by preaching class war." Mesmerized by Lenin's strength and determination, charmed by Trotsky's eloquence, John

Reed spent the critical weeks of October–November 1917 in a state of euphoria, dreaming utopian daydreams. He was convinced that with the Bolshevik victory the millennium was around the corner. For him the Revolution was "one of the most marvelous mankind ever embarked upon, sweeping into history at the head of toiling masses, and staking everything on their vast desires. Already the machinery had been set up by which the land of the great estates could be distributed among peasants. The Factory-Shop Committees and Trade Unions were there to put into operation workers' control of industry."

While watching in Moscow the funeral of the 500 Bolshevik casualties of the Revolution, a ceremony at which the Orthodox clergy refused to officiate, John Reed remarked: "I suddenly realized that the devout Russian people no longer needed priests to pray them into heaven. On earth they were building a kingdom more bright than any heaven had to offer. . . ."

Ten Days That Shook the World was first published in 1919 by Boni and Liveright and then in 1934 and 1935 by International Publishers. A paperback edition is also available. Lenin wrote a warm introduction to the first edition. Soon the book was translated into Russian and published in large editions. In the 1920s the Soviet director Sergei Eisenstein based one of his movies on Reed's book and gave it the same title. Banned under Stalin because it stressed Trotsky's role, the book was reissued in the Soviet Union after 1956.

The passage given below constitutes the bulk of Chapter 5, "Plunging Ahead." It describes the first day of the Bolsheviks in power, Thursday, November 8 (October 26), 1917. Despite the uncritical enthusiasm of the author for the Bolshevik Revolution, or perhaps because of it, the passage conveys better than any other the sense of drama and excitement and the mood of great expectations that permeated the first days of the Bolshevik rule.

★ ★ ★ ★ ★

Thursday, November 8 [October 26]. Day broke on a city in the wildest excitement and confusion, a whole nation heaving up in long hissing swells of storm. Superficially all was quiet; hundreds of thousands of people retired at a prudent hour, got up early, and went to work. In Petrograd the street-cars were running, the stores and restaurants open, theatres going, an exhibition of paintings advertised. . . . All the complex routine of common life —humdrum even in war-time—proceeded as usual. Nothing is so astounding as the vitality of the social organism—how it persists, feeding itself, clothing itself, amusing itself, in the face of the worst calamities. . . .

The air was full of rumours about Kerensky, who was said to have raised the Front, and to be leading a great army against the capital. *Volia Naroda*[1] published a *prikaz* launched by him at Pskov:

> The disorders caused by the insane attempt of the Bolsheviki place the country on the verge of a precipice, and demand the effort of our entire will, our courage and the devotion of every one of us, to win through the terrible trial which the fatherland is undergoing. . . .
>
> Until the declaration of the composition of the new Government— if one is formed—every one ought to remain at his post and fulfil his duty toward bleeding Russia. It must be remembered that the least interference with existing Army organisations can bring on irreparable misfortunes, by opening the Front to the enemy. Therefore it is indispensable to preserve at any price the morale of the troops, by assuring complete order and the preservation of the Army from new shocks, and by maintaining absolute confidence between officers and their subordinates. I order all the chiefs and Commissars, in the name of the safety of the country, to stay at their posts, as I myself retain the post of Supreme Commander, until the Provisional Government of the Republic shall declare its will. . . .

In answer, this placard on all the walls:

FROM THE
ALL-RUSSIAN CONGRESS OF SOVIETS

The ex-Ministers Konovalov, Kishkin, Terestchenko, Maliantovitch, Nikitin and others have been arrested by the Military Revolutionary Committee. Kerensky has fled. All Army organi-

---

[1] *Volia Naroda* (People's Freedom), a Petrograd daily supporting the Provisional Government; *Prikaz*: order, command.

sations are ordered to take every measure for the immediate arrest of Kerensky and his conveyance to Petrograd.

All assistance given to Kerensky will be punished as a serious crime against the state.

With brakes released the Military Revolutionary Committee whirled, throwing off orders, appeals, decrees, like sparks. . . . Kornilov was ordered brought to Petrograd. Members of the Peasant Land Committees imprisoned by the Provisional Government were declared free. Capital punishment in the army was abolished. Government employees were ordered to continue their work, and threatened with severe penalties if they refused. All pillage, disorder and speculation were forbidden under pain of death. Temporary Commissars were appointed to the various Ministries: Foreign Affairs, Vuritsky and Trotzky; Interior and Justice, Rykov; Labor, Shliapnikov; Finance, Menzhinsky; Public Welfare, Madam Kollontai; Commerce, Ways and Communications, Riazanov; Navy, the sailor Korbir; Posts and Telegraphs, Spiro; Theaters, Muraviov; State Printing Office, Gherbychev; for the City of Petrograd, Lieutenant Neserov; for the Northern Front, Pozern. . . .

To the Army, appeal to set up Military Revolutionary Committees. To the railway workers, to maintain order, especially not to delay the transport of food to the cities and the front. . . . In return, they were promised representation in the Ministry of Ways and Communications.

Cossack brothers! (said one proclamation). You are being led against Petrograd. They want to force you into battle with the revolutionary workers and soldiers of the capital. Do not believe a word that is said to our common enemies, the land-owners and the capitalists.

At our Congress are represented all the conscious organisations of workers, soldiers and peasants of Russia. The Congress wishes also to welcome into its midst the worker-Cossacks. The Generals of the Black Band, henchmen of the land-owners, of Nicolai the Cruel, are our enemies.

They tell you that the Soviets wish to confiscate the lands of the

Cossacks. This is a lie. It is only from the great Cossack landlords that the Revolution will confiscate the land to give it to the people.

Organise Soviets of Cossacks' Deputies! Join with the Soviets of Workers' and Soldiers' Deputies!

Show the Black Band that you are not traitors to the People, and that you do not wish to be cursed by the whole of revolutionary Russia! . . .

Cossack brothers, execute no orders of the enemies of the people. Send your delegates to Petrograd to talk it over with us. . . . The Cossacks of the Petrograd garrison, to their honour, have not justified the hope of the People's enemies. . . .

Cossack brothers! The All-Russian Congress of Soviets extends to you a fraternal hand. Long live the brotherhood of the Cossacks with the soldiers, workers and peasants of all Russia!

On the other side, what a storm of proclamations posted up, hand-bills scattered everywhere, newspapers—screaming and cursing and prophesying evil. Now raged the battle of the printing press—all other weapons being in the hands of the Soviets.

First, the appeal of the Committee for Salvation of Country and Revolution,[2] flung broadcasts over Russia and Europe:

TO THE CITIZENS
OF THE RUSSIAN REPUBLIC!

Contrary to the will of the revolutionary masses, on November seventh [October 25] the Bolsheviki of Petrograd criminally arrested part of the Provisional Government, dispersed the Council of the Republic, and proclaimed an illegal power. Such violence committed against the Government of revolutionary Russia at the

---

[2] The Committee for Salvation of the Country and the Revolution was hastily formed, as a reaction to the Bolshevik coup, during the night of November 7–8 (October 25–26). It was headed by N. D. Avksentiev (1878–1943), a prominent leader of the Socialist Revolutionary Party, and president of the Council of the Republic. The Committee was composed of representatives from the Kadet, Socialist Revolutionary, and Menshevik parties. It was also joined by some non-partisan elements representing the Municipal Duma, the cooperatives and some trade unions. The main task of the Committee was to galvanize into action the anti-Bolshevik opposition and to organize military resistance against them.

moment of its greatest external danger, is an indescribable crime against the fatherland.

The insurrection of the Bolsheviki deals a mortal blow to the cause of national defence, and postpones immeasurably the moment of peace so greatly desired.

Civil war, begun by the Bolsheviki, threatens to deliver the country to the horrors of anarchy and counter-revolution, and cause the failure of the Constituent Assembly, which must affirm the republican régime and transmit to the People forever their right to the land.

Preserving the continuity of the only legal Governmental power, the Committee for Salvation of Country and Revolution, established on the night of November 7th, takes the initiative in forming a new Provisional Government; which, basing itself on the forces of democracy, will conduct the country to the Constituent Assembly and save it from anarchy and counter-revolution. The Committee for Salvation summons you, citizens, to refuse to recognise the power of violence. Do not obey its orders!

Rise for the defence of the country and Revolution!

Support the Committee for Salvation!

Signed by the Council of the Russian Republic, the Municipal Duma of Petrograd, the *Tsay-ee-kah* (*First Congress*),[3] the Executive Committee of the Peasants' Soviets, and from the Congress itself the Front group, the factions of Socialist Revolutionaries, Mensheviki, Populist Socialists, Unified Social Democrats, and the group "Yedinstvo."[4]

Then posters from the Socialist Revolutionary party, the Men-

[3] *Tsay-ee-kah*: the Russian colloquial abbreviation of Central Executive Committee of the Soviet and Workers' and Soldiers' Deputies; it was chosen by the First Congress dominated by the Mensheviks and the Right Social Revolutionaries. The Second Congress met on October 25 (November 7) and was controlled by the Bolsheviks.
[4] "*Yedinstvo*" (unity), a small Social Democratic group composed mainly of the personal followers of G. V. Plekhanov (1856–1918), a leading Marxist theoretician and Menshevik, hence an opponent of Lenin.

sheviki *oborontsi*,[5] Peasants' Soviets again; from the Central Army Committee,[6] the *Tsentroflot*. . . .[7]

. . . Famine will crush Petrograd! (they cried). The German armies will trample on our liberty. Black Hundred [8] *pogroms* will spread over Russia, if we all—conscious workers, soldiers, citizens—do not unite. . . .

Do not trust the promises of the Bolsheviki! The promise of immediate peace—is a lie! The promise of bread—a hoax! The promise of land—a fairy tale! . . .

They were all in this manner.

Comrades! You have been basely and cruelly deceived! The seizure of power has been accomplished by the Bolsheviki alone. . . . They concealed their plot from the other Socialist parties composing the Soviet. . . .

You have been promised land and freedom, but the counter-revolution will profit by the anarchy called forth by the Bolsheviki, and will deprive you of land and freedom. . . .

The newspapers were as violent.

Our duty (said the *Dielo Naroda*) is to unmask these traitors to the working class. Our duty is to mobilise all our forces and mount guard over the cause of the Revolution! . . .

Izviestia, for the last time speaking in the name of the old *Tsay-ee-kah*, threatened awful retribution.

As for the Congress of Soviets, we affirm that there has been no Congress of Soviets! We affirm that it was merely a private conference

[5] *Oborontsi* (or defensists), a Menshevik faction that supported Russian war effort as long as it was necessary to defend the country against foreign aggression. Many Mensheviks, including G. V. Plekhanov, shared this point of view.
[6] The Central Army Committee was the apex of the pyramid of the army committees formed by the soldiers at the beginning of the Revolution. Every company, battalion, regiment, brigade, division and army corps had its committee. Over all of them was the Central Army Committee.
[7] Parallel to the army committees, fleet committees were set up in the Navy. The *Tsentroflot* (literally: Center Fleet) was the counterpart of the Central Army Committee.
[8] Black Hundreds, a right-wing, reactionary, anti-Semitic group founded during the Revolution of 1905. Some of the Jewish pogroms were engineered, or at least instigated, by the Black Hundreds.

of the Bolshevik faction! And in that case, they have no right to cancel the powers of the *Tsay-ee-kah*. . . .

. . . . .

Rabotchi Put blossomed out as *Pravda*, Lenin's newspaper which had been suppressed in July. It crowed, bristling:

Workers, soldiers, peasants! In March you struck down the tyranny of the clique of nobles. Yesterday you struck down the tyranny of the bourgeois gang. . . .
The first task now is to guard the approaches to Petrograd.
The second is definitely to disarm the counter-revolutionary elements of Petrograd.
The third is definitely to organise the revolutionary power and assure the realisation of the popular programme. . . .

What few Cadet organs appeared, and the bourgeoisie generally, adopted a detached, ironical attitude toward the whole business, a sort of contemptuous "I-told-you-so" to the other parties. Influential Cadets were to be seen hovering around the Municipal Duma, and on the outskirts of the Committee for Salvation. Other than that, the bourgeoisie lay low, biding its hour—which could not be far off. That the Bolsheviki would remain in power longer than three days never occurred to anybody—except perhaps to Lenin, Trotzky, the Petrograd workers and the simpler soldiers. . . .
In the high, amphitheatrical Nicolai Hall that afternoon I saw the Duma sitting in *permanence*, tempestuous, grouping around it all the forces of opposition. The old Mayor, Schreider, majestic with his white hair and beard, was describing his visit to Smolny the night before, to protest in the name of the Municipal Self-Government. "The Duma, being the only existing legal Government in the city, elected by equal, direct and secret suffrage, would not recognise the new power," he had told Trotzky. And Trotzky had answered, "There is a constitutional remedy for that. The Duma can be dissolved and re-elected. . . ." At this report there was a furious outcry.
"If one recognises a Government by bayonet," continued the old man, addressing the Duma, "well, we have one; but I consider legitimate only a Government recognised by the people, by the

majority, and not one created by the usurpation of a minority!"
Wild applause on all benches except those of the Bolsheviki. Amid
renewed tumult the Mayor announced that the Bolsheviki already
were violating Municipal autonomy by appointing Commissars in
many departments.

The Bolshevik speaker shouted, trying to make himself heard,
that the decisions of the Congress of Soviets meant that all Russia
backed up the action of the Bolsheviki.

"You!" he cried. "You are not the real representative of the
people of Petrograd!" Shrieks of "Insult! Insult!" The old Mayor,
with dignity, reminded him that the Duma was elected by the
freest possible popular vote. "Yes," he answered, "but that was a
long time ago—like the *Tsay-ee-kah*—like the Army Committee."

"There has been no new Congress of Soviets!" they yelled at
him.

"The Bolshevik faction refuses to remain any longer in this
nest of counter-revolution—" Uproar. "—and we demand a re-
election of the Duma. . . ." Whereupon the Bolsheviki left the
chamber, followed by cries of "German agents! Down with the
traitors!"

Shingariov,[9] Cadet, then demanded that all Municipal function-
aries who had consented to be Commissars of the Military Revolutionary Committee be discharged from their position and indicted.
Schreider was on his feet, putting a motion to the effect that the
Duma protested against the menace of the Bolsheviki to dissolve
it, and as the legal representative of the population, it would
refuse to leave its post.

Outside, the Alexander Hall was crowded for the meeting of
the Committee for Salvation, and Skobeliev was again speaking.
"Never yet," he said, "was the fate of the Revolution so acute,
never yet did the question of the existence of the Russian state
excite so much anxiety, never yet did history put so harshly and
categorically the question—is Russia to be or not to be! The great
hour for the salvation of the Revolution has arrived, and in con-

[9] A. I. Shingarev (1860–1918), a leading member of the Kadet Party, minister of finance of the Provisional Government (March–May) and of agriculture (May–July 1917).

sciousness thereof we observe the close union of the live forces of the revolutionary democracy, by whose organised will a centre for the salvation of the country and the Revolution has already been created. . . ." And much of the same sort. "We shall die sooner than surrender our post!"

Amid violent applause it was announced that the Union of Railway Workers had joined the Committee for Salvation. A few moments later the Post and Telegraph Employees came in; then some Mensheviki Internationalists[10] entered the hall, to cheers. The Railway men said they did not recognise the Bolsheviki and had taken the entire railroad apparatus into their own hands, refusing to entrust it to any usurpatory power. The Telegraphers' delegate declared that the operators had flatly refused to work their instruments as long as the Bolshevik Commissar was in the office. The Postmen would not deliver or accept mail at Smolny. . . . All the Smolny telephones were cut off. With great glee it was reported how Uritzky had gone to the Ministry of Foreign Affairs to demand the secret treaties, and how Neratov had put him out. The Government employees were all stopping work. . . .

It was war—war deliberately planned, Russian fashion; war by strike and sabotage. As we sat there the chairman read a list of names and assignments; so-and-so was to make the round of the Ministries; another was to visit the banks; some ten or twelve were to work the barracks and persuade the soldiers to remain neutral—"Russian soldiers, do not shed the blood of your brothers!"; a committee was to go and confer with Kerensky; still others were despatched to provincial cities, to form branches of the Committee for Salvation, and link together the anti-Bolshevik elements.

The crowd was in high spirits. "These Bolsheviki *will* try to dictate to the intelligentzia? We'll show them!" . . . Nothing could be more striking than the contrast between this assemblage and the Congress of Soviets. There, great masses of shabby sol-

[10] Mensheviki Internationalists or Social Democratic Internationalists formed a radical left wing of the Menshevik Party, and were led by L. Martov (Y. O. Tsederbaum) and Maxim Gorky (A. M. Peshkov, 1868–1936). The group opposed all coalition with the propertied classes, yet was unwilling to cooperate with the Bolsheviks and opposed their dictatorship.

diers, grimy workmen, peasants—poor men, bent and scarred in the brute struggle for existence; here the Menshevik and Social Revolutionary leaders—Avksentievs, Dans, Liebers—the former Socialist Ministers—Skobelievs, Tchernovs—rubbed shoulders with Cadets like oily Shatsky, sleek Vinaver; with journalists, students, intellectuals of almost all camps. This Duma crowd was well-fed, well-dressed; I did not see more than three proletarians among them all. . . .

News came. Kornilov's faithful *Tekhintsi*[11] had slaughtered his guards at Bykhov,[12] and he had escaped. Kaledin was marching north. . . . The Soviet of Moscow had set up a Military Revolutionary Committee, and was negotiating with the commandant of the city for possession of the arsenal, so that the workers might be armed.

With these facts was mixed an astounding jumble of rumours, distortions, and plain lies. For instance, an intelligent young Cadet, formerly private secretary to Miliukov and then to Terestchenko, drew us aside and told us all about the taking of the Winter Palace.

"The Bolsheviki were led by German and Austrian officers," he affirmed.

"Is that so?" we replied, politely. "How do you know?"

"A friend of mine was there and saw them."

"How could he tell they were German officers?"

"Oh, because they wore German uniforms!"

There were hundreds of such absurd tales, and they were not only solemnly published by the anti-Bolshevik press, but believed by the most unlikely persons—Socialist Revolutionaries and Mensheviki who had always been distinguished by their sober devotion to facts. . . .

But more serious were the stories of Bolshevik violence and terrorism. For example, it was said and printed that the Red Guards had not only thoroughly looted the Winter Palace, but

[11] *Tekhintsi*, General Kornilov's faithful bodyguard composed of Mohammedan tribesmen from Central Asia.
[12] Bykhov, the town where the Provisional Government interned General Kornilov and some of his associates.

that they had massacred the *yunkers*[13] after disarming them, had killed some of the Ministers in cold blood; and as for the women soldiers, most of them had been violated, and many had committed suicide because of the tortures they had gone through. . . . All these stories were swallowed whole by the crowd in the Duma. And worse still, the mothers and fathers of the students and of the women read these frightful details, *often accompanied by lists of names,* and toward nightfall the Duma began to be besieged by frantic citizens. . . .

A typical case is that of Prince Tumanov,[14] whose body, it was announced in many newspapers, had been found floating in the Moika Canal. A few hours later this was denied by the Prince's family, who added that the Prince was under arrest, so the press identified the dead man as General Demissov. The General having also come to life, we investigated, and could find no trace of any body having been found whatever. . . .

As we left the Duma building two boy scouts were distributing hand-bills to the enormous crowd which blocked the Nevsky in front of the door—a crowd composed almost entirely of business men, shop-keepers, *tchinovniki,*[15] clerks. One read:

FROM THE MUNICIPAL DUMA

The Municipal Duma in its meeting of October 26 [October 13], in view of the events of the day decrees: To announce the inviolability of private dwellings. Through the House Committees it calls upon the population of the town of Petrograd to meet with decisive repulse all attempts to enter by force private apartments, not stopping at the use of arms, in the interests of the self-defence of citizens.

Up on the corner of the Liteiny,[16] five or six Red Guards and a

[13] *Yunkers:* Cadet officers.
[14] Prince Tumanov was a member of the Military Committee of the Duma and assistant minister of war (May–August, 1917); later on he was actually assassinated by the Bolsheviks.
[15] *Tchinovniki:* governmental officials (*tchin:* rank).
[16] Liteiny (Prospect): one of the main streets of Petrograd.

couple of sailors had surrounded a news-dealer and were demanding that he hand over his copies of the Menshevik *Rabotchaya Gazeta* (Workers' Gazette). Angrily he shouted at them, shaking his fist, as one of the sailors tore the papers from his stand. An ugly crowd gathered around, abusing the patrol. One little workman kept explaining doggedly to the people and the news-dealer, over and over again, "It has Kerensky's proclamation in it. It says we killed Russian people. It will make bloodshed. . . ."

Smolny was tenser than ever, if that were possible. The same running men in the dark corridors, squads of workers with rifles, leaders with bulging portfolios arguing, explaining, giving orders as they hurried anxiously along, surrounded by friends and lieutenants. Men literally out of themselves, living prodigies of sleeplessness and work—men unshaven, filthy, with burning eyes, who drove upon their fixed purpose full speed on engines of exaltation. So much they had to do, so much! Take over the Government, organise the City, keep the garrison loyal, fight the Duma and the Committee for Salvation, keep out the Germans, prepare to do battle with Kerensky, inform the provinces what had happened, propagandise from Archangel to Vladivostok. . . . Government and Municipal employees refusing to obey their Commissars, post and telegraph refusing them communication, railroads stonily ignoring their appeals for trains, Kerensky coming, the garrison not altogether to be trusted, the Cossacks waiting to come out. . . . Against them not only the organised bourgeoisie, but all the other Socialist parties except the Left Socialist Revolutionaries, a few Mensheviki Internationalists and the Social Democrat Internationalists,[17] and even they undecided whether to stand by or not. With them, it is true, the workers and the soldier-masses—the peasants an unknown quantity—but after all the Bolsheviki were a political faction not rich in trained and educated men. . . .

Riazanov was coming up the front steps, explaining in a sort of humourous panic that he, Commissar of Commerce, knew nothing whatever of business. In the upstairs café sat a man all by him-

[17] Social Democratic Internationalists, another name for Menshevik Internationalists.

self in the corner, in a goat-skin cape and clothes which had been —I was going to say "slept in," but of course he hadn't slept—and a three days' growth of beard. He was anxiously figuring on a dirty envelope, and biting his pencil meanwhile. This was Menzhinsky,[18] Commissar of Finance, whose qualifications were that he had once been clerk in a French bank. . . . And these four half-running down the hall from the office of the Military Revolutionary Committee, and scribbling on bits of paper as they run—these were Commissars despatched to the four corners of Russia to carry the news, argue, or fight—with whatever arguments or weapons came to hand. . . .

The Congress was to meet at one o'clock, and long since the great meetinghall had filled, but by seven there was yet no sign of the presidium. . . . The Bolshevik and Left Social Revolutionary[19] factions were in session in their own rooms. All the livelong afternoon Lenin and Trotzky had fought against compromise. A considerable part of the Bolsheviki were in favor of giving way so far as to create a joint all-Socialist government. "We can't hold on!" they cried. "Too much is against us. We haven't got the men. We will be isolated, and the whole thing will fall." . . .

But Lenin, with Trotzky beside him, stood firm as a rock. "Let the compromisers accept our programme and they can come in! We won't give way an inch. If there are comrades here who haven't the courage and the will to dare what we dare, let them leave with the rest of the cowards and conciliators! Backed by the workers and soldiers we shall go on."

At five minutes past seven came word from the Left Socialist Revolutionaries to say that they would remain in the Military Revolutionary Committee.

"See!" said Lenin. "They are following!"

A little later, as we sat at the press table in the big hall, an

[18] V. R. Menzhinsky (1874–1934), one of the chiefs of the Secret Police (CHEKA-GPU); its chief from 1926 to 1934.
[19] Left Social Revolutionary faction, or the left wing of the Social Revolutionary Party, split in the fall of 1917 from the main body and threw its support to the Bolsheviks.

Anarchist who was writing for the bourgeois papers proposed to me that we go and find out what had become of the presidium. There was nobody in the *Tsay-ee-kah* office, nor in the bureau of the Petrograd Soviet. From room to room we wandered, through vast Smolny. Nobody seemed to have the slightest idea where to find the governing body of the Congress. As we went my companion described his ancient revolutionary activities, his long and pleasant exile in France. . . . As for the Bolsheviki, he confided to me that they were common, rude, ignorant persons, without aesthetic sensibilities. He was a real specimen of the Russian intelligentzia. . . . So we came at last to Room 17, office of the Military Revolutionary Committee, and stood there in the midst of all the furious coming and going. The door opened, and out shot a squat, flat-faced man in a uniform without insignia, who seemed to be smiling—which smile, after a minute, one saw to be the fixed grin of extreme fatigue. It was Krylenko.[20]

My friend, who was a dapper, civilized-looking young man, gave a cry of pleasure and stepped forward.

"Nicolai Vasilievitch!" he said, holding out his hand. "Don't you remember me, comrade? We were in prison together."

Krylenko made an effort and concentrated his mind and sight. "Why yes," he answered finally, looking the other up and down with an expression of great friendliness. "You are S———. Zdra'stvuitye!"[21] They kissed. "What are you doing in all this?" He waved his arm around.

"Oh, I'm just looking on. . . . You seem very successful."

"Yes," replied Krylenko, with a sort of doggedness, "the proletarian Revolution is a great success." He laughed. "Perhaps—perhaps, however, we'll meet in prison again!"

When we got out into the corridor again my friend went on with his explanations. "You see, I'm a follower of Kropotkin. To us the Revolution is a great failure; it has not aroused the patriot-

[20] N. V. Krylenko (1885–1938?), a prominent Bolshevik; conscripted into the army, he organized Communist propaganda among soldiers. On December 8 (November 25), 1917, Lenin appointed him commander in chief of all armed forces.

[21] "*Zdra'stvuitye!*": "Greetings!" or "How are you!"

ism of the masses. Of course that only proves that the people are not ready for Revolution. . . ."

It was just 8:40 when a thundering wave of cheers announced the entrance of the presidium, with Lenin—great Lenin—among them. A short, stocky figure, with a big head set down in his shoulders, bald and bulging. Little eyes, a snubbish nose, wide, generous mouth, and heavy chin; clean-shaven now, but already beginning to bristle with the well-known beard of his past and future. Dressed in shabby clothes, his trousers much too long for him. Unimpressive, to be the idol of a mob, loved and revered as perhaps few leaders in history have been. A strange popular leader —a leader purely by virtue of intellect; colourless, humourless, uncompromising and detached, without picturesque idiosyncrasies— but with the power of explaining profound ideas in simple terms, of analysing a concrete situation. And combined with shrewdness, the greatest intellectual audacity.

Kameniev was reading the report of the actions of the Military Revolutionary Committee; abolition of capital punishment in the Army, restoration of the free right of propaganda, release of officers and soldiers arrested for political crimes, orders to arrest Kerensky and confiscation of food supplies in private store-houses. . . . Tremendous applause.

Again the representative of the *Bund*.[22] The uncompromising attitude of the Bolsheviki would mean the crushing of the Revolution; therefore, the *Bund* delegates must refuse any longer to sit in the Congress. Cries from the audience, "We thought you walked out last night! How many more times are you going to walk out?"

Then the representative of the Mensheviki Internationalists. Shouts, "What! You here still?" The speaker explained that only part of the Mensheviki Internationalists left the Congress; the rest were going to stay——

"We consider it dangerous and perhaps even mortal for the

[22] *Bund*, a Jewish labor and Socialist Party in Russia, Poland, and Lithuania founded in 1897; it oscillated between the Bolsheviks and the Mensheviks.

Revolution to transfer the power to the Soviets"—Interruptions—
"but we feel it our duty to remain in the Congress and vote
against the transfer here!"

Other speakers followed, apparently without any order. A delegate of the coal miners of the Don Basin called upon the Congress
to take measures against Kaledin, who might cut off coal and food
from the capital. Several soldiers just arrived from the Front
brought the enthusiastic greetings of their regiments. . . . Now
Lenin, gripping the edge of the reading stand, letting his little
winking eyes travel over the crowd as he stood there waiting, apparently oblivious to the long-rolling ovation, which lasted several
minutes. When it finished, he said simply, "We shall now proceed
to construct the Socialist order!" Again that overwhelming human
roar.

"The first thing is the adoption of practical measures to realise
peace. . . . We shall offer peace to the peoples of all the belligerent countries upon the basis of the Soviet terms—no annexations,
no indemnities, and the right of self-determination of peoples. At
the same time, according to our promise, we shall publish and
repudiate the secret treaties. . . . The question of War and Peace
is so clear that I think that I may, without preamble, read the
project of a Proclamation to the Peoples of All the Belligerent
Countries. . . ."

His great mouth, seeming to smile, opened wide as he spoke;
his voice was hoarse—not unpleasantly so, but as if it had hard-
ened that way after years and years of speaking—and went on
monotonously, with the effect of being able to go on forever. . . .
For emphasis he bent forward slightly. No gestures. And before
him, a thousand simple faces looking up in intent adoration.

PROCLAMATION TO THE
PEOPLES AND GOVERNMENTS
OF ALL THE BELLIGERENT NATIONS

The Workers' and Peasants' Government, created by the revolution of November 6 and 7 [October 24 and 25] and based on the

Soviets of Workers', Soldiers' and Peasants' Deputies, proposed to all the belligerent peoples and to their Governments to begin immediately negotiations for a just and democratic peace.

The Government means by a just and democratic peace, which is desired by the immense majority of the workers and the labouring classes, exhausted and depleted by the war—that peace which the Russian workers and peasants, after having struck down the Tsarist monarchy, have not ceased to demand categorically— immediate peace without annexations (that is to say, without conquest of foreign territory, without forcible annexation of other nationalities), and without indemnities.

The Government of Russia proposes to all the belligerent peoples immediately to conclude such a peace, by showing themselves willing to enter upon the decisive steps of negotiations aiming at such a peace, at once, without the slightest delay, before the definitive ratification of all the conditions of such a peace by the authorised assemblies of the people of all countries and of all nationalities.

By annexation or conquest of foreign territory, the Government means—conformably to the conception of democratic rights in general, and the rights of the working-class in particular—all union to a great and strong State of a small or weak nationality, without the voluntary, clear and precise expression of its consent and desire; whatever be the moment when such an annexation by force was accomplished, whatever be the degree of civilisation of the nation annexed by force or maintained outside the frontiers of another State, no matter if that nation be in Europe or in the far countries across the sea.

If any nation is retained by force within the limits of another State; if, in spite of the desire expressed by it (it matters little if that desire be expressed by the press, by popular meetings, decisions of political parties, or by disorders and riots against national oppression), that nation is not given the right of deciding by free vote—without the slightest constraint, after the complete departure of the armed forces of the nation which has annexed it or wishes to annex it or is stronger in general—the form of its national and political organisation, such a union constitutes an annexation—that is to say, conquest and an act of violence.

To continue this war in order to permit the strong and rich nations to divide among themselves the weak and conquered nationalities is considered by the Government the greatest possible crime against humanity; and the Government solemnly proclaims its decision to sign a treaty of peace which will put an end to this war upon the above conditions, equally fair for all nationalities without exception.

The Government abolishes secret diplomacy, expressing before the whole country its firm decision to conduct all the negotiations in the light of day before the people, and will proceed immediately to the full publication of all secret treaties confirmed or concluded by the Government of land-owners and capitalists, from March until November 7 [October 25], 1917. All the clauses of the secret treaties which, as occur in a majority of cases, have for their object to procure advantages and privileges for Russian capitalists, to maintain or augment the annexations of the Russian imperialists, are denounced by the Government immediately and without discussion.

In proposing to all Governments and all peoples to engage in public negotiations for peace, the Government declares itself ready to carry on these negotiations by telegraph, by post, or by pourparlers between the representatives of the different countries, or at a conference of these representatives. To facilitate these pourparlers, the Government appoints its authorised representatives in the neutral countries.

The Government proposes to all the Governments and to the peoples of all the belligerent countries to conclude an immediate armistice, at the same time suggesting that the armistice ought to last three months, during which time it is perfectly possible, not only to hold the necessary pourparlers between the representatives of all the nations and nationalities without exception drawn into the war or forced to take part in it, but also to convoke authorised assemblies of representatives of the people of all countries, for the purpose of the definite acceptance of the conditions of peace.

In addressing this offer of peace to the Governments and to the peoples of all the belligerent countries, the Provisional Workers' and Peasants' Government of Russia addresses equally and in particular the conscious workers of the three nations most devoted to humanity and the three most important nations among those taking part in the present war—England, France, and Germany. The workers of these countries have rendered the greatest services to the cause of progress and of Socialism. The splendid examples of the Chartists movement in England, the series of revolutions, of world-wide historical significance, accomplished by the French proletariat —and finally, in Germany, the historic struggle against the Laws of Exception, an example for the workers of the whole world of prolonged and stubborn action, and the creation of the formidable organisations of Germany proletarians—all these models of proletarian heroism, these monuments of history, are for us a sure guarantee that the workers of these countries will understand the duty imposed upon them to liberate humanity from the horrors and consequences of war; and that these workers, by decisive, energetic and continued action, will help us to bring to a successful conclusion the cause of peace—and at the same time, the cause of the liberation of the exploited working masses from all slavery and all exploitation.

When the grave thunder of applause had died away, Lenin spoke again:

"We propose to the Congress to ratify this declaration. We address ourselves to the Governments as well as to the peoples, for a declaration which would be addressed only to the peoples of the belligerent countries might delay the conclusion of peace. The conditions of peace, drawn up during the armistice, will be ratified by the Constituent Assembly. In fixing the duration of the armistice at three months, we desire to give to the peoples as long a rest as possible after this bloody extermination, and ample time for them to elect their representatives. This proposal of peace will meet with resistance on the part of the imperialist governments— we don't fool ourselves on that score. But we hope that revolution will soon break out in all the belligerent countries; that is why we address ourselves especially to the workers of France, England and Germany. . . .

"The revolution of November 6 and 7," he ended, "has opened the era of the Social Revolution. . . . The labour movement, in the name of peace and Socialism, shall win, and fulfil its destiny. . . ."

There was something quiet and powerful in all this, which stirred the souls of men. It was understandable why people believed when Lenin spoke. . . .

By crowd vote it was quickly decided that only representatives of political factions should be allowed to speak on the motion and that speakers should be limited to fifteen minutes.

First Karelin for the Left Socialist Revolutionaries. "Our faction had no opportunity to propose amendments to the text of the proclamation; it is a private document of the Bolsheviki. But we will vote for it because we agree with its spirit. . . ."

For the Social Democratic Internationalists Kramarov, long, stoop-shouldered and near-sighted—destined to achieve some notoriety as the Clown of the Opposition. Only a Government composed of all the Socialist parties, he said, could possess the authority to take such important action. If a Socialist coalition were formed, his faction would support the entire programme; if not, only part of it. As for the proclamation, the Internationalists were in thorough accord with its main points. . . .

Then one after another, amid rising enthusiasm; Ukrainean Social Democracy, support; Lithuanian Social Democracy, support; Populist Socialists,[23] support; Polish Social Democracy,[24] support; Polish Socialists,[25] support—but would prefer a Socialist

[23] Populist Socialist or *Trudoviki* (Labor Group), the native party of Kerensky, a small group of mild Socialists representing largely peasant interests.
[24] Polish Social Democracy—Social Democracy of Poland and Lithuania, founded in 1893; allied with the Bolsheviks; the native party of F. E. Dzierzynski (Dzerzhinsky), Rosa Luxemburg (1871–1919), and K. B. Radek (1885–1947).
[25] Polish Socialists—Polish Socialist Party (better known by its Polish initials PPS), founded in 1892, strongly patriotic and opposed to the Social Democracy of Poland and Lithuania, and consequently to the Bolshevik. The voice of support of the Bolsheviks registered here came from a few individual members who happened to be present at the Second Congress of the Soviets and not from official representatives of the Party.

coalition; Lettish Social Democracy, support. . . . Something was kindled in these men. One spoke of the "coming World-Revolution, of which we are the advance-guard"; another of "the new age of brotherhood, when all the peoples will become one great family. . . ." An individual member claimed the floor. "There is contradiction here," he said. "First you offer peace without annexations and indemnities, and then you say you will consider all peace offers. To consider means to accept. . . ."

Lenin was on his feet. "We want a just peace, but we are not afraid of a revolutionary war. . . . Probably the imperialist Governments will not answer our appeal—but we shall not issue an ultimatum to which it will be easy to say no. . . . If the German proletariat realises that we are ready to consider all offers of peace, that will perhaps be the last drop which overflows the bowl—revolution will break out in Germany. . . .

"We consent to examine all conditions of peace, but that doesn't mean that we shall accept them. . . . For some of our terms we shall fight to the end—but possibly for others will find it impossible to continue the war. . . . Above all, we want to finish the war. . . ."

It was exactly 10:35 when Kameniev asked all in favour of the proclamation to hold up their cards. One delegate dared to raise his hand against, but the sudden sharp outburst around him brought it swiftly down. . . . Unanimous.

Suddenly, by common impulse, we found ourselves on our feet, mumbling together into the smooth lifting unison of the *Internationale*. A grizzled old soldier was sobbing like a child. Alexandra Kollontai rapidly winked the tears back. The immense sound rolled through the hall, burst windows and doors and seared into the quiet sky. "The war is ended! The war is ended!" said a young workman near me, his face shining. And when it was over, as we stood there in a kind of awkward hush, some one in the back of the room shouted, "Comrades! Let us remember those who have died for liberty!" So we began to sing the "Funeral March," that slow, melancholy and yet triumphant chant, so Russian and so moving. The *Internationale* is an alien air, after all. The "Funeral

March" seemed the very soul of those dark masses whose delegates sat in this hall, building from their obscure visions a new Russia —and perhaps more.

You fell in the fatal fight
For the liberty of the people, for the honour of the people . . .
You gave up your lives and everything dear to you,
You suffered in horrible prisons,
You went to exile in chains. . . .

Without a word you carried your chains because you could not ignore
    your suffering brothers,
Because you believed that justice is stronger than the sword. . . .
The time will come when your surrendered life will count.
That time is near; when tyranny falls the people will rise, great and
    free!
Farewell brothers, you chose a noble path,
You are followed by the new and fresh army ready to die and to suf-
    fer. . . .

Farewell, brothers, you chose a noble path,
At your grave we swear to fight, to work for freedom and the people's
    happiness. . . .

For this did they lie there, the martyrs of March, in their cold Brotherhood Grave on Mars Field; for this thousands and tens of thousands had died in the prisons, in exile, in Siberian mines. It had not come as they expected it would come, nor as the intelligentzia desired it; but it had come—rough, strong, impatient of formulas, contemptuous of sentimentalism; *real.* . . .

Lenin was reading the Decree on Land:

1. All private ownership of land is abolished immediately without compensation.
2. All land-owners' estates, and all lands belonging to the Crown, to monasteries, church lands with all their live stock and inventoried property, buildings and all appurtenances, are trans-

ferred to the disposition of the township Land Committees and the district Soviets of Peasants' Deputies until the Constituent Assembly meets.

3. Any damage whatever done to the confiscated property which from now on belongs to the whole People, is regarded as a serious crime, punishable by the revolutionary tribunals. The district Soviets of Peasants' Deputies shall take all necessary measures for the observance of the strictest order during the taking over of the land-owners' estates, for the determination of the dimensions of the plots of land and which of them are subject to confiscation, for the drawing up of an inventory of the entire confiscated property, and for the strictest revolutionary protection of all the farming property on the land, with all buildings, implements, cattle, supplies of products, etc., passing into the hands of the People.

4. For guidance during the realisation of the great land reforms until their final resolution by the Constituent Assembly, shall serve the following peasant *nakaz* (instructions), drawn up on the basis of 242 local peasant *nakazi* by the editorial board of the "*Izviestia* of the All-Russian Soviet of Peasants' Deputies," and published in No. 88 of said "*Izviestia*" (Petrograd, No. 88, August 19, 1917).

The lands of peasants and of Cossacks serving in the Army shall not be confiscated.

"This is not," explained Lenin, "the project of former Minister Tchernov, who spoke of 'erecting a frame-work' and tried to realise reforms from above. From below, on the spot, will be decided the questions of division of the land. The amount of land received by each peasant will vary according to the locality. . . .

"Under the Provisional Government, the *pomieshtchiki*[26] flatly refused to obey the orders of the Land Committees—those Land Committees projected by Lvov, brought into existence by Shingariov, and administered by Kerensky!"

Before the debates could begin a man forced his way violently through the crowd in the aisle and climbed upon the platform.

[26] *Pomieshtchiki*: landowners.

It was Pianikh, member of the Executive Committee of the Peasants' Soviets, and he was mad clean through.

"The Executive Committee of the All-Russian Soviets of Peasants' Deputies protests against the arrest of our comrades, the Ministers Salazkin and Mazlov!" [27] he flung harshly in the faces of the crowd. "We demand their instant release! They are now in Peter-Paul fortress. We must have immediate action! There is not a moment to lose!"

Another followed him, a soldier with disordered beard and flaming eyes. "You sit here and talk about giving the land to the peasants, and you commit an act of tyrants and usurpers against the peasants' chosen representatives! I tell you—" he raised his fist, "if one hair of their heads is harmed, you'll have a revolt on your hands!" The crowd stirred confusedly.

Then up rose Trotzky, calm and venomous, conscious of power, greeted with a roar. "Yesterday the Military Revolutionary Committee decided to release the Socialist Revolutionary and Menshevik Ministers, Mazlov, Salazkin, Gvozdov and Maliantovitch[28] —on principle. That they are still in Peter-Paul is only because we have had so much to do. . . . They will, however, be detained at their homes under arrest until we have investigated their complicity in the treacherous acts of Kerensky during the Kornilov affair!"

"Never," shouted Pianikh, "in any revolution have such things been seen as go on here!"

"You are mistaken," responded Trotzky. "Such things have been seen even in this revolution. Hundreds of our comrades were arrested in the July days. . . . When Comrade Kollontai was released from prison by the doctor's orders, Avksentiev placed at

[27] S. S. Salazkin, a former *Zemstvo* worker, minister of education (September–October 1917). S. L. Maslov, member of the right faction of the Socialist Revolutionary Party, minister of agriculture (October 1917); P. N. Maliantovich, Menshevik minister of justice of the Provisional Government (September–October 1917).

[28] K. A. Gvozdov, Menshevik chairman of the Labor Group of the Central War Industry Committee, member of the Executive Committee of the Petrograd Soviet, minister of labor (September–October 1917). P. N. Maliantovitch, Menshevik, minister of justice (September–October 1917).

her door two former agents of the Tsar's secret police!" The peasants withdrew, muttering, followed by ironical hoots.

The representative of the Left Socialist Revolutionaries spoke on the Land Decree. While agreeing in principle, his faction could not vote on the question until after discussion. The Peasants' Soviets should be consulted. . . .

The Mensheviki Internationalists, too, insisted on a party caucus.

Then the leader of the Maximalists,[29] the Anarchist wing of the peasants: "We must do honour to a political party which puts such an act into effect the first day, without jawing about it!"

A typical peasant was in the tribute, long hair, boots and sheepskin coat, bowing to all corners of the hall. "I wish you well, comrades and citizens," he said. "There are some Cadets walking around outside. You arrested our Socialist peasants—why not arrest them?"

This was the signal for a debate of excited peasants. It was precisely like the debate of soldiers of the night before. Here were the real proletarians of the land. . . .

"Those members of our Executive Committee, Avksentiev and the rest, whom we thought were the peasants' protectors—they are only Cadets too! Arrest them! Arrest them!"

Another, "Who are these Pianikhs, these Avksentievs? They are not peasants at all! They only wag their tails!"

How the crowd rose to them, recognising brothers!

The Left Socialist Revolutionaries proposed a half-hour intermission. As the delegates streamed out, Lenin stood up in his place.

"We must not lose time, comrades! News all-important to Russia must be on the press to-morrow morning. No delay!"

And above the hot discussion, argument, shuffling of feet could be heard the voice of an emissary of the Military Revolutionary Committee, crying, "Fifteen agitators wanted in room 17 at once! To go to the Front!". . .

---

[29] Maximalists, a small offshoot of the Socialist Revolutionary Party, demanding the immediate application of the maximum Socialist program.

It was almost two hours and a half later that the delegates came straggling back, the presidium mounted the platform, and the session recommenced by the reading of telegrams from regiment after regiment, announcing their adhesion to the Military Revolutionary Committee.

In leisurely manner the meeting gathered momentum. A delegate from the Russian troops on the Macedonian front spoke bitterly of their situation. "We suffer there more from the friendship of our 'Allies' than from the enemy," he said. Representatives of the Tenth and Twelfth Armies, just arrived in hot haste, reported, "We support you with all our strength!" A peasant-soldier protested against the release of "the traitor Socialists, Mazlov and Salazkin"; as for the Executive Committee of the Peasants' Soviets, it should be arrested *en masse!* Here was real revolutionary talk. . . . A deputy from the Russian Army in Persia declared he was instructed to demand all power to the Soviets. . . . A Ukrainean officer, speaking in his native tongue: "There is no nationalism in this crisis. . . . *Da zdravstvuyet* the proletarian dictatorship of all lands!" Such a deluge of high and hot thoughts that surely Russia would never again be dumb!

Kameniev remarked that the anti-Bolshevik forces were trying to stir up disorders everywhere, and read an appeal of the Congress to all the Soviets of Russia:

The All-Russian Congress of Soviets of Workers' and Soldiers' Deputies, including some Peasants' Deputies, calls upon the local Soviets to take immediate energetic measures to oppose all counter-revolutionary anti-Jewish action and all *pogroms*, whatever they may be. The honour of the Workers', Peasants' and Soldiers' Revolution demands that no *pogrom* be tolerated.

The Red Guard of Petrograd, the revolutionary garrison and the sailors have maintained complete order in the capital.

Workers, soldiers and peasants, you should follow everywhere the example of the workers and soldiers of Petrograd.

Comrade soldiers and Cossacks, on us falls the duty of assuring real revolutionary order.

All revolutionary Russia and the entire world have their eyes on us. . . .

At two o'clock the Land Decree was put to vote, with only one against and the peasant delegates wild with joy. . . . So plunged the Bolsheviki ahead, irresistible, over-riding hesitations and opposition—the only people in Russia who had a definite programme of action while the others talked for eight long months.

Now arose a soldier, gaunt, ragged and eloquent, to protest against the clause of the *Nakaz*[30] tending to deprive military deserters from a share in village land allotments. Bawled at and hissed at first, his simple, moving speech finally made silence. "Forced against his will into the butchery of the trenches," he cried, "which you yourselves, in the Peace decree, have voted senseless as well as horrible, he greeted the Revolution with hope of peace and freedom. Peace? The Government of Kerensky forced him again to go forward into Galicia to slaughter and be slaughtered; to his pleas for peace, Terestchenko simply laughed. . . . Freedom? Under Kerensky he found his Committees suppressed, his newspapers cut off, his party speakers put in prison. . . . At home in his village, the landlords were defying his Land Committees, jailing his comrades. . . . In Petrograd the bourgeoisie, in alliance with the Germans, were sabotaging the food and ammunition for the Army. . . . He was without boots, or clothes. . . . Who forced him to desert? The Government of Kerensky, which you have overthrown!" At the end there was applause.

But another soldier hotly denounced it: "The Government of Kerensky is not a screen behind which can be hidden dirty work like desertion! Deserters are scoundrels, who run away home and leave their comrades to die in the trenches alone! Every deserter is a traitor, and should be punished. . . ." Uproar, shouts of *"Do volno! Teesche!"* [31] Kameniev hastily proposed to leave the matter to the Government for decision.

At 2:30 A.M. fell a tense hush. Kameniev was reading the decree of the Constitution of Power:

Until the meeting of the Constituent Assembly, a provisional Workers' and Peasants' Government is formed, which shall be named the Council of People's Commissars.

---

[30] *Nakaz*: decree.
[31] *"Do volno! Teesche!"*: "Enough! Silence!"

The administration of the different branches of state activity shall be intrusted to commissions, whose composition shall be regulated to ensure the carrying out of the programme of the Congress, in close union with the mass organisations of working-men, working-women, sailors, soldiers, peasants and clerical employees. The governmental power is vested in a collegium made up of the chairmen of these commissions, that is to say, the Council of People's Commissars.

Control over the activities of the People's Commissars, and the right to replace them, shall belong to the All-Russian Congress of Soviets of Workers', Peasants' and Soldiers' Deputies, and its Central Executive Committee.

Still silence; as he read the list of Commissars, bursts of applause after each name, Lenin's and Trotzky's especially.

President of the Council: Vladimir Ulianov (Lenin)
Interior: A. E. Rykov
Agriculture: V. P. Miliutin
Labour: A. G. Shliapnikov
Military and Naval Affairs—a committee composed of V. A.
    Ovseenko (Antonov), N. V. Krylenko, and F. M. Dybenko.
Commerce and Industry: V. P. Nogin
Popular Education: A. V. Lunatcharsky
Finance: E. E. Skvortsov (Stepanov)
Foreign Affairs: L. D. Bronstein (Trotzky)
Justice: G. E. Oppokov (Lomov)
Supplies: E. A. Teodorovitch
Post and Telegraph: N. P. Avilov (Gliebov)
Chairman for Nationalities: L. V. Djougashvili (Stalin)
Railroads: To be filled later.

There were bayonets at the edges of the room, bayonets pricking up among the delegates; the Military Revolutionary Committee was arming everybody, Bolshevism was arming for the decisive battle with Kerensky, the sound of whose trumpets came up the southwest wind. . . .

Chronological Table

	1917	
	Old Style	New Style
Mutiny of the Petrograd Garrison	February 27	March 12
Negotiations begin between Duma and Soviet	February 28	March 13
Army Order No. 1	March 1	March 14
Provisional Government set up; Nicholas II abdicates	March 2	March 15
Lenin returns to Petrograd	April 3	April 16
The July Offensive	June 17–July 1	July 1–July 14
Bolshevik uprising in Petrograd	July 3–4	July 16–17
The Kornilov mutiny	August 25–30	September 7–12
Petrograd Garrison sides with the Soviet	October 21	November 3
Bolsheviks begin coup d'etat	October 24	November 6
Winter Palace captured	October 25	November 7
Soviet Government proclaimed	October 26	November 8

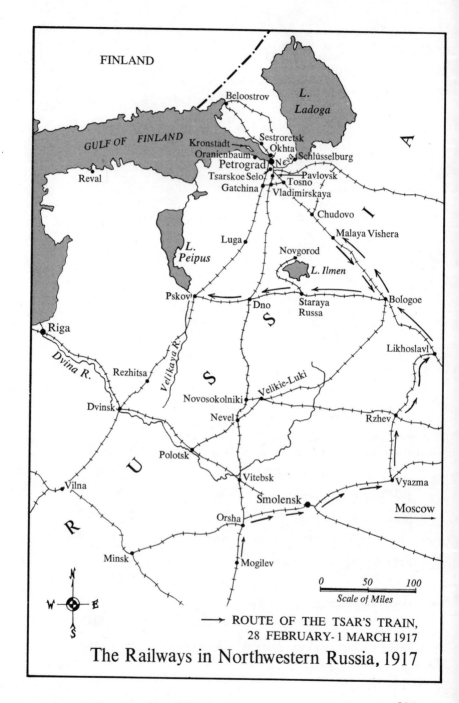

FINLAND

GULF OF FINLAND

Beloostrov

L. Ladoga

Kronstadt
Oranienbaum
Sestroretsk
Okhta
Schlüsselburg
Petrograd   Neva
Reval
Tsarskoe Selo   Pavlovsk
Gatchina   Tosno
Vladimirskaya

Chudovo

Malaya Vishera

Luga

L. Peipus

Novgorod

L. Ilmen

Pskov   Dno   Staraya Russa   Bologoe

Riga

Likhoslavl

Dvina R.

Rezhitsa

Velikaya R.

Novosokolniki   Velikie-Luki

Dvinsk   Nevel   Rzhev

Polotsk

Vyazma

Vilna   Vitebsk

Smolensk   Moscow

Orsha

Minsk

Mogilev

| 0 | 50 | 100 |
Scale of Miles

→ ROUTE OF THE TSAR'S TRAIN,
28 FEBRUARY- 1 MARCH 1917

The Railways in Northwestern Russia, 1917

214

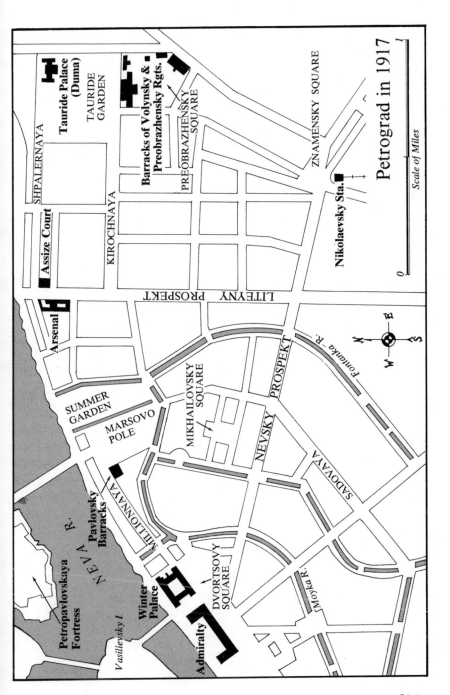

Petrograd in 1917

Scale of Miles

0 — 1

Tauride Palace (Duma)

TAURIDE GARDEN

Barracks of Volynsky & Preobrazhensky Rgts.

PREOBRAZHENSKY SQUARE

ZNAMENSKY SQUARE

SHPALERNAYA

Assize Court

KIROCHNAYA

Nikolaevsky Sta.

Arsenal

LITEYNY PROSPEKT

SUMMER GARDEN

MARSOVO POLE

MIKHAILOVSKY SQUARE

NEVSKY PROSPEKT

Fontanka R.

SADOVAYA

Pavlovsky Barracks

MILLIONNAYA

NEVA R.

Petropavlovskaya Fortress

Vasilievsky I.

Winter Palace

DVORTSOVY SQUARE

Moyka R.

Admiralty

215

Bibliography

I. Principal Bibliographic Guides

Hammond, Thomas T., ed. *Soviet Foreign Relations and World Communism*, pp. 19–24. Princeton, 1965.

Horecky, Paul L., ed. *Basic Russian Publications*, pp. 81–83. Chicago, 1962.

——. *Russia and the Soviet Union. A Bibliographic Guide to Western Language Publications*, pp. 112–119. Chicago, 1965.

Morley, Charles. *Guide to Research in Russian History*, pp. 102–105. Syracuse, N.Y., 1951. (Also available in microfilm-xerographic reprint, Ann Arbor, 1965.) This book is especially useful for research on the Russian Revolution.

Simmons, J. S. G., ed. *Guide to Russian Reference Books*. Vol. 2, *History, Historical Sciences, Ethnography, Geography*, pp. 61–69. Stanford, 1964.

Zaleski, Eugene. *Mouvements Ouvrier et Socialistes (Chronologie et Bibliography)*. Vol. 2, *1908–1917*. Paris, 1956.

II. Principal Collections of Source Material

Browder, Robert P. and Kerensky, A. F., eds. *The Russian Provisional Government, 1917: Documents,* 3 vols. Stanford, 1961.

Bunyan, J. and Fisher, H. H., eds. *The Bolshevik Revolution, 1917–1918: Documents and Materials.* Stanford, 1934.

Daniels, Robert V., ed. *Documentary History of Communism.* New York, 1960.

Gankin, O. H. and Fisher, H. H., eds. *The Bolsheviks and World War. The Origin of the Third International.* Stanford, 1940.

Golder, Frank A., ed. *Documents of Russian History, 1914–1917.* New York, 1927.

Jacob, Dan N., ed. *Communist Manifesto and Related Documents.* New York, 1961.

Kohn, Hans, ed. *The Mind of Modern Russia.* New Brunswick, 1955.

Lenin, V. I. *Selected Works,* 2 vols. New York, 1947.

Meisel, James H. and Kozera, E. S. *Materials for the Study of the Soviet System.* Ann Arbor, 1950.

III. Memoirs, Monographs and Basic Background Books

Abramovitch, R. R. *The Soviet Revolution, 1917–1939.* New York, 1962.

Anet, Claude (Schaeffer, Jean). *La Revolution Russe,* 4 vols. Paris, 1918–1919.

Arendt, Hannah. *The Origins of Totalitarianism.* New York, 1960.

Berdyaev, Nicolas. *The Origins of Russian Communism.* London, 1948.

Berlin, Isaiah. *Karl Marx.* London, 1948.

Billington, James H. *Mikhailovsky and Russian Populism.* New York, 1958.

Buchanan, Sir George. *My Mission to Russia and Other Diplomatic Memoirs,* 2 vols. Boston, 1923.

Burdzialov, E. N. *Vtoraia Russkaia Revolutsiia.* Moscow, 1967.

Carmichael, Joel. *A Short History of the Russian Revolution.* New York, 1958.

Carr, Edward H. *The Bolshevik Revolution, 1917–1923*, 3 vols. New York, 1951–1953.

Chamberlin, William Henry. *The Russian Revolution*, 2 vols. New York, 1935.

Charques, Richard. *The Twilight of Imperial Russia*. London, 1959.

Churchill, Winston S. *The Unknown War: The Eastern Front*. New Haven, 1931.

Chernov, Victor. *The Great Russian Revolution*. New Haven, 1936.

Curtiss, J. S. *The Russian Revolution, 1917*. Princeton, 1957.

Daniels, Robert V. *The Nature of Communism*. New York, 1962.

———. *The Red October*. New York, 1967.

Deutscher, Isaak. *The Prophet Armed. Trotsky: 1879–1921*. New York, 1954.

———. *Stalin: A Political Biography*. New York, 1949.

Dziewanowski, M. K. *The Communist Party of Poland. An Outline of History*. Cambridge, Mass., 1959.

———. *Joseph Pilsudski, 1918–1922*. Stanford, 1969.

Fainsod, Merle. *How Russia is Ruled*. Cambridge, Mass., 1967.

———. *International Socialism and the World War*. Cambridge, Mass., 1935.

Fischer, Louis. *The Soviets in World Affairs*. New York, 1960.

Francis, David R. *Russia from the American Embassy*. New York, 1921.

Friedrich, Carl J. and Brzezinski, Zbigniew K. *Totalitarian Dictatorship and Autocracy*. Cambridge, Mass., 1956.

Golovin, N. N. *The Russian Army in the World War*. New Haven, 1931.

Gorian, Waldemar, ed. *The Soviet Union: Background, Ideology, Reality*. Notre Dame, 1951.

Florinsky, Michael T. *The End of the Russian Empire*. New Haven, 1931.

Haimson, Leopold H. *The Russian Marxism and the Origins of Bolshevism*. Cambridge, Mass., 1955.

Hare, Richard. *Pioneers of Russian Social Thought*. London, 1951.

Hunt, R. N. Carew. *The Theory and Practice of Communism*. London, 1957.

Katkov, George. *Russia 1917: The February Revolution*. London, 1967.

Kazemzadeh, Firuz. *The Struggle for Transcaucasia, 1917–1921*. New York, 1951.

Kennan, George F. *Soviet Russian Relation, 1917–1920*. Vol. 1, *Russia Leaves The War*. Princeton, 1956.

Kerensky, Alexander. *The Catastrophe*. New York, 1927.

————. *The Crucification of Liberty*. New York, 1934.

————. *Russia and History's Turning Point*. New York, 1965.

Lockhart, Bruce H. B. *Memoirs of a British Agent*. New York, 1932.

Malia, Martin E. *Alexander Herzen and the Birth of Russian Socialism, 1812–1855*. Cambridge, Mass., 1961.

Marcuse, Herbert. *Soviet Marxism: A Critical Survey*. New York, 1961.

Maynard, John. *Russia in Flux*. New York, 1959.

Meyer, Alfred G. *Leninism*. Cambridge, Mass., 1957.

————. *Marxism*. Cambridge, Mass., 1954.

Miliukov, Paul. *Istoriia Vtoroi Ruskoi Revolutsii*, 3 vols. Sofia, 1921–1924.

Moorehead, Alan. *The Russian Revolution*. New York, 1955.

Nolde, B. E. *Russia in the Economic War*. New Haven, 1928.

Noulens, Joseph. *Mon Ambassade en Russie Sovietique, 1917–1919*, 2 vols. Paris, 1933.

Paleologue, Maurice. *An Ambassador's Memoirs*, 3 vols. London, 1923–1925.

Pares, Sir Bernard. *The Fall of the Russian Monarchy*. New York, 1934.

Pipes, Richard. *The Formation of the Soviet Union. Communism and Nationalism, 1917–1923*. Cambridge, Mass., 1954.

Pipes, Richard, ed. *Revolutionary Russia*. Cambridge, Mass., 1968.

————. *Social Democracy and the St. Petersburg Labor Movement, 1885–1897*. Cambridge, Mass., 1963.

Pokrovsky, M. N. *Ocherki Po Istorii Oktiabr'skoi Revolutsii*. Moscow, 1924.

Price, Morgan Philip. *My Reminiscences of the Russian Revolution*. London, 1921.

Radkey, Oliver H. *The Election to the Russian Constituent Assembly of 1917*. Cambridge, Mass., 1950.

———. *The Agrarian Foes of Bolshevism. Promise and Default of the Russian Socialist Revolutionaries. February to October 1917*. New York, 1958.

Reed, John. *Ten Days That Shook the World*. New York, 1919.

Reshetar, John S., Jr. *The Ukrainian Revolution, 1917–1920. A Study in Nationalism*. Princeton, 1952.

Rodzianko, M. V. *The Reign of Rasputin: An Empire's Collapse*. London, 1927.

Schapiro, Leonard. *The Origin of the Communist Autocracy, 1917–1922*. Cambridge, Mass., 1955.

Seton-Watson, Hugh. *The Decline of Imperial Russia*. London, 1952.

Shub, David. *Lenin*. New York, 1948.

Smith, Jay C., Jr. *The Russian Struggle for Power, 1914–1917*. New York, 1956.

Souvarine, Boris. *Stalin*. New York, 1939.

(Stalin, Joseph). *History of the Communist Party of the Soviet Union (Bolsheviks)*. New York, 1939. (Official history, a major part of the writing of which is attributed to Stalin.)

Stalin, Joseph. *Leninism*. 2 vols. London, 1940.

Sukhanov, N. N. (Himmer, N. N.). *The Russian Revolution, 1917: A Personal Record*. New York, 1955.

Talmon, Jacob L. *Political Messianism: The Romantic Phase*. New York, 1960.

———. *The Rise of Totalitarian Democracy*. Boston, 1952.

Treadgold, Donald W. *Lenin and His Rivals*. New York, 1955.

———. *Twentieth Century Russia*. Chicago, 1959.

Trotsky, Leon. *The History of the Russian Revolution*, 3 vols. New York, 1932.

————. *My Life*. New York, 1930.

————. *Stalin*. New York, 1941.

Tsereteli, Iraklii. *Vospominania o Fevralskoi Revolutsii*. Paris, 1963.

Tucker, Robert. *Philosophy and Myth in Karl Marx*. Cambridge, Mass., 1961.

Ulam, Adam B. *Expansion and Coexistence. Soviet Foreign Policy, 1917–1967*. Cambridge, Mass., 1968.

————. *The Unfinished Revolution*. New York, 1960.

Vakar, Nicholas P. *Belorussia*. Cambridge, Mass., 1956.

Venturi, Franco. *Roots of Revolution: History of the Populist and Socialist Movements in 19th Century Russia*. Garden City, 1947.

Warth, Robert D. *The Allies and the Russian Revolution: From the Fall of the Monarchy to the Peace of Brest Litovsk*. Durham, 1954.

Wetter, Gustavo A. *Dialectical Materialism*. New York, 1959.

Wheeler-Bennett, J. W. *The Forgotten Peace: Brest-Litovsk, March, 1918*. New York, 1939.

Wilson, Edmund. *To the Finland Station*. Garden City, 1947.

Wolfe, Bertram D. *Three Who Made a Revolution*. New York, 1948.

Yarmolinsky, Avram. *Road to Revolution*. New York, 1959.